HAGS

HAGS

The demonisation of middle-aged women

VICTORIA SMITH

FLEET
2023

FLEET

First published in Great Britain in 2023 by Fleet

3 5 7 9 10 8 6 4

A CIP catalogue record for this book
is available from the British Library.

Hardback ISBN 978-0-349-72696-0
Trade Paperback ISBN 978-0-349-72697-7

Typeset in Bembo by M Rules
Printed and bound in Great Britain by Clays Ltd, Elcograf S.p.A.

Papers used by Fleet are from well-managed forests
and other responsible sources.

Fleet
An imprint of
Little, Brown Book Group
Carmelite House
50 Victoria Embankment
London EC4Y 0DZ

An Hachette UK Company
www.hachette.co.uk

www.hachette.co.uk

To *all* the hags, past, present and in waiting

CONTENTS

INTRODUCTION

In fairy-tales, witches always wear silly black hats and black cloaks, and they ride on broomsticks. But this is not a fairy-tale. This is about REAL WITCHES.

Roald Dahl, *The Witches*

When we read 'witches' for 'women', we gain a fuller comprehension of the cruelties inflicted by the church on this portion of humanity.

Matilda Joslyn Gage, *Women, Church and State*

Say what you like about the anti-feminist backlash that dominated the late eighties, but it produced some excellent, unwittingly hilarious films. The greatest of these is *Fatal Attraction*.

Psychobitch Alex, played by Glenn Close, just can't take the hint when Michael Douglas's Dan tries to drop her following a weekend's hot sex. For all the righteous, legitimate feminist criticism of the film (director Adrian Lyne claimed to have based Alex on single women who were 'overcompensating for not being men') and for all the times boorish men have described perfectly sane women as 'bunny boilers' (referencing Alex's decision to stick Dan's daughter's pet rabbit on the hob), I love this film. Indeed, the older I get, the more I see Alex join the ranks of women in film and literature – murderous spinsters, evil stepmothers – whom I'm supposed to find obscene, but whose grievances suddenly seem entirely reasonable. Never is this more true than when Close delivers the line 'I'm not going to be *ignored*'.

For a while this line formed the basis of a running joke between me and an old schoolfriend. We'd add the acronym INGTBI to the end of emails, especially if the recipient happened to be the kind of man who'd use the term 'bunny boiler'. Then I noticed other women my age had a particular fondness for that scene, too. 'I just want to be part of your life,' pleads Alex, her voice rising. 'You won't answer my calls, you've changed your number. I mean, I'm not going to be *ignored*, Dan!' It speaks to us, especially with that stress on the penultimate word.

I am not suggesting all menopausal women – or even just the ones with whom I associate – identify with murderous stalkers. It's a metaphor (a menophor, if you will). It captures that feeling of having been fucked then ghosted by life itself. Feminism won't answer our calls, it's changed its number. When we protest, it tells us, in full-on patronising Michael Douglas mode, 'you don't get it, you just don't get it'. This is middle-aged womanhood in a nutshell, and there's no way of responding to the situation which will not be read as sinister, entitled and/or insane.

The cliché of middle-aged womanhood is that it's a time when we 'become invisible'. Alas, superpower fans, this does not happen. We are still here, same as always; it's just that we're being ignored. Other people are actively choosing not to acknowledge or value us. This ignoring is often talked of as a minor issue, perhaps even a perk of becoming decrepit (hey, at least we don't get catcalled any more!). Meaningful, positive attention is not on the cards for us; the implication is that any irritation we might now feel amounts to a hypocritical resentment at no longer being treated as sex objects. This trivialises what is being done to us and – bonus sexism – implies younger women secretly love being treated like pieces of meat and miss it when it's gone.

I write as one who fell for this. Mistakenly believing my impending 'invisibility' would indeed be a matter of escaping objectification, I assumed it would not bother me. I even allowed myself to feel a little superior to women who seemed more reluctant to let nature take its course. But this active ignoring is not the same as the end of objectification. You're still an object; you've just changed in status from painting or sculpture to, say, hat stand.

I have felt the shift over the past five or six years, as I've progressed from early to late forties: men my age or older speak to women younger than us both as though they are peers, while I am barely there at all. I struggle to edge into the conversation; I feel small and merely tolerated, as if I have walked in on a discussion not meant for me. Attempting to make myself heard feels ridiculous, as though I'm kidding myself that I've still 'got it', only now realising that 'it' incorporates my right to interact with others in public space.

In 1978 Susan Sontag coined the term 'the double standard of aging' to describe the way in which ageist sexism/sexist ageism impacts the status of women, particularly with regard to physical appearance. Since then, the pressure on women to look younger has not eased off; if anything, the increasing variety of ways in which to 'get work done' (for those who can afford it) has made the standard even more unforgiving.

Research is conducted, not just into double, but triple or more 'standards' faced by women as sexism and ageism intersect with lookism, classism, racism and other forms of discrimination. At forty-seven I am already beyond the age at which women reach their highest career earnings; were I a man I would, on average, have another ten years to go before reaching this peak. A BBC/Ofcom review in autumn 2018 found the under-representation of women on screen to be entirely down to low proportions of women in older age bands. As Nicky Clark, founder of the Acting Your Age campaign, documents, between 2000 and 2021 the average age for a male actor nominated for a BAFTA remained in the mid-forties, while for their female counterparts it fell to early thirties. She has also found that only 9 per cent of UK audiences can recognise more than fifteen women over forty-five, compared to 48 per cent when the question relates to men. The belief that we have less to offer, deserve fewer rewards and should ideally not be seen at all remains widespread.

This is frustrating not just because the problem itself – being ignored – defies attempts to draw attention to it, but because there are reasons why women my age might feel we have more to contribute than ever. As Rachel Shabi put it in a 2021 *Guardian* piece, 'women reach forty and hit their stride ... only to be cruelly shoved aside'. Disorientating though this is, I do not think it is random. The idea that middle-aged (and older) women's perspectives might be of value, not just on the male-default assumption that knowledge builds over time but because of what it means to experience sexism as a cumulative process across the female lifecycle, is of little interest even to mainstream feminism. This is humiliating and enraging, but should one push back, one risks only making it worse.

As luck would have it, I appear to have hit middle age at a point where efforts to counteract the ignoring of older women are being eagerly slapped down in the name of kind, virtuous conduct (though to be fair, the more I research, the more I find every era has its hag/shrew/mother-in-law/scold figure to wield piously against the inappropriately audible/visible older woman). In today's iteration of ageist sexism, 'complaining to the manager' and 'being entitled' have been identified as the key sins committed by middle-aged women, particularly (but not exclusively) white ones. Middle-aged women are, apparently, 'the worst online trolls', 'the worst drunks', or simply 'the worst'.

Naturally I have asked myself whether this is just one of these things that happens as you get older and find yourself out of touch with the Youth of Today. You no longer like the right music, your taste in clothing offends, people make Halloween masks based on your face and carry effigies of women like you being guillotined on protest marches. I've been told that 'suck my dick, you dried-up hag' is a gender-neutral insult, and that my own experiences of what it is to inhabit the social category 'woman' have been overwritten by fresher, more authentic ones. I've seriously asked myself whether trying to exist in public space, speak up for my cohort, meet with them, talk about the things we have learned, is actually the female equivalent of buying a massive, shiny motorbike and trading in your wife for a junior colleague half her age. For middle-aged women, could simply retaining an inner life and wanting to express it not constitute its own rather undignified midlife crisis? Who wants to be one of those 'women who dare to keep existing, speaking, and asking to see the manager, after their reproductive peak'? Wouldn't it be less embarrassing all round for us to hold our tongues?

That would, of course, be convenient. 'Yeah,' one interviewee tells me, 'because we're supposed to just fade away. And I don't think it's an accident that this is exactly the point where a woman's not-giving-a-fuckness really starts to kick in. Everyone's like, "we can't hear you". Or it's "we can hear you, but you're completely wrong and fortunately everyone like you is going to die out soon".' The cohort of women who report being talked over and ignored – who are demonstrably erased from public life and media representation – just so happen to be the cohort of women other people would like to shut up just that little bit more. Not only are we made to feel greedy and superfluous when we want to participate in everyday human interactions (rather than quietly getting on with our disproportionate share of unpaid labour), we are told 'yes, you are greedy and superfluous' when we do so. There is a cultural narrative which seeks to justify not only ignoring older women but demonising us when we act in ways which cannot be ignored (just like Alex, even though we're not actually cooking family pets). A moral case is being made for silencing us, one which scapegoats us for bad behaviour which is not unique to our group and makes crimes of traits that in other people would be seen as independence, self-assertion or empowerment. After two brief decades of being told 'you go, girl!', suddenly it's 'hang on, we didn't mean *you!*'

All in all, it's enough to drive any woman Alexwards. Writing this book is my alternative to boiling the bunny.

INGTBI.

Defining hag hate

People are dismissive of older women. We know this already, not least because many of us have been dismissive of older women before realising – too late! – that we'd become such creatures ourselves. I often feel like the person in that well-known meme: 'I never thought leopards would eat *my* face,' sobs woman who voted for the Leopards Eating People's Faces Party. I never saw the vilification of older women as something that could happen to me because I felt – in a way that is inexplicable but not uncommon in the face of suffering that could one day be yours – that the villains had brought it on themselves. I'm not alone in having thought this way. It's one of patriarchy's perfect self-perpetuating cycles: the demonisation of older women ensures we do not wish to identify with or learn from them, so cannot gain any knowledge to prepare us for our own experience of ageing. Instead we turn away from our future selves.*

In approaching this topic now, I do not wish merely to present the myriad ways in which older women are belittled, undermined or misrepresented. This is not intended as a compendium of ageism-flavoured misogyny/misogyny-flavoured ageism, served up for the sole purpose of proving it exists (and getting cross about it, though there will be that). I want to draw links between past and present, with feminist history and politics, in order to ask why this particular separation of women from other women and their own older selves keeps happening, and what's different – or not – in how it is manifested today. Middle-aged women are not just a particular type of woman; to many we represent an important stage in political narratives regarding the nature of womanhood, and of progress and decline. Ageist misogyny has always existed; what I think is different now, and what makes it more intractable, is that it frequently masquerades as feminism.

Right now we are experiencing a backlash against feminist gains, and middle-aged women form a perfect target for

---

* This is not true of all younger women, some of whom I have interviewed in the process of writing this book, and some of whom suggested the hostility and disidentification of their peers is not as sincere as it may seem. I do not want to suggest all younger women are as I was; they are not. What I would say is that I understand those who are.

hostility. As the philosopher Kate Manne argues, you do not need to express misogynistic views or behave in a misogynistic manner towards all women all the time in order to chip away at the freedom of women as a class: 'one woman can often serve as a stand-in or representative for a whole host of others in the misogynist imagination'. Men who hate middle-aged women hate all women; nonetheless, in their everyday interactions it can be useful for them to grant younger ones a temporary reprieve.

To be openly, consistently anti-feminist can be socially and politically inconvenient. Rather than attack feminism itself – something which, according to the viewpoint your politics requires you to endorse, is either 'on the right side of history' or has already taken over – it is easier to weed out the women who have aged beyond feminism's promise and been found wanting. In this way, younger women can be told certain forms of misogynist aggression and marginalisation are a temporary measure; it will not happen to them because they are different. This assurance hints at a stance many of us have detected in recent years within otherwise progressive circles: feminism will be great, once we've cleared away the debris, the old women, the bad feminists. Once we're rid of the bigots who spoil the party, bad fairies at the christening, our purified souls will ascend to feminist heaven. The process will be painful, but it's the right thing, the feminist thing, to do, because after the witches are burned, women will be worthy of the equality they've always craved. The trouble is that there are so many witches, and yes, the majority might share certain qualities – not least in terms of age and social role – with innocent victims of witch trials of yore, but that's just coincidence. This time the witches are guilty as charged.

The ageist misogyny directed at middle-aged women today – or hag hate, as I have come to think of it – is insidious because it enables deeply regressive beliefs about what women should be (young, beautiful, feminine, fertile, fuckable) to be recast as progressive. There are those who will claim that it's not middle-aged women who are the problem, just *these* middle-aged women, here, now, who are *particularly* trouble-some. It's regrettable, but Generation X women just so happen to fit a template which is every misogynist's dream, while also possessing enough freedom to make the misogyny they do experience look like something they have chosen, either in return for other privileges or because they are simply too ignorant to understand how misogyny works. Older women, just by virtue of being older, are associated with a 'more sexist' past and thus appear complicit in a sexism which is on its way out. They are 'dinosaurs'. Raging against them can feel like a break with the patriarchal past. The target of misogyny becomes an emblem for it. Get rid of her, and the problem is solved.

Who can be a perpetrator of hag hate? Anyone at all. There are the men, of course, and these include both the tradition-alists, who slot us into the battleaxe/mother-in-law/shrew categories, and the self-styled progressives, who prefer to portray us as ill-educated bigots, essentialist mummies or mis-erable prudes. The first group has tended to see this as a fixed stage, with shrewishness eventually coming to all women, while the latter favours the more feminism-friendly cohort-based analysis, suggesting that once we are gone an all-new, better brand of middle-aged woman will come to take our place. Both portrayals of older women, while superficially dif-ferent, serve a similar purpose, policing the divisions between generations of women and ensuring women's accumulated work and experiences can be easily dismissed.

The internalised ageist misogyny of women themselves – both younger ones who do not want to acknowledge the thread that connects them to older women, and older ones who do not wish to be seen as 'like all the others' – develops in proximity to male power. Difficult truths about the oppression of women – that, unlike other oppressed groups, we are not a minority, and that the particular nature of our oppression is shaped by the status of the men in our lives, some of whom we may love – influence the way in which internalised misogyny and ageism interact. Discomfort with our own powerlessness and dependency on the men of our own social milieu can translate into rage at the older woman who is like us, but more embedded, more complicit, the Aunt Lydia to our Offred. It can feel as though the only way to access true sisterhood is by rejecting her.

If misogyny differs from other forms of oppression due to women's relationships with men, then ageism differs from other forms of discrimination due to the fact all of us will experience both sides of the young/old divide. Unless we die young, each young person slowly becomes an old one, and there is no way around this, no means of changing direction or halting the course.* This difference informs the themes which have emerged as I have explored the topic: shame, fear, privilege, dependency, memory, progress versus regression, renewal versus legacy. Both political and deeply personal, these themes are woven through not just how we relate to other people, but how we relate to our own histories and bodies. The older woman, to quote the title of Marilyn Pearsall's 1997 anthology of feminist writing on ageing, is 'the other within us'. If we are taught to fear her, we are taught to fear our future selves.

From the moment we are born female, we are conditioned to feel ashamed not just of our appearance, our biology and

---

* Or, as many have observed, this starts out as a slow transition, then suddenly appears to have happened all at once.

our desires, but also of other women and our connection to them. A measure of this shame is the hesitation I felt at even typing 'born female', as if to state that innate bond is to tie women down, lumping them together with creatures they might not wish to be. It is impossible to have a feminist class politics as long as we are in denial over what it is we have in common. More than that, it is impossible to feel honestly, truly at one with yourself and the space you occupy as long as you are living in fear of your own potential, the woman you might become. As a form of pseudo-feminism, hag hate provides a means to pacify that fear and shame by projecting it onto the older woman, as though by doing so one has found a way to be delivered from her fate. It's a shaky means – deep down, we all know we will age, too – hence if we are going to disidentify, we must disidentify hard. We must find or manufacture differences that appear impossible to overcome.

That feminism has a tendency to trash the past, setting fire to its own legacy in order to start afresh – a process Susan Faludi has dubbed its 'ritual matricide' – is hardly a new observation. What I had not understood is how closely connected this is to our knowledge that, in the eyes of mainstream society, the not-young woman becomes trash herself. Women who went before us are an embarrassment. In late 2020 a tweet comparing Covid-19 to feminism went viral, declaring both to have 'problematic second waves'. The young female tweeter gained multiple likes and follows, which may be of less practical use than the equal pay legislation and domestic violence shelters created by second-wavers, but at least they are clean. The longer you live, and the harder you fight, the dirtier your hands become.

Hag hate is related to loser stigma. This is touched on in Caitlin Moran's 2011 bestseller *How to Be a Woman*, in which she argues that 'most sexism is down to men being accustomed to us being the losers'. I know this feeling of loser-dom, the way in which it can creep up on you, whispering in your ear 'maybe women don't have power because we're genuinely inferior'. Once you start down that road, you begin to wonder whether women really count as victims of oppression at all. A temporary solution can be to concede that women *were* inferior, but won't be in future. We're not victims so much as failures, and as long as our failure can be treated as generation- rather than lifecycle-specific – something that describes us, as opposed to something done to us – the promise of a better, more equal future can be dangled in front of those who come after. All they have to do is be nothing like us (we could tell them that's what we were advised, too, but we're losers, so we would say that).

In the chapters that follow, I'm going to look at a number of areas – beauty, the body, unpaid work, progress, sex, community, power, violence – in terms of how they are experienced by women in midlife, and how other groups exploit, scapegoat and demonise middle-aged women in order to preserve favoured narratives. Misogyny is not just hatred enacted on women, but the means of defending stories about what women are in order to entrench male dominance. Nice men are as likely as unrepentant sexists to have their stories; younger women turn to them, too. The middle-aged woman becomes a repository of sorts, a holding area for ugliness, female inferiority, bigotry, failure, obsolescence, not just to indulge the traditionalist, but so that the progressive might see himself creating space around her in which others can flourish. After decades of feminism being sold as a project which can only be good for men, the expectation that men sacrifice space themselves, taking ownership of their own dirt and failings, is unthinkable. In this sense, 'being hag' is another form of housework, a way of keeping things – in this case, the progress narrative of gender liberation – neat and tidy despite mounting evidence that things are not going women's way.

In the words of Arch Hag J. K. Rowling, 'We're living through the most misogynistic period I've experienced [...] Everywhere, women are being told to shut up and sit down, or else.' Some women, in some locations, have made significant gains over the course of the past century, but the pushback is enormous, facilitated by the tech industry and made palatable to those with progressive leanings by the spectre of bad women who are undeserving of feminism's spoils. This is not the gentle resistance of an unreconstructed minority, but a slick, rebranded backlash which actively seeks to incite and legitimise fear and disgust. Just as hardcore pornography does with regard to young female bodies, hag hate provides a 'culturally approved script' to legitimise extreme fantasies of violence against older women. As was the case in historical witch hunts, pornographic violence against women can be made to seem virtuous; the worse the things you want to do to her, the worse she is, and older women are being made to look very bad indeed.

My intention is not to suggest older women are politically pure. We are people with flaws like everyone else. What I challenge is the way in which our flaws are used to further beliefs about women which are then used to withhold power from us, make us unsafe and keep us divided. Misogyny directed at older women is not just one particular flavour of misogyny. It is, in the end, a catch-all, a misogyny directed if not at the self you already are, then the one you will one day be. It's hatred not just of women in the world as they are now, but of dreams, hopes and desires. It clouds our vision by making us ashamed to see our reflections.

Who is a hag?

This book is for all women because the demonisation of older women affects all women. It interrupts the passing down of knowledge and undermines the foundations of a consistent, inclusive feminist politics, one that reaches across the divisions constructed by our complex allegiances to the men of our own culture and class. Younger women are being disadvantaged by the relationships they will not form and the stories they will not hear. 'The generation gap,' wrote Audre Lorde, 'is an important tool for any repressive society [...] We find ourselves having to repeat and relearn the same old lessons over and over that our mothers did because we do not pass on what we have learned, or because we are unable to listen.' There are vast bodies of feminist scholarship in economics, politics, literary studies, philosophy, science and history, and countless models for revolutionary activism, which women either do not know about or are taught to dismiss because they are the work of woman past, and woman past does not count. This harms all of us.

Nonetheless, the main focus of this book is a particular cohort of women at a particular point in time: middle-aged women as opposed to those who are simply older. I am thinking of Generation X women, those born between 1965 and 1980, who at the time of writing will be in their forties and fifties. Generational boundaries are to a degree arbitrary (a Generation Xer born in 1980 will have more in common with a Millennial born in 1981 than an Xer born in 1965). A good deal will be relevant to older women in general, and sometimes to younger women who find their conduct has put them on the fast track to hagdom (in *Difficult Women*, Helen Lewis recalls being told 'I was out of touch because I was middle-aged' at the age of twenty-nine). Nonetheless, there are two reasons why I want to prioritise my own generation of women (I was born in 1975) when discussing what it means to be a hag.

The first is cohort-specific: that is, to do with what it means to belong to that group of women who started to come of age just as feminism's second wave had crashed in the eighties. Although often lumped together with second-wavers on account of being 'old', today's middle-aged women were not the contemporaries of second-wave feminists but the first batch of young women to deal with this iteration of feminism's aftermath. Rebecca Walker, daughter of the novelist and activist Alice Walker, wrote the essay 'Becoming the Third Wave' for *Ms* magazine in 1992, calling for a new age of activism for a new generation. For all its optimism, this 'new' feminism found its identity in pushing back against the 'old', on both personal (familial) levels and structural ones. The post-'sex wars' period of the nineties saw the rise of raunch feminism, do-me feminism, power feminism, post-feminism, girl power and a whole host of other capitalist misappropriations of women's liberation. Much of what we learned about feminism's very recent past was inaccurate, just as much of what is told about us is inaccurate today. There are three interesting stories here: first, how the lives of older women were presented to us, shaping our identities not in dialogue with but in opposition to them, as though the principal gain of our mothers' feminism was that it might enable us to be better (more sexually available, more intelligent, less complicit) than them; second, what it means to grow up both benefiting from and feeling driven to disidentify from a female legacy; third, what it now means to try to pass on one's own knowledge and experience at a time when the entire concept of women having any single thing in common is considered unfashionably second wave.

Generation X – 'a low-slung, straight-line bridge between two noisy behemoths', the Boomers and the Millennials – carries its own weird problem-child status into feminism itself. Slackers to the last, many of us were too enamoured with disidentification to forge an independent identity for ourselves, and now find ourselves told that the viewpoints it has taken us half a lifetime to work towards are on the verge of dying out. These days I find myself wanting to tell younger women that I was finding second-wavers problematic before they were born. If anyone tried to kill the mother, it was my generation. The trouble is, we still got older, and experiences – some of them specific to our generation, but others more specific to our sex – changed us and our politics. The ageist misogyny we encounter now is not our fault – it was in the air we breathed – but it has flourished in attitudes we helped to shape.

The second reason for this book's focus on middle-aged women is to do with the simple fact that we are not the same as old women.* One particularly insidious form of ageism is that which conflates the experiences of any person over forty into one great mass of 'being not-young'. Issues such as the care crisis and the feminisation of poverty affect middle-aged and old women differently, in some cases furthering divisions between us. Feminist analysis must avoid replicating the ageism often found in business and advertising, whereby women under fifty are subdivided into different groups with specific desires, while those over fifty are one undifferentiated market segment. There is as much of an age gap between me and women in their early twenties as there is between me and the contributors to *Not Dead Yet*, Renate Klein and Susan

---

* As if to demonstrate what the latter are up against, here I have misgivings about using what should be the perfectly neutral term 'old women', given the ageist and sexist associations ('you're like an old woman' etc.).

Hawthorne's 2021 anthology of feminist writing in which every contributor was aged over seventy. My experience of feminism, of the body, of being read as 'not young' and of cumulative inequality is different from theirs. While I'm keen to make use of the knowledge and insights of the women who went before me, the differences between us are also part of how and why women struggle to pass on a female and feminist legacy.

My experience of being a middle-aged woman is significantly affected by the fact that I am white, middle class, heterosexual and have children. I list these things neither to downplay the social and embodied experiences middle-aged women share, nor in an effort to absolve myself for any implicit or explicit bias in the pages that follow. The privilege of women such as myself means that we are often viewed as the default middle-aged woman. It also means that our privilege can be a conduit through which to attack all middle-aged women (I know numerous working-class lesbians and child-free women who have found themselves treated as honorary heterosexual middle-class mummies in the name of hag hate). While this does not make being viewed as the default middle-aged women any less advantageous, it does make the work of challenging hag hate more complex and fraught. I will outline some particular areas of concern below, and in more detail in Chapter Seven, but know that this cannot form the basis of a back-covering exercise.

In writing about middle-aged womanhood I am writing about a life stage shaped by the accumulation of experiences, responsibilities and dependencies. By the time they reach their mid-forties, around 80 per cent of UK women will have had at least one child, an experience which will have had a significant effect on their bodies, finances, relationships and social status. This still leaves another 20 per cent who do not have children, and face other forms of discrimination and social censure. 'If a woman has kids, she will always be a mother,' writes Dorthe Nors, 'but a woman who has chosen not to procreate and who now no longer is young and sexy is perceived by many as a pointless being.' I do not wish to downplay the challenges faced by middle-aged women who do not have children, whether or not by choice. Nor do I wish to conflate middle-aged womanhood with older motherhood. However, both the practical marginalisation of women who become mothers (again, whether or not by choice) and readings of middle-aged women through the lens of maternal stereotype influence how all older women are viewed. Not all of us are mothers, but almost all younger adults experience their closest relationship with a middle-aged woman via their mothers. The all-powerful Eternal Mummy – be she nurturing and caring, or judgemental and restrictive – has a face like ours.

In addition, I believe that the physical, social, economic and psychological impact of pregnancy, birth and caring for offspring has to form part of the knowledge base that is shared between women across generations. These experiences are not meaningless, and it would be a mistake to exclude them from any analysis of the female lifecycle, as though by shaving off any experience not shared by all female people we reach something perfect and pure (which would be patriarchy's ideal woman, for she has no experiences around which to form either an inner life or a collective politics). For many women, the visceral experiences of pregnancy and birth, not to mention the long-term aftermath, transform their understanding of sex, gender and the body. These are not the only experiences that might do so, but they help us to understand why older women might have different views to younger ones on, for instance, the political salience of biological sex. It is more than a matter of older women having views that are 'out of date'. Older women have views that are informed by a variety of different experiences, and these experiences deserve to be understood not as creating bias or triggering prejudice, but as adding to a lifetime's knowledge base. Chapters Three and Six look particularly closely at middle-aged women as mothers of older children (in the first case, in relation to their role as carers, and in the second, as a political group).

I am conscious that some older women may feel that their own views have not been influenced by the ageing process, and that accusations of being 'out of touch' or on 'the wrong side of history' apply to some older women, but not them. They may even feel that questioning the demonisation of other older women is 'playing the ageist misogyny card'. That is their right and I would not wish to taint the politically pure by lumping them together with hags like me. I would, however, argue that as long as being middle aged and female is associated with having the 'wrong' views, it is not acceptable to deny feminists the right to ask why some middle-aged women might hold views that others present as wrong, or to examine what these views really are and how far they may have been misrepresented. Otherwise we are left with Schrödinger's middle-aged hag, who is allowed to exist when others attack her, but not when she is defending herself, whereupon she shifts from known type to isolated individual.

At times – particularly in Chapter Seven – this book focuses on the experiences of white middle-aged women.* There are a number of 'progressive' criticisms of middle-aged women which are specific to white women, particularly in relation to the 'Karen' figure, whom dictionary.com describes as 'an obnoxious, angry, entitled, and often racist middle-aged white woman who uses her privilege to get her way or police other

---

* There will be other times when it does so as a consequence of my own unconscious bias, for which I apologise. Here, however, the focus is deliberate.

people's behaviours'. Although there is a part of me that would very much like to use my own white privilege to gloss over this part of hag hate, I would rather risk accusations of Karen-ing myself than pretend this is not an issue. I am afraid of getting things wrong, and I will get things wrong, but to have the choice not to lay oneself on the line – or to simply offer up other white women for a kicking, in the hope that this makes me look less racist – is itself a facet of white privilege. It's easy for women like me to become the middle-class, left-wing version of the conservative white woman described by Lorde, who deludes herself that 'if you are good enough, pretty enough, sweet enough, quiet enough, teach the children to behave, hate the right people, and marry the right men, then you will be allowed to co-exist with patriarchy in relative peace'. It's equally untrue that if you are performatively apologetic enough, self-censoring enough, teach the children that reproductive biology doesn't exist, hate the right other white women, and worship the right ageing leftist white men, then you will be allowed to exist in public without being seen to get your privileged white hands dirty. Our hands are already dirty. We owe less privileged women more than fudging arguments in the hope no one finds us problematic. That unproblematic ship has already sailed.

Ageing is not a great leveller between women. Some of the differences between us can become more stark; for instance, if I am to write of 'pension poverty' or the 'feminisation of poverty' as it accumulates over a lifetime, these phrases can mask the way in which middle-class women like me do not experience the same precarity, exploitation and deprivation that build over the lifetimes of working-class women. The experience of motherhood, the age at which one might first become a mother, and the size and structure of one's family will be influenced by factors such as race, socio-economic status and sexual orientation. 'Class and racial privileges serve to undercut the ability of women to see themselves as part of a coherent group, which, in fact, they are not, since women uniquely of all oppressed groups occur in all strata of society,' wrote Gerda Lerner in *The Creation of Patriarchy*. Ageism is weaponised against women to prevent us from seeing what we have in common and thereby developing a feminist conscious-ness, but in order to resist we must recognise the differences between us. When I write about middle-aged women, I will not always be writing about all middle-aged women. To claim otherwise would be to misrepresent and exclude purely for the sake of a neatly packaged argument.

Many of the writers who have had the greatest impact on my thinking about women and ageing – women such as Adrienne Rich, Audre Lorde, Sheila Jeffreys and Baba Copper – are lesbians, but the perspective from which I write is heterosexual. To me this is significant because much of what I feel heterosexual women experience when we hit middle age – the spite that arises when men deem us to have served our purpose and wonder why we are still here – les-bians experience much earlier, and more harshly due to their uncompromising withdrawal from men. I regret that this is not something I noticed earlier, and that from a lesbian per-spective, some of what I describe may prompt the question 'it took you that long to catch on?' I'm afraid it did, and for that I am sorry.

That said, from an early age, girls are taught to apologise a great deal: for taking up space, for having needs of our own, for just not being male. Apology as female affect can function as a defence strategy, signalling to men that we know our place, that we are no threat, that, maybe, they can afford to grant us a little more room. Older women tend to be less reflexively apologetic, for numerous reasons: our forced exit

from a sexual marketplace which directed us towards prioritising men's needs in return for higher status, our increased
reliance on female networks, perhaps even hormonal changes.
'I don't want to do performative kindness,' one friend tells
me. 'As you get older, there's less time to fuck about.' The
flipside of this is that when we say sorry, we mean it. We're
less likely to recite the social justice catechisms, falling over
ourselves to make sure no one thinks we are terrible people
(we're hags, so they're going to think we're terrible anyway).
It is for this reason that, while I apologise for any ways in
which the chapters that follow misread or exclude some
groups of middle-aged women, or make sweeping statements
about middle-aged womanhood that really apply only to a
subgroup, I do not apologise for the overall intent, which is
to centre and prioritise middle-aged women in the context of
the oppression of women as a class.

We matter. Middle-aged women do not have to represent,
include or step aside for every other person before we claim
space for ourselves.

The hag and her imitators

There will be some who argue there's never been a better
time to be an ageing hag. 'Hags are cool, man,' writes Caitlin
Moran in 2020's *More Than a Woman*. I get this, I really do.
The figure of the witch or hag has long served as, to quote
Kristen J. Sollée, 'a martyr mascot for the women's movement'. There's something deliciously confrontational about
the darkness and ugliness of witches in a world where women
are expected to be pretty, compliant and eternally young. As
the historian Susannah Lipscomb puts it, 'the powerless have
always wanted to be feared'.

It might seem particularly fitting for today's middle-aged women – the cohort for whom 'ironic' sexism was invented – to seek to embrace the status that's going to be imposed on us anyway. When I see articles claiming that 'women are invoking the witch to find their power in a patriarchal society' there's a part of me that thinks, Yes! Just like we used to! Only with Wonderbras! And when British *Vogue* starts to enthuse over the way in which 'women are reclaiming this once heretic identity', I'm reminded of all the dogged 'reclaiming' of my Britpop years. 'Long gone are the antiquated stereotypes of witches practising black magic (bad), or white magic (good); modern witches can be whatever they choose.' It seems choice feminism didn't die; she just put on a pointy hat.

'It's a far cry from the Salem Witch trials,' adds *Vogue*, helpfully. This is, I think, part of the problem with any willed reclamation of the hag. A chosen identity is never the same as a social reality, just as a chosen aesthetic cannot dictate how others perceive you. I fear the 'witchcore' of Gen Z TikTokers may not convey the same message on a woman in her forties or fifties, especially if her way of being a 'feisty independent woman' involves disagreeing with said TikTokers about literally anything to do with womanhood. It's all fun and games till the moment you find yourself tied to the ducking stool, wondering how you got there. I recall that sensation from my own flirtations with raunch feminism, when I'd realise a simulation of rebellion had gone too far, and that I was about to be punished for behaving as though the game really was one I could win. That moment when you suddenly see it's not bantz; call yourself what you like, but when others call you a witch or a slut, they mean it. We can act as though the words can be fully reclaimed, but they can't. Those who dislike and fear us are using them too.

As Mary Beard points out in *Women & Power*, 'we have

not got anywhere near subverting those foundational stories of power that serve to keep women out of it, and turning them to our own advantage'. Referring to the example of Medusa, she notes that 'despite the well-known feminist attempts over the last fifty years or more to reclaim [her] for female power [...] it has made not a blind bit of difference to the way she has been used in attacks on female politicians'. As with Gorgons, so with hags. This book is not a celebration of our hag status. Both the history of witch hunts and the witch figure in fairy tales tell us something about attitudes to older women which have not gone away. She is presumed to be powerful – or privileged, one might now say – all the better to vilify her.

There is a generational aspect to hag-shaming that gets lost when younger feminists 'invoke the witch as a statement of strength and empowerment'. As soon as your edginess can be subsumed into a mainstream narrative, particularly one which venerates youth, it isn't edginess any more. 'Like many millennial women,' writes Sollée, 'I see a reclamation of female power in the witch, slut, and feminist identities.' Yet to me the first two look less like identities, more like imposed statuses; less like a reclamation of power, more like a drain on our resources. It is easier to fetishise the trappings of stigma than it is to embrace those to whom it is genuinely attached. Today's resurgence of interest in transgressive womanhood permits a superficial indulgence of difference which does little to change the underlying power structure.

When I picture today's hag, I don't see someone who is an easily defined outsider, neat to categorise and ripe for rehabilitation, but someone who inhabits an uneasy space between perfectly mundane and beyond the pale. She's not called Maleficent or Serafina or Elphaba, but Sharon or Carol or, yes, Karen. The older woman with the bad haircut who talks too much, who oscillates between seeming to have infinite power and having none at all. The woman who inspires disgust in those who pride themselves on rising above such instinctive responses. The woman who unsettles stable categories not by what she wears or what she asks to be called, but by refusing to efface herself beyond the age of thirty-five.

We love the idea of the outspoken, boundary-defying woman in stories, rather than in the (ageing, decaying) flesh. Reworked fairy tales, feminist dystopias, historical rehabilitations – too often these enable a performative embrace of the Bad Woman, who is, inevitably, not all that bad by modern-day standards. There's comfort in believing that we, unlike the villains of our tales, would find space in our hearts for the condemned witch. This celebration of a stylised female darkness demands no moral or social compromise on our part. It allows us to see ourselves as people who would speak up on behalf of the outsider, should the need arise. So convinced are we of this, we can treat every real-life woman accused of witchery as a real witch – otherwise, wouldn't we have said something? In the world of fiction we might see numerous new books – Madeline Miller's *Circe*, Alix E. Harrow's *The Once and Future Witches*, the reworked folk-tale anthology *Hag*, Kiran Millwood Hargrave's *The Mercies* – which explore the relationship between femaleness, witchcraft, creativity and demonisation, but this does not necessarily make for an easy working environment for the older female author.

There's a bloodlessness to the liberal feminist rehabilitation of the witch. When the actress Emma Watson, presenting an award at the 2022 BAFTAs, declared she was 'here for *all* of the witches', this was taken to be a dig at the older, supposedly 'exclusionary' J. K. Rowling. Yet in taking on the role of the younger woman denouncing the older woman who nurtured her, Watson was really signalling that *she* wasn't a witch: *I only played Hermione. Burn the author, not me.*

Commercialised hag culture has given us a love of women talking about women talking – but not a love of women talking about anything else. Misogyny flourishes in spaces where it can be made to appear virtuous. It takes far more courage to defend the women of Mumsnet or the latest victim of internet hag-shaming than it does to cheer on the garrulous hag of folklore. As long as this narrative of subversion is strictly controlled, any liberation it provides is illusory. I suspect one of the reasons that it is easy for younger feminists to defend the fictional or historical hag is precisely because she isn't here now. In fairy tales, the only good mother is a dead one; in feminism, the only good older feminist is a dead witch. Through her, you can imagine a world in which older women are not just powerful but are able to have strong bonds with their younger counterparts. The dead witch's wickedness is perfectly contained; living, breathing hags are, by contrast, too messy and flawed. They just won't stick to the script.

Are middle-aged women women?

And now, some housekeeping. In recent years it has become customary to introduce any work self-centred enough to focus on mere women with musings on what a woman even is. The same is not done for books on men (or, as they're usually known, books). It is women who are obliged to justify their existence by qualifying it to within an inch of its life. Best get on with it, then.

As has been made clear, this book is about a particular subset of this already shonky category: the middle-aged woman. For this group, the question 'what is a woman anyway?' brings its own unique set of challenges. It won't do to start with what *sort* of woman we are, leading to a shamefaced, if cursory, analysis of whom this includes and whom it excludes. First we must establish whether being female and middle aged means we count as women to start with.

It might surprise you to learn that there's a body of literature that insists we do not. In his 1966, pro-HRT bestseller *Feminine Forever*, the physician Robert A. Wilson proposed that menopause makes a woman 'the equivalent of a eunuch', with women approaching their fifties experiencing 'the death of their own womanhood during what should be their best years'. Such a view was backed up by the psychiatrist David R. Reuben in 1969's *Everything You Always Wanted to Know About Sex But Were Afraid to Ask*. According to Reuben, the postmenopausal woman comes 'as close as she can to being a man' (but before you get excited, there are limits: 'not really a man, but no longer a functional woman'). HRT, then in its infancy, promised to make us poor castrates real women again, thus equating womanhood with femininity. It would be good to think that over fifty years later we've moved on from such regressive beliefs, but I am not sure that is true.

'What I'm witnessing,' Lucy, an academic in her fifties, tells me, 'is just the shrinking and shrinking of what is interpretable as a woman.' As the philosopher Janet Radcliffe Richards put it, 'much of what is believed about women stems from what is wanted of women'. Are women complete human beings, with our own socialised and embodied experiences, our stories forever changing as we move through time? Or are we a cobbled-together, pick-and-mix range of woman-y offerings, most of which fall into decay as we age? Is a woman really a woman when there's nothing more for men to take from or project onto her? When she might, in fact, seem to be on the verge of living for herself?

In 1991's *The Change*, Germaine Greer argued that men 'see menopause as the cancellation of the only important female functions, namely attracting, stimulating, gratifying and nurturing men and/or children'. While some might counter that the 2020s are witnessing a brave new womanhood free-for-all, what we find, on closer inspection, is the reinscription of a social construct to exclude what older women are, and include everything we are not. The groundwork for this was already laid with the alliterative *Feminine Forever*; then as now, it's all about the Fs. The one F all middle-aged women retain – femaleness – pales into insignificance with the loss of the Fs that matter most to patriarchy: fertility, femininity, fuckability. Standards for 'being a woman' are more rigid than ever; it's just that the 'female' part has been more fully excised, all the better to dismiss those of us whose very existence might put all the other Fs in question (if the unfeminine are women, too, then there's nothing essentially feminine about women at all).

This book argues that ageing while female remains a deeply unsettling transgression, albeit not one that those who tend to celebrate transgression are wont to celebrate very much. At a time when the very meaning of 'woman' is being openly debated, older women are well and truly screwing things up. Neither reproductively useful enough for conservative definitions, nor feminine enough for social or pornified ones, here we are, still insisting on both our humanity and our womanhood. It is inconvenient, to say the least, even if recent years have witnessed some valiant attempts to square the circle. In her 2019 memoir *Flash Count Diary*, Darcey Steinke describes how 'during menopause I slip out from under a claustrophobic femininity. But I also don't feel fully masculine. I feel in the middle, a third gender. They.' You and me both, Darcey. Only this dutiful handing back of the woman card does not strike me as altogether different from being stripped of it by hormone-toting physicians and psychiatrists half a century ago. Both are responses to the fact, not that we are no longer women but that, as women, we are no longer what men want us to be. And in certain men, this provokes rage.

Perhaps you are thinking, sure, but it isn't all *that* bad. We often hear that middle-aged women are 'finally' finding a voice, in much the same way that masculinity is 'now' in crisis, and young people are 'suddenly' rejecting traditional gender roles. 'The days when women of a certain age were expected to fade into the wallpaper, wearing beige Crimplene and accepting they had reached their sell-by date, are no more than a memory,' reports a *Guardian* article from 1999, when I was twenty-four and quite oblivious to whatever middle-aged woman-quake was apparently on the horizon. Now, more than two decades later, the *Telegraph* reports that 'menopause is having a MeToo moment'. Numerous how-to guides are appearing to once more defend a woman's right to exist as a biological entity moving through time. The central message seems to be 'we're not that bad. With a bit of spit and polish, and maybe some needles, we might even be desirable again! Triple-F womanhood – or a simulation of the fertile, feminine, fuckable self – is ours for the taking.' The inherent classism of this (being a middle-aged woman who doesn't 'seem' middle aged costs money) isn't the only, or even the main problem. It's that we were fine to begin with. Today's middle-aged woman isn't a new, improved version of yesterday's, who never quite made the womanhood grade. We have always been fine. That we do not see this is testimony to the way in which the patriarchal tail is still wagging the womanhood dog.

Women are not supposed to be what older women are, and middle-aged women occupy a particularly discomfiting, in-between space. As my friend Marina says, 'when you are no longer desirable for sexual service and no longer capable of reproductive labour, what are you for? The expectation is that you disappear, and the fact that we don't disappear freaks people out.' We are uncanny, causing discomfort by failing to conform to the standards others have set for us. We are also, most inconveniently, the future of each and every woman on the planet.

1

UGLY HAG

Is a woman entirely alive, or only the parts of her that are young and 'beautiful'?

Naomi Wolf, *The Beauty Myth*

Of course it's true that now that I'm older, I'm wise and sage and mellow. And it's also true that I honestly do understand just what matters in life. But guess what? It's my neck.

Nora Ephron, *I Feel Bad About My Neck*

I did not plan to devote the first chapter of this book to beauty and its decline. This is, I told myself, a serious analysis of the social and political status of middle-aged women, not another 'pro-age' guide to making oneself marginally less repulsive to polite society. Beauty is transient and frivolous, and I know nothing about peels, fillers or a host of other 'non-invasive' treatments guaranteed to turn a hot flush into a sexy glow. I was tempted to skip the topic, heading straight for meatier matters: work, money, sex, violence, death. But a woman's appearance is also a meaty matter, perhaps the meatiest of all.

Female flesh, notes Eimear McBride, undergoes a process of 'meatification' under the male gaze. We, as older women, do not escape this; rather, we are 'persistently reminded of the undesirability of [our] brand of meatiness'. We might not think we have chosen to gain those extra grey hairs, pounds and wrinkles, but our changing presentation will be considered no less offensive for it. 'If it is a gaffe to be plain,' writes Jane Shilling in her memoir of middle age, *The Stranger in the Mirror*, 'it is a pure affront to grow older.'

One is not born, but becomes, a middle-aged woman, and it starts on the outside. First the neck, then the mouth, then the daily surprise of body parts that you never felt were particularly 'young' suddenly being no longer so. You can claim not to care, which might be possible if you live in complete isolation from the rest of human society. If not, you must join the rest of us, knowing that how we look as women situates us in relation to everyone else, locating us in a hierarchy and determining our position in the marketplace of the three Fs. It shapes our interactions and dictates what we must do to be noticed, and how our words and actions are perceived thereafter. It influences how we feel and what we believe, not because we are vain or trivial, but because it alters what cut of meat we are on the patriarchal table.

Enter any branch of Boots or Superdrug and behold how many treatments there are for that terrible sickness, growing old while female. It doesn't matter that none of the treatments work. Buying them is a ritual act of submission. That serum won't transform your face, but handing over the cash shows willing. It's a joke, but one in which we tread a very fine line between 'laughing with' and 'being laughed at'. We might never have wanted to attract male attention, or we might have long ceased wanting any more, but a sizeable number of us continue to behave 'as if'. The performance of 'vanity' is both a form of degradation and an attempt to maintain status; the one informs the other in a feedback loop of ever-increasing shame.

It ought to have got easier. It is more than thirty years since Naomi Wolf wrote *The Beauty Myth*, more than two hundred since Mary Wollstonecraft picked apart the gilded-cage bullshit that is femininity in *A Vindication of the Rights of Woman*. Yet somehow it's got harder, and it's the narrative that says we're more tolerant of self-expression that makes it so. Treatments abound; we're now 'allowed' to be more sexy; no one judges the woman who's had 'work done'. We try to be supportive of everyone's right to look like their 'true self'. Only the path to universal acceptance is not so straightforward, not least because it turns out that few people think their true self looks like a middle-aged woman. If self-presentation is a facet of social identity, what does it mean to move through the world as a woman who has aged beyond how she might imagine her 'true self' to appear? If identity is fluid and malleable, why would anyone consent to look frumpy, unfashionable, out of time, if that isn't who she really is? Like many older women, I catch glimpses of myself and think, no, that isn't me. This person I see is coded so differently from the self I imagine myself to be.

It's not that we are entirely misread. Even if one grants that one is not the sum of one's looks, it is true that looking older, for women, signals a change in our perspective. How can you not be a different person when your relationship with others has altered so dramatically? Except now this change in perspective merges with contemporary beliefs about choice and identity. Women I have spoken to have described the way in which their middle-aged appearance is used to dismiss their politics, in much the same way 'hairy-legged' feminists and 'ugly' suffragettes were written off in years gone by. There are memes that connect our haircuts and body shapes to bigotry, revealing the conviction that what has aged us is not time but our belonging to a cohort of women who are politically beyond redemption (unlike the next batch, who will remain forever young, both morally and aesthetically).

This chapter contains no hints on how to ward off the seven signs of ageing. On the plus side, it will explain why having saggy tits makes you evil and why your failure to maintain a sufficiently feminine appearance constitutes an attack on everyone else's right to be themselves. I do not make the rules here; I'm just explaining how they work.

Are we the baddies?

It started for me with Snow White. It's tragic how often this is the case, that moment when you rediscover the fairy tale, only to realise you've switched sides. Elissa Melamed's 1983 book *Mirror, Mirror: The Terror of Not Being Young* opens with just such a shock discovery: 'I who was Snow White had turned into the stepmother! How had this happened?' Forty years later, I am embarrassed to confess that I, too, first confronted the approach of middle age via the exact same realisation. How derivative! Then again, as long as we fear the wicked stepmother, we are condemned to repeat her mistakes.

I wasn't even that old when it happened. It was my thirty-seventh birthday, and my partner and I had gone to see the film *Snow White and the Huntsman*, Rupert Sanders's retelling of the traditional tale, starring Kristen Stewart as a feisty, sword-wielding Snow White, and Charlize Theron, fourteen years her senior, as the evil queen Ravenna. It was pitched as a feminist reworking, as all such reworkings are, overwriting the apparently simplistic politics of the original story. Where once there were witches, now there are complex female characters with troubled inner lives (who are also witches). The longer I sat through the film, and it is long, the more my discomfort grew. There was a feminism, but it was no longer mine.

Theron plays a woman fighting the ravages of time. Ha! Aren't we all? Although it's probably worse when you're a Hollywood actress. Probably worse, too, when you're in a film about a woman trying to cling on to youth and beauty, which your mother has taught you is 'your ultimate power and only protection'. Worse still if the means by which your character seeks to maintain her beauty are unremittingly evil, involving the abuse of younger characters played by younger actresses. There's a scene in which Theron's Ravenna literally sucks the youth and beauty out of model Lily Cole, twelve years her junior. That might have been the point at which I started to suspect the whole thing was a massive act of trolling on the part of studio execs, an explicit endorsement of the 'double standard of aging', making a morality tale – a feminist one, no less – of the threat of obsolescence and the corresponding sin of resistance.

Such trolling is not particularly new. In 1950's *Sunset Boulevard* the slippage between Norma Desmond as charac-ter and Gloria Swanson as fifty-year-old actress veers towards directorial sadism. Create and perpetuate a problem – in this case, the combination of ageism and misogyny which edges women out of the representational field – then get a woman to simultaneously live and perform it for your amusement. Older women in the act of resisting their own sidelining are to be pitied, but also demonised. It could even be argued that traditional fairy tales explored the theme in ways that are more nuanced and complex than we see in their updatings. In the wicked witch and the ugly stepmother we see the usurped woman cling to power. That power, in the original telling, may have been a matter of life and death, survival versus destitution. What's being passed down is a double-edged warning: beware the older woman because you are not her, but also because you will become her, and your feistiness alone cannot save you.

I have come to realise that a common theme in the all-new feminist, progressive sidelining of the hag is this: you are not hated because you are an older woman – for that would be wrong and regressive – but because you have failed to remain a young one. Stewart's character, the younger woman, the new feminism, serves to absorb any accusations of sexism. Her Snow White is more than her beauty; she engages in physical combat and does not marry a handsome prince. Yet the alignment of youth and beauty with virtue and courage remains. It just so happens that those who best represent a politics which doesn't privilege youth and beauty are young and beautiful themselves.

When Ravenna is murdering Snow White's father, she tells him, 'Men use women. They ruin us and when they are finished with us, they toss us to the dogs like scraps.' Given that this was a film in which a not-even-middle-aged actress was being presented with computer-generated images of her face at 'no longer suitable for lead roles' stage under the guise of her character's 'true nature' being revealed, I found her character's rage pretty on point. Munching my popcorn, I wondered at how things which sound a little extreme, perhaps even man-hating, when you are younger can start to make sense once you notice your own jawline start to droop – when you are, as several interviewees have put it to me, on the verge of 'exiting the market'. I left the cinema feeling deeply unsettled. That strange *Am I the baddie?* sensation that comes over you when you know what side you're supposed to be on yet can't quite get with it. I've had that more and more over the decade that's followed.

On the one hand it seemed churlish to dismiss Snow White – the feistiness! The sword! – just because of the 'age thing'. Indeed, that felt like just the sort of thing some bitter hag would do. I was suddenly very aware of what my increasing age might mean in terms of my right to question anything that looked suspiciously like old-style sexism with a thin coating of feminist gloss. Recalling my own resentment of those who poured cold water over the raunch feminism of my nineties youth, I pictured a younger me dismissing my older self as a frumpy traditionalist who secretly had issues with Stewart's non-conforming character. On the other hand, I was pretty sure that whatever the film offered, it was not a sustainable vision of liberation. Not so much a folk tale mapping complex social roles as a male fantasy of women scrapping it out, the old representing badness, bitterness, regression, quite deserving of being slaughtered – in a move handily taught to Snow White by the Huntsman – in the end. Easier by far to hate and reject an evil queen than to see beyond to the forces acting upon her.

What disturbed me most was how perfectly the film laid out Ravenna's – Theron's, my own – dilemma, that of the ageing woman who has no choice other than to be seen, and just left it there. The problem is not 'simply' that of how we look or whether we are desired, but the interplay of beliefs about beauty, conservatism, progress and obsolescence. It's not that the injustice of the beauty myth goes unnamed, but on naming it we project the blame back onto its victims. Now that you can be anyone – in a visual, virtual age when

surely magic is real – today's older women must have chosen
to be wicked.

The Halloween mask is you

Charlize Theron was born in 1975, the same year as me, and
as *Apprentice*-contestant-turned-professional-offence-giver
Katie Hopkins, best known for hawking self-consciously bigoted views on race, feminism, religion and anything else likely
to cause distress to others. If you were to rank me in terms of
conformity to conventional beauty standards and how old I
actually appear, you would place me on the side of Hopkins,
not Theron. And in terms of politics and moral outlook?
Would it depend on what I say and do, or how I look?

In 2019 a quotation from Roald Dahl's *The Twits* started to
appear in memes relating to Hopkins, with pictures showing
her face at different ages:

> If a person has ugly thoughts, it begins to show on the face.
> And when that person has ugly thoughts every day, every
> week, every year, the face gets uglier and uglier until it gets
> so ugly that you can hardly look at it.

The implication was that by her mid-forties, Hopkins now
looked hag-like, older than her years, because of all her 'ugly
thoughts'. Of course, it's just a joke – why not have a dig at a
woman's appearance if you think she's so beyond the pale it
doesn't matter? Indeed, isn't that the kind of thing Hopkins
would do herself? Except it sits alongside a growing online
trend for mocking the appearance of middle-aged women
on the basis that their presumed non-progressive views make
them fair game.

Perhaps they have 'TERF bangs' (fringes denoting exclusionary views about gender). Or maybe a 'Karen haircut' (a bleached bob that is a sure sign of middle-aged entitlement, and quite probably racism). Or even 'suburban wine mom bodies' (imperfect post-partum abs which prove they voted for Trump in 2016, even if they've lived in Surbiton all their lives). Once upon a time getting a bad haircut might just have meant having to purchase a fetching hat; now a woman might find herself having to record and distribute a public statement claiming a rare mismatch between politics and frumpy appearance. And woe betide any group of women attending an Edinburgh Fringe event while looking insufficiently hip and youthful; they might stand accused of emitting 'TERF vibes'.

To be fair to the Dahl quote, it goes on to say that it doesn't matter how far a person strays from conventional standards of attractiveness as long as they possess inner virtue. This is not what people are suggesting when they share photos of Hopkins. The opportunity to make a moral case for ridiculing and expressing disgust at the appearance of older women is the point. It is lucky that today's progressive misogynists found a middle-aged woman with genuinely objectionable views, otherwise they would have had to invent her.

The belief that, for women, old equates to ugly, and ugly equates to morally depraved, is not new. Neither are the ways in which it is justified. Describing thirteenth-century representations of the virtues of Silence and Obedience, Marina Warner notes that 'to look fair and speak fair are linked feminine virtues; to look foul and speak foul equally; the hag curses, the scold is ugly'. This is convenient, particularly if speaking 'foul' constitutes saying things which displease or disrupt the dominant social order. 'Ugliness' – which, for women, is the very fact of ageing – is construed not as a natural process but a punishment for going against one's 'true', feminine nature: 'When the object of desire raised her voice, her desirability decreased; speaking implied unruliness, disobedience. And the penalty for this [...] was the appearance of physical decay. Decrepitude enciphered ugliness, ugliness unloveliness, unloveliness unwomanliness, unwomanliness infertility: a state of being against nature.' Say the wrong thing and you will enter the wasteland of infertility and obsolescence. Yet despite centuries of warnings, we older women keep doing it.

A century ago, anti-suffragette propaganda depicted those demanding the vote as 'ugly manly harridans', contrasted with feminine ladies who understood their true role. More recently, the scholar and broadcaster Mary Beard, subjected to an appalling degree of misogynist abuse for her allegedly 'witchy' appearance, has described how older women's voices and looks are used to discredit their views: 'It is still the case that when listeners hear a female voice, they do not hear a voice that connotes authority [...] And it is not just voice: you can add in the craggy or wrinkled faces that signal mature wisdom in the case of a bloke, but "past-my-use-by-date" in the case of a woman.' What is particularly striking is the way in which cause and effect constantly swap places, a sleight of hand that means you can never quite pin down the original sin. I am used to being told by men's rights activists that bitterness over my innate ugliness and consequent lack of appeal to men must have driven me to feminism. Yet I also encounter men on the left, many of whom consider themselves feminist allies, who are entirely comfortable with suggesting that the politics of today's middle-aged women is what makes them unattractive. 'I'm guessing late 50s,' as one of them tweets in response to one woman's views on sex and gender, 'all dried-Fairy liquid hair and saggy-faced delightfulness. Hate makes them ugly.' A woman might now be permitted to hold political views, but they must remain in constant dialogue with her perceived position on the sexual marketplace. In this way, deferring to the opinions of a self-styled progressive male half one's age can constitute a form of political Botox, a conservative act in both senses of the word.

Sagginess, of face and especially of tit, appears to be a particularly egregious moral failing. Julie Bindel describes a scene at Manchester Pride in 2018, where 'one of the organisers said of a small group of lesbians who were demanding better representation and inclusivity at Pride events, that they should be dragged off by their "saggy tits"'. Twitter is awash with invective regarding the sins of the sagging woman: 'the biggest haters on social media are saggy middle aged and older women with bible verses in their bios and awful haircuts'; 'Calm your saggy tits, Karen'; 'Middle aged women are THE worst and rudest people to serve ever, all angry at the world because their faces have gone saggy'; 'The Lord was holding me back at the nail salon while middle-aged, anti-mask, saggy-titty, white women kept going on and on about refusing to wear masks ...' The media and communications professor Sarah Pedersen tells me of interviewing an older feminist, who described being sent rape threats while also being told 'I wouldn't want to rape you. You're all saggy. Nobody would rape you.' In her song 'Better Than You', performed on Channel 4's *Friday Night Live*, the trans comedian Jordan Gray included the line 'I'm a perfect woman – my tits will never shrink', defending it on the basis this was satire and self-mockery. But how is it satire if it reflects what is genuinely believed about women whose breasts have aged? Isn't the real target of mockery the sinfully shrivelled?

As someone who has breastfed three children and still expresses political opinions, I am obviously one of the damned. This association between saggy breasts and evil is age-old, even if universal access to porn means breast expectations have never been more unrealistic. Warner describes how 'in medieval representations, the Devil at his work of temptation sometimes mirrors Eve's own face, but he also often has wrinkled female dugs'. In René d'Anjou's *Livre du cœur d'Amour épris* the figure of jealousy has 'dugs big and soft and hanging on her belly', while the thirteenth-century comedy *De vetula* bemoans the differences between younger and older female bodies: 'the aged crowd of parts betrays the old woman: the fibrous neck, the sharp points of her shoulder blades, the rocky chest, the breast with loosened skin. Not a breast, but as empty and soft as the bags of shepherds' (tell me about it).

Saggy tit-haters old and new have always found serious, utterly straight-faced moral justifications for their mockery. The modern tit-phobes are particularly impressive. There they are, totally oblivious to anything so regressive as sex difference, yet there's something about the breasts of a woman beyond the age of fertility and fuckability that really freaks them out. At the same time, it is very hard to challenge ageist, sexist mockery of one's appearance that has been tied to a moral cause. While you may think you are arguing about one thing – the demonisation of older women for no longer meeting achingly patriarchal beauty standards – said appearance has been made inseparable from a rag-bag of views on race, gender identity, sexual orientation, politics etc., which you are allegedly 'defending' the moment you speak out. With hindsight the self-styled progressive can say, 'Well, the suffragettes were on the right side of history after all, so it's perfectly obvious that postcards depicting them with werewolf teeth and grotesque, howling mouths were driven by misogyny.' But now? That same progressive would never think himself naive enough to believe hate literally makes a woman ugly, or that all older women are ugly because they all harbour hateful views. Thus if he suggests this, we must accept it is just a metaphor, the discourse, a meme, or, as one might have said fifteen years ago, bantz (and anyhow, he might counter, if your biggest problem is being called ugly, how privileged are you?).

It's embarrassing to make a fuss about the moralistic lookism older women face. Not only will you attract more critiques of your own appearance, but in speaking at all you could be accused of proving your critics right. In the figure of 'Karen', for instance, the very act of complaining is conflated with an ugliness specific to middle-aged white women. In 2020 the make-up artist Jason Adcock went so far as to create a $180 latex Halloween mask based on the face of 'Karen', 'an angry, middle-aged white woman'. I think this is a big deal. As a child I had a Halloween mask based on the green face of the Wicked Witch of the West; as an (intermittently) 'angry, middle-aged white woman', I am now told no disguise is necessary. I am the caricature, the more so if I object to it. There is a detailed discussion to be had about the relationship between privilege and the behaviour of white women, and the ways in which certain terms might capture it (Chapter Seven looks more closely at the use of 'Karen'). Nonetheless, all we have here is a man, Adcock, who has made a grotesque mask (plus an extra-grotesque 'Covid Karen' variation) which mocks a face one might see on a woman out shopping, picking up children, or, God forbid, making a complaint that is perfectly legitimate (and perhaps even necessitating a conversation with a manager).

Adcock claims that '"Karen" is transcendent of all gender and size. She is just a modern-day tyrant. Anybody evil can be a Karen.' This is wheedling nonsense, reminiscent of claims that because not all people burned as witches were older women, the intersection of misogyny and ageism was not a significant factor in history's hag panics. Witches, and Karens, have a face, and it is that of a woman who no longer embodies the three Fs. It is the face of a female person who has out-stayed her welcome. How then should we read accusations of her being too loud, too entitled, just too damn present?

Younger white women are not treated as ready-made, walking, talking Halloween grotesques. Witchiness, for such women, is a performance and a choice. Recent books with titles such as *Becoming Dangerous: Witchy Femmes, Queer Conjurers, and Magical Rebels* and *Basic Witches: How to Summon Success, Banish Drama, and Raise Hell with Your Coven* present the witch as a cross between self-help heroine and cool feminist sorceress. Prettified ugliness and uglified prettiness, rebellion you can purchase along with crystals and incense, is not a challenge to the social order. The same goes for the so-called 'sex-positive' witchiness celebrated by Kristen J. Sollée in *Witches, Sluts, Feminists: Conjuring the Sex Positive*, which goes from acknowledging women have been demonised for their sexuality to pretending today's witch-hunter can be owned by offering up (young) female flesh as a marketable commodity. 'At the nexus of the witch and slut identities is sex work', writes Sollée. I really doubt the average patriarch is quaking in his boots. This is a hollowing-out of transgression, leaving only the surface trappings.

I wouldn't know whether Katie Hopkins and I look older than our actual ages, because such a concept has become meaningless. Gloria Steinem, when told by a reporter that she didn't look forty, famously responded 'this is what forty looks like – we've been lying for so long, who would know?' It's a witty retort, although half a century later, forty looks differ-ent again. As women no longer knock years off their actual ages, but instead 'have work done', we have moved in reverse.

Instead of thinking it normal for a woman in her thirties to look like someone much older, we set a standard for looking the 'right' age which few older women can meet. When *Sex and the City* was rebooted for the 2020s as *And Just Like That . . .*, much was made of the fact that the now middle-aged characters were older than those in the first season of 1980s sitcom *The Golden Girls* yet looked much younger. 'Amazing how different our view of women that age is now,' tweeted the writer Flora Gill, herself in her early thirties. Our view, or our expectations?

Achieving the right look is, as ever, a question of time, money and inclination, yet the old-new lookism means it can be read as one of virtue, compassion and care. It is easier to justify lookism – and the attendant moral judgements – if you can convince yourself that looking like a middle-aged woman is a genuine choice.

How 'trying not to look your age' became 'being your true self'

In many of the guides I consult on menopause, midlife, *that* time, the women on the covers, my peers, do not look like me. They look younger, even though they tend to be slightly older, and I guess this is the point. They don't look young, but polished, preserved, 'well kept'. Inoffensive, insofar as any woman over forty might be such. They are saying, 'Yes, I know I have crossed the line, but please, don't judge me too much.' They want, I think, not to be desired, but forgiven.

These books do not market themselves as guides to passing as twenty-five. It's all about being your best you, using whatever raw materials you have available, supplementing with whatever else you can afford. This is presented as something one does for one's own benefit, but scratch the surface and you'll find a moral imperative. 'New possibilities for women quickly become new obligations,' wrote Wolf in *The Beauty Myth*. 'It is a short step from "anything can be done for beauty" to "anything *must* be done".' Never was this more true than today, when the lessons of Wolf's text – still brilliant, whatever one makes of the author's subsequent career trajectory – have been grossly distorted, obligation recast as self-expression, compliance as rebellion.

The Beauty Myth was a formative text for my generation of women. It might have been slipshod in its use of statistics on anorexia, and said things that had been said before, but the key points it made remain vital and true. Hatred of one's own body is an insidious trap; a choice is not freely made if the alternatives are exclusion and alienation; the pain of plastic surgery is extreme and unjustifiable; the more modifications that can be made to female bodies, the more will be expected of them; the myth pushes younger women to disidentify with older ones. None of these things has been disproven, but each and every one has, in the years since the book's publication, been undercut by a 'feminist' reworking seasoned with misogyny: no one should be 'trapped' in a body in which they do not feel at home; no one should be denied 'choices' which liberate them; the psychological pain of not having surgery is extreme and unjustifiable; the more modifications that can be made to female bodies, the less stigmatised such modifications should be; older women don't get it – how could they? They're still stuck in 1990, the year of the book's publication.

In its 2019 audit, the British Association of Aesthetic Plastic Surgeons reported that 'women underwent 92 per cent of all cosmetic procedures recorded'. As though somehow, quite reasonably, we are the ones most in need of repair. Almost three decades after Wolf noted the way in which cosmetic surgery could be repackaged as progress, BAAPS boasted that the rising trend for women going under the knife was partly 'driven by the openness of celebrities like Jane Fonda who recently admitted to having surgery over several decades to enhance her looks and prolong her career'. I find this quite a staggering admission. You need to be cut and fixed if you want to keep your foot in the door – if you're a woman, and if you can afford it. Yet mainstream feminist rage at this is almost non-existent. The US National Organization for Women did, in 2009, express concern at a proposal that elective cosmetic surgery be subject to an additional tax to help finance universal healthcare, on the basis that this would be punishing women for responding to the fact that they were already being punished for getting older. This is true and logical, but shows how what starts out as a temporary measure, a way of coping with rather than ending injustice, soon becomes 'just the way things are', or even 'what women want'. This has in turn allowed the normalisation of surgery to be recast as a growing 'openness', allowing women to 'admit' to undergoing treatment, as though the issue was never prejudice against women but prejudice against facelifts themselves.

No one wants to shame a woman for the moves she has made when forced to play a game according to someone else's rules, but criticising the rules is easily conflated with criticising the player. This is a ploy which extends into multiple areas in which women make choices, from traditional housewifery to sex work. Those of us who question the conditions under which women make decisions which limit or harm them are deemed to be invalidating the women themselves, due to some inexplicable, innate discomfort or phobia regarding children, sex or even silicone. It becomes increasingly impossible to question anything other than the most obvious expressions of male rage, lest one be committing the crime of 'denying agency'. Everything comes down to being yourself, and the right to be yourself is far more sacred than any Generation X anguish over the divisive class politics of women getting their faces injected with poison.

In 2011's *How to Be a Woman*, Caitlin Moran – another woman of 1975 vintage – is critical of the idea of ever having 'work done'. She describes herself at the age of thirty-five, observing older, wealthy women who 'all look the same': 'As you progress through the decades – from the jolly, untroubled gals in their twenties, towards the grande dames in their forties, fifties and sixties – the women in the room just look more and more scared. To be as privileged and safe as they are – but to still go through such painful, expensive procedures – gives the impression of a room full of fear. Female fear.' Moran's ordering of the ages, from the carefree to the fearful, reminds me of a quote from Germaine Greer's *The Female Eunuch*: 'young and pretty women may delude themselves about the amount of abuse meted out to women, for as long as they remain so they escape most of it'. While I don't think this is wholly true (young women have enough to contend with), both quotes illustrate the way in which women's status as objects beneath the male gaze imposes a decline narrative on the female lifecycle, a narrative in which we are constantly losing, and any act of resistance might serve only to highlight our status as losers.

A decade after *How to Be a Woman*, in *More Than a Woman*, Moran backtracks on having 'work done', having had Botox herself. Her reasons are twofold: the treatment is much less noticeable and more effective than a decade before, and the objective is not to look younger or more beautiful, but less 'sad' – to have a face that reflects the way she feels inside. I talk to Laura, aged forty-nine, who gives a similar justification for her Botox treatments: 'It looks like you're more unhappy when your mouth looks downturned. Everyone's got different-shaped mouths but I can see that mine will go downward as I age. I'd have to smile more in order to more accurately reflect how I feel.'

Perhaps this is true for me, too. Perhaps I do look more unhappy, at least in terms of how female facial expressions are read in our current environment. There is, nonetheless, something about women my age turning to Botox to look 'less sad' that makes me think of all the years we've had to put up with men demanding that we give them a smile. Our faces at whatever age have been supposed to put others at their ease, regardless of our inner emotions; equivalent numbers of middle-aged men are not getting themselves treated in order to look less angry, aggressive or miserable. Botox might allow some of us to avoid joining the ranks of those middle-aged hags deemed to be 'all angry at the world because their faces have gone saggy' – but isn't the problem the limited emotional range we assign to all women, whatever their age? If we can't tell whether a woman is happy or sad the moment her frown lines deepen or her jawline starts to droop, it could be our sensitivity to female emotions that is in need of fine-tuning. The fact that, as Phoebe Maltz Bovy writes, 'changes to facial features that happen naturally with age read, on women, as anger', might constitute an issue not with women's natural faces, but with their unnaturally low status.

Over the past thirty years, we have moved from attacking the cosmetic surgery industry at the root to pretending we can magically distinguish between the 'anti-ageing' practices we undertake to look young and pretty (vain and deluded!), those we undertake to keep resembling our true, happy selves (sort-of acceptable!) and those we undertake to avoid getting sidelined and sacked (understandable, but also enraging!). None of this has made looking older any more acceptable. On the contrary, it has added a form of moral gymnastics to the practical work Nora Ephron wryly termed 'maintenance'. You are generously 'allowed' to participate in the practices once identified as symptomatic of women's oppression provided you can offer a suitably cerebral or economically valid justification. At the same time, failure to participate in these practices will result in even harsher criticism than before (since it has been agreed that they are no longer oppressive per se).

I understand the sense of alienation that comes from suddenly being reminded that you do not look like the person you picture in your head. I understand why attempting to reclaim a 'truer' image of oneself can feel like an act of empowerment, a fundamentally human raging against the dying of the light. However, the 'true self' justification for battling the ravages of time seems to me tied to something far more insidious: the misogynistic message that a woman who matters wouldn't look like you.

It's your duty to be beautiful: femininity versus femaleness

> *Keep young and beautiful*
> *It's your duty to be beautiful*
> *Keep young and beautiful*
> *If you want to be loved.*

AL DUBIN, 'KEEP YOUNG AND BEAUTIFUL'

The psychologist Ann E. Gerike has proposed that 'the fact that women expend far more time, money, and effort in attempts to retain a youthful appearance than men do' may be seen as a form of 'emotional caretaking'. This suggests that 'maintenance', for older women, is not just about trying to keep hold of one's status as a prime cut of meat, but bolstering men's views of themselves as prime cuts, too. Beauty, like gender, is relational; women have been obliged to remain forever young so that men can delude themselves that they are not ageing themselves. If, as Virginia Woolf wrote in *A Room of One's Own*, women have served 'as looking-glasses possessing the magic and delicious power of reflecting the figure of man at twice its natural size', we have also been obliged to reflect our male contemporaries at half their natural ages.

Understanding beauty and youthfulness as duties is important. On the first Women's Liberation March in London, on 6 March 1971, feminists chose to broadcast the 1933 song 'Keep Young and Beautiful' from a gramophone pushed in a pram. It was a sharp, funny way of capturing the fact that, for women, conforming to ever-changing standards of femininity and fuckability is not a matter of choice, self-expression or desire; it is a moral obligation, and one forever at odds with women's economic, physical and social reality. Women can never win, but any failure to do so is considered not just pitiable but offensive, deserving of exclusion from the realm of those who are valued and loved.

In the half-century since the 1971 march, this message has become distorted. More than that: the 'duty' towards the male gaze has been recast as a 'duty' towards a supposedly beleaguered femininity – one which the new feminism supports. The outcome is the same: the woman who fails to 'keep young and beautiful' is a faulty looking-glass, whose insistence that she still exists as a woman puts the standards by which others identify themselves in question. This is particularly problematic at a time when attacks on women and attacks on femininity are conflated in a feminist-sounding rhetoric which creates the impression that older feminists never had a serious power analysis, but just thought lipstick and facelifts a bit silly and beneath them.

In the run-up to the 2020 US presidential election, Alexandria Ocasio-Cortez posted a much-praised video of herself applying skincare treatments and make-up while apparently demolishing the patriarchy. 'There's this really false idea,' she says, mid-application of a vitamin C serum, 'that if you care about make-up, or if your interests are in beauty and fashion, that's somehow frivolous.' She is right to question this. Being obsessed with make-up isn't just about being obsessed with make-up, any more than being obsessed with football is just about being obsessed with feet and balls. Both things are politically significant. However, she then goes on to claim that the reason why it is 'so important to share these things' is that 'femininity has power, and in politics there is so much criticism and nitpicking about how women and femme people present ourselves'. It's a curious double argument: femininity does indeed have power, but who is wielding it and whom do they control?

What Ocasio-Cortez offers is a reversal of the original feminist critique of femininity: in this new version, you're not being forced into the feminine corner because it is a means of marking those such as you as inferior, but you're considered inferior because you're feminine. It's an attempt to reclaim femininity 'as a form of self-expression', one which makes no distinction between those upon whom femininity is forced and those from who it is withheld, or the unequal power distribution between the two groups. Perhaps it is easier to engage in such 'reclaiming' when you are yourself young and beautiful. But is this genuinely challenging oppressive norms, or is it twisting the argument to avoid taking responsibility for those instances in which you are able to benefit from them?

At this juncture it would of course be useful to define what femininity is. Useful, but impossible. A set of stereotypes? An innate affinity for a particular group of qualities? The Barbie-pink end of a gender spectrum? Or merely a synonym for 'femaleness' or 'womanhood', on the basis that reproductive biology is of no consequence? For many people, I sense it's the temporary, culturally bound stereotypes associated with women and girls that they want, with the others cast aside. High heels are feminine, unpaid domestic shitwork is not (although servitude is definitely feminine, hence domestic shitwork done in high heels probably gets a pass). Youth is feminine; middle and old age are not. If femininity is fragile, misunderstood and stigmatised, then those who do it the greatest violence are older women. More than anyone else, we tear strips off the notion of an essential 'womanly' quality transcending the baseness of female biology. We don't mean to do this; it's just who we are.

Old-style, unfeminine feminism proposed that femininity's function was to create arbitrary distinctions between male and female people to enable the former to exploit the latter as reproductive and sexual resources. As Janet Radcliffe Richards put it, 'All the fuss about femininity (and to a lesser degree masculinity) is obviously not about inherent differences between the sexes. It must [. . .] be about what it is thought that the sexes ought to be like, and about what measures need to be taken to achieve whatever that is.' In this view, perceptions of masculinity and femininity are not about personal preferences or self-expression but justifying and enforcing the low status of female people in relation to male people. Hence a logical follow-on might be that decoupling the concept of femininity from femaleness – after which femininity ceases to be a meaningful concept – should constitute a feminist objective. Yet this is not an objective shared by all.

My own generation – those who came after the second wave – were taught to be dubious of old-style feminism's critique of femininity. It was presented to us not as a politically coherent assault on gender stereotyping and gender as a social hierarchy, but an arbitrary attack on harmless lifestyle choices. 'The new feminist,' proclaimed Natasha Walter in 1999's *The New Feminism*, 'is a confident creature, who both embraces and exceeds old notions of femininity. She may be feminine in her dress, or feminine in her desire for marriage and children, but she is feminist in her commitment to equality.' Somehow it felt as though this was the new challenge: overcoming the misguided fretfulness that had led our foremothers to make such a big deal about tarting oneself up a bit. It's a feeling that has embedded itself deeper within mainstream feminism, even as those who first embraced it have outgrown it. In 2007's *Whipping Girl*, the trans writer Julia Serano decries an earlier feminism's 'scapegoating of femininity', accusing earlier feminists of 'buying into traditionally sexist notions about femininity – that it is artificial, contrived, and frivolous'. A 2020 anthology goes by the title *Feminists Don't Wear Pink (and Other Lies)*, reducing a complex analysis of coercion, performance and complicity to crass caricature. In her 2004 book *Not My Mother's Sister*, the gender studies professor Astrid Henry quotes from a 1992 essay by a former member of the queer activist group ACT UP: 'in those heady days, it was all too easy for us girls to dismiss the older lesbian feminists as flabby ferocious frumps'. This finds an echo in Walter's assurance that 'the old myths about feminists, that they all wear dungarees and are lesbians and socialists, must be buried for good'. The original, solid feminist critique of femininity – already extant in 1792's *A Vindication of the Rights of Woman* – is all but lost, with the determination to shatter a social hierarchy replaced by a vague, hand-waving promise to 'live beyond the binary' (without getting rid of said binary. Careful now.)

All this has led mainstream feminism to a state of analytical incoherence. On the one hand, gender stereotyping in toys and marketing is worse than it has ever been, a problem widely condemned by feminists young and old, along with the bizarre ritual that is the antenatal gender-reveal party. At the same time, femininity itself is strangely sacrosanct. Several of the middle-aged women I talk to confess to feeling that stereotypes have eased for boys and tightened for girls since they were young: 'It's a remarkable historical change from when girls used to have, I think, a much wider range ... where girls once had more freedom they have less, and boys have more'; 'All the girls at my daughter's school have to have long hair. They just wouldn't be girls if they didn't. I look back at my school days, and we could be ordinary.'

I don't think we can understand levels of antipathy towards middle-aged women, particularly in relation to our appearance, without relating it to this tension as it manifests itself in the supposedly more gender-enlightened 2020s. Middle-aged womanhood, and especially menopause, has long been associated with visual 'defeminisation'. As discussed in the introduction, the psychiatrist David Reuben argued that the postmenopausal woman comes 'as close as she can to being a man', while Robert Wilson characterised post-menopausal women as 'castrates', with a pap smear count apparently answering 'one of the most crucial questions that ever confronts a woman – it tells her whether her body is still feminine, or whether it is gradually turning neuter'. As the philosopher Jacquelyn N. Zita notes, 'From this perspective [...] menopause is a deviance from the gendered norm of true femininity.' Half a century later, this deviance is not being celebrated as a bold rejection of the gender binary. On the contrary, it is more resented than ever. Middle-aged women are not gender rebels so much as spoilsports who expose the entire gender dance as a sham. When J. K. Rowling lunched with a group of middle-aged feminist activists in early 2022, one response to pictures shared on social media was 'trans women look more like women than they do'.

By slowly morphing into creatures who look less and behave less 'like women' – with our increased facial hair, our thickening waistlines, our coarsening skin, our greater independence – today's middle-aged women expose (once again) the femininity template as unfit for purpose. Only we are doing so just as it is being fully rehabilitated, treated as a 'power' that needs nothing more than to be made available for all. Some older women are duly apologetic for making such a terrible faux pas in the new gender landscape. 'In menopause, femininity strains, splits at the seams, and what once seemed natural now has to be constructed,' writes Darcy Steinke in *Flash Count Diary*. Rather than view this as a problem with femininity itself, Steinke attempts to position this as an endorsement of Judith Butler's view of gender as unstable, 'an identity tenuously constituted in time'. This is a bit like being given a doll-sized dress you must wear for life and insisting the entire problem is your too-big body. The femininity dress has never truly fitted, but rather than declare it a useless sort of garment for capturing an ever-changing self – a real, live woman, moving through time – you must blame your own body for splitting the seams.

As long as a 'progressive' vision of gender venerates femininity, visibly ageing while female will constitute a particularly egregious failure to do one's 'duty' as patriarchal looking-glass. Older women disrupt the re-emergence of womanhood as unencumbered, shame-free, vitamin C serum-enriched empowerment merely by existing in our saggy, non-pornified bodies. When I was young enough not to be a target, una-shamedly sexist men mocked older women as hatchet-faced battle-axes. Now more liberal – or even 'feminist' – men join in, on the grounds that this is not attacking women per se, but rehabilitating supposedly 'stigmatised' notions of how women should be. Don't judge a woman for conforming to a youth-obsessed fantasy of sexy girlhood; judge an older woman for undermining it with her (definitely prudish) lined mouth and (quite obviously exclusionary) haircut.

'The mythology of temptation,' writes Greer in *The Change*, 'is full of beautiful maidens who turn into hell hags with no more gruesome attributes than the normal attributes of age.' We have not moved on from this. We have simply rebranded the first group feminists; the second group is made up of conservative killjoys who cling to the past, squatting in womanhood despite the space now being reserved for the young and the pretty, the feminine and the femme. But where else are we to go? Writing on the invisibility of middle-aged women, Dorthe Nors recalls asking an older feminist what she would say is the strangest thing about becoming an older woman: 'And she answered: Woman?! I'm no longer a woman, and then she laughed her heart out, because what else can you do.'

'Some sort of bad spell'

In *The Stranger in the Mirror*, Jane Shilling describes herself as a teenager, comparing pictures of her mother at the same age with the forty-something woman she sees before her:

> The tender coltishness of the early photographs has van-ished. [...] It looks [...] as though some sort of bad spell

was cast over the golden-haired teenager with the kitten
and terrier and the pretty French penfriend in the album
pictures. As though a spiteful magician had come along
and shut her up in a carapace of thickened limbs and mot-
tled skin, from which only her heavy-lidded Bette Davis
eyes peer out, myopic but still recognisable, behind the big
lenses of her spectacles. Whatever the sums say, whatever
the photographic evidence, I am quite certain that the same
spell is not going to be cast over me.

Shilling's teenage self struggles to understand 'how someone can get up in the mornings, contemplate their reflection
in the mirror, even draw breath, looking as my mother does'.
A culture that continues to prize youth and beauty in
women – one which has found ever more convoluted ways in
which to defend lookism on the grounds of self-expression,
and to align visible ageing with political ugliness – is a culture
in which men can divide and rule. It primes younger women
to fear and blame older women for their diminished status. It
puts us in flight from our future selves, and makes us unwilling to acknowledge the female thread that connects us. We tell
ourselves 'the same spell is not going to be cast over me', right
up to the moment when we, too, find Snow White has become
the Evil Queen. As the philosopher Clare Chambers writes,
'beauty thus acts as a way of disrupting solidarity between
women, which might develop into consciousness-raising and
resistance. It [...] provides a way of disempowering women
as they age – a process that might otherwise increase their
power and status.'
    We know that in politics, appearance matters. 'In an age
that worshipped outward beauty and equated it with inward
virtue,' writes the witchcraft historian Anne Llewellyn
Barstow of the early modern period, 'an ugly old woman

was seen as evil, and therefore as a witch.' Only we are more sophisticated than that. In an age that is just as obsessed with beauty and keeping women in check, but in which naked misogyny is deemed ugly, a more circuitous route is needed in order to police women as they age. Naturally it would be too obvious and crude to declare women witches because they have failed to keep young and beautiful. Instead we posit correlations – between sagginess and bitterness, or bad hair and entitlement – while never quite claiming a causal relationship between a woman looking like a witch and her actually being one (the Karen mask can represent 'anyone'). Yet – and here is the twist – a causal relationship between looking older and holding different, inconvenient beliefs, beliefs the dominant culture might find unacceptable, does exist.

On the one hand, it is true that the inner lives of middle-aged women are misrepresented because we no longer look like our younger selves. On the other, those of us who no longer fall into the feminine, fertile and fuckable category do see the world differently because our relationship with said world, and our place in it, have changed. This is why it becomes so important for those wishing to maintain the status quo to use beauty as a means to make women mistrustful of one another. That way, we don't listen to what insights older women may have gained due to their being on the other side of the Snow White/Evil Queen divide. Instead, this change in perspective is used against us.

Here's one example: in the summer of 2021, newspapers were eager to report that 'the biggest online trolls' were middle-aged women. Only we're not. As you might expect, in a virtual world that accommodates revenge porn, Gamergate and 4Chan, the antics of women such as myself are comparatively tame. It turns out we're (possibly) more likely to be a bit mean about certain lifestyle influencers on Instagram.

Nonetheless, this didn't prevent a slew of articles suggesting that our rampant trollishness arises from bitterness at our own fading beauty. The *Telegraph* quoted the retired psychotherapist Dr Sheri Jacobson: 'At some point, middle-aged women get to a place where they realise that their youth isn't coming back. So when bloggers promote a lifestyle that is very much unattainable it can trigger aspects of envy and jealousy.' Writing in *i*, Esther Walker adopted a self-analytical approach: 'Sure, I had bad thoughts about other people when I was young, too, but I had the consolation of also being young, with bouncy skin and dewy eyes [...] The trick is to understand the bad feelings come from within, not without [...] Your anger is just collateral damage from your reverse pubescence.' The messaging is all very *Snow White and the Huntsman*. Got that, ladies? Don't be the witch in front of the mirror, plotting Kristen Stewart's doom!

The belief that middle-aged women respond to being cast out from the patriarchal meat market by becoming embittered hags hellbent on destroying younger women is as present on social media as it is in traditional fairy tales. If only we 'fucking cunting jealous cows' would just pipe down and 'enjoy [our] saggy tits and menopause'. This reliance on 'jealousy' is a convenient way of overlooking the real side-effect of no longer being deemed a prime cut: no longer regarding yourself as meat at all. Having spent half your life being told you might cease to exist the moment your 'value' drops, you find that, actually, you're as real as you ever were. It is, as Walker writes, a difficult transition, but it is also one which reveals a woman for what she is: the complete human beneath the layers of artifice, a whole person who cannot be made to vanish, no matter how pointedly she is ignored. The flipside of the discrimination women face upon having 'lost their market value' is no longer having anything to lose by refusing to play by the market's rules. From the perspective of those who value these rules the most, this makes middle-aged women dangerous, capable of leading younger women astray.

'You know you are less attractive,' my friend Juliet, fifty, tells me. 'You've lost that currency. I went through a little bit of feeling sad. Then I went through a bit of liberation, because I thought of the stress I felt. Before, I had to uphold something, I had to try to be more attractive than I was, I was on that treadmill thinking, That's part of why I'm valued and part of why people might want me. And then that value started to ebb away and now I think that's in direct correlation to how many fucks I give. Because my currency is much more about who I am, not what people see when they look at me, and I feel an urgency to respect myself more. Respecting myself, regardless of how people see me, has such a higher currency than in my twenties and thirties, even my early forties. Nature abhors a vacuum, right? So when the looks go, what's going to come in its place?'

For all the talk of bitterness and envy, the people who feel worst about their appearance are not middle-aged women but those who have not got there yet, who feel, as Jane Shilling once did, that it cannot be possible to get out of bed looking the way we do. The degree to which we older women hate the way we look is exaggerated, all the better to misrepresent our justified anger at the social and economic marginalisation that comes from looking older as foolish pique at no longer being deemed fuckable. I do resent what has happened to me – but not for the reasons men tend to think. If we could explain this to younger women, how might this change both their wariness of us and their attitudes towards their own bodies? What might this do for female solidarity and for individual confidence?

According to the 2020 Women and Equalities Committee Body Image Survey, young people hate their bodies more than older people, and women more than men. This does not surprise me at all. Mainstream feminism has spent decades demanding that beauty standards become 'more inclusive', yet if I flick through a magazine or walk through a shopping centre, the female bodies I see in advertising are even younger, thinner, more compliant, than those I encountered when I was in the throes of my own teenage body-hate. It is as though the conflation of 'young' with 'progressive' has created a loophole that allows underaged, underfed, over-waxed bodies to pass as something other than the same old regressive ideal. What's more, there is always a term – usually one that ends in '-shaming' – that makes any concern an older woman expresses regarding the beauty, plastic surgery or porn industries sound as though it is motivated by Evil Queen spite. As long as feminine primping is misrepresented as power, those still clinging to the possibility of one day being 'good enough' can be persuaded that older women just don't want them to be powerful when we no longer stand a chance ourselves. How can we tell them that this 'power' is illusory, looking the way we do? How can we make them believe us, the hags?

Negative attitudes towards our appearance hurt younger women more deeply than they hurt us, because we are over the worst. The spiteful magician cast his spell, and we got up the next morning, same as always. What if younger women knew it would always be thus? What if myths about beauty and envy no longer disrupted the lines of communication, and younger women were equipped to focus their energies on their real enemies, not their future selves?

Whatever we call our witches, as long as we are stuck in the same fairy tale, progressing towards the Snow White to Evil Queen epiphany, women will remain alienated not just from one another but our own reflections. Imagine a world in which this wasn't the case, in which the sight of shelf after shelf of magic potions promising to 'cure' female ageing was not treated as perfectly normal but truly absurd, in which we were free to feel compassion for ourselves at every life stage instead of retreating into fantasy. As Juliet puts it, 'As time passes, looks stop being so important because they've gone anyway, so what's in the vacuum? It is more empathy. And there is absolutely no time to fuck about telling stories.'

2

BEASTLY HAG

You can denounce me as much as you like but you cannot deny my life's work of living somehow inside this female body. You cannot tell me it's not real. It's as real as it gets.

Suzanne Moore, 'Why I Had to Leave *The Guardian*'

... the traditional status conferred upon women's bodies everywhere: not that of the simple, physical manifestation of their humanity but an object of unpardonable inconvenience, comprised of just so much meat.

Eimear McBride, *Something Out of Place*

My early understanding of feminism was as of an escape hatch. Bide your time while they frogmarch you towards that biology-as-destiny, honour-and-obey, barefoot-and-pregnant cell, pick your moment, and go, go, go. I did not grow up around feminists, but I knew that feminism existed, ready to save me from the fate of the women around me, the not-feminists, with their silences, their housekeeping money, their *well, if she would nag him, what did she expect?* That would never be me. I would never be a not-man, a mirror, a shadow; I'd be a not-one-of-those-women instead.

I never thought of this as hating women. On the contrary, I loved them, if only in terms of our potential, the creatures we could be, rather than the ones we were and had been. Such thinking exerts a heavy psychological toll. It is agonising to feel the threat embedded deep within you, that fatal flaw, the horrific possibility that if you are not careful, you, too, will become 'one of them'. How best to destroy the older woman, 'the victim in ourselves, the unfree woman, the martyr'? Starve her out, cut her out, deny her name, exorcise her as you enumerate each and every one of her sins. Yet unless you stop time in the most extreme way possible – none of the severe anorexics I knew made it beyond the age of thirty-five, and even then they looked ancient, mummified – you will descend into hagdom, too.

Like many young women, I spent my teenage years on the run from myself, starving away each marker of femaleness, cutting the threads one by one: *I will not be that, or that, or that*. As Marya Hornbacher puts it in her memoir *Wasted*, 'I had no patience for my body. I wanted it to go away so that I could be a pure mind, a walking brain.' Anything but a female organism, anything but that. Decades later, thinking of the body, *being it*, I see my teenage self before me and find it hard to believe she can be anything but disgusted at my fall from grace into undifferentiated middle-aged womanhood. It turns out I never was going to live for ever, untouchable, on books, black coffee and air. Instead I thickened, bled, allowed the boundaries between self and other to blur.

The only location from which to articulate the truth of being middle-aged and female is a middle-aged female body. It's a body that undermines one's credibility before one even gets started. The meanings ascribed to older female bodies – decline, dependency, the end of reproductive potential – challenge political narratives which champion self-definition, self-sufficiency and freedom of choice, whether such narratives be rooted in liberal feminism or patriarchal individualism. The body that has a female story defies both conservative 'sex neutrality' – that is, treating male bodies and lifecycles as a neutral default – and progressive attempts to decouple social and political identities from biological sex. At a time when 'biological essentialist' – ruefully described by Maureen Freely as 'what you are if you assume that there are any attributes common to all women' – is the ultimate woke insult, what could be more biologically essentialist, more of an admission of defeat before the arc of progress, than physically ageing while female?

The experience of living in a female body is marked by instability and change in a way that living in a male body is not: menstruation, gestation, lactation, menopause, years in which you are one thing and then suddenly are not. It is marked by meanings imposed from without (what do breasts 'mean'? Whom are they 'for'?) It can be marked by self-hatred, which becomes indistinguishable from hatred of other, potential bodies (the older/younger one, the fatter/thinner one, the fertile/infertile one). What we do to our bodies and how we speak of them situates other women in relation to us, and vice versa (if resisting growth is an expression of self, what do you imply about the selves who grow? Is what one 'allows' one's own body to do also consent for what is done to it?). Female embodiment is deeply political, but so, too, is flight from it. There is no way of removing oneself from the conversation entirely, and it's one that is inextricably linked to how we feel about ageing, because female embodiment is movement through time.

There are particular reasons why contemporary antipathy towards middle-aged women focuses on the body. The menopause – that big flashing sign telling everyone YOUR TIME HERE IS FINITE – is an obvious one. The difference in male and female reproductive lifespans creates the illusion that only women 'really' age (men live, then die), and it's one that persists even in those who claim not to notice which class of people does and does not get pregnant. At the same time, the onset of menopause can be the point at which many of us become more invested in an understanding of our own body story, and how it has shaped our lives. Alas, the 2020s may not be an optimum time to be doing such a thing.

This chapter explores how three fundamental human fears relating to the body – fear of inferiority, fear of change, fear of our own mortality – influence how we respond to older women. Ageist misogyny offers a temporary 'solution' to these fears, with ageing hags being cast as flesh-burdened obstacles to equality, stability and transcendence. In this way, hag hate performs an important function both psychologically and practically, easing anxiety while removing the need to take responsibility for one's own body and those of other people. The long-term impact is that women are robbed both of the conceptual frameworks and narrative structures with which to tell their own body stories, and the means to organise politically in order to change the conditions in which these stories play out.

Fear of inferiority

In 2009, Tampax launched an advertising campaign based on the theme 'Outsmart Mother Nature'. In TV commercials and posters, Mother Nature – played by an actress in fifties-stye clothing, 'her pinched face suggesting a sinister edge' – would attempt to thwart a younger woman by presenting her with her period, only to be foiled by the arrival of nature-defying Tampax Pearl tampons. 'Cut Mother Nature down to size!', one poster advised, depicting the older woman about to be squashed by oversized sanitary protection.

Prodding and poking at female anxieties – about appearance, about motherhood, about ageing, about one's tenuous status as a human being – is an effective strategy for advertisers. Female biology, with all its mess and inconvenience, is easy to sell as an outdated concept, the lingering fetish of those too old, too set in their ways and/or too dumb to realise that it's already been tamed, not least by the products you are offering. The Tampax campaign was clever; what's being sold is not just an object to insert into your vagina to soak up blood but an overcoming. Mother Nature is standing not for new life and creativity but corporeal (whisper it, *female*) limitation. Worried about 'nature' screwing you over, the same way it screwed over your mother and her mother before her? Then crush the older woman you see ahead of you, preferably with a massive, plastic-wrapped applicator tampon.

It is not difficult to fall into the trap of thinking that having a female body necessarily renders you inferior. 'The body,' wrote Adrienne Rich, 'has been made so problematic for women that it has often seemed easier to shrug it off and travel as a disembodied spirit.' *Of Woman Born* was published in 1976, but Rich could just as well have been writing today. The anxiety she captures, driving 'many intellectual and creative women [to insist] that they were "human beings" first and women only incidentally', was familiar to me in the nineties, and I sense it in younger women right now, those who see, as I did, 'any appeal to the physical as a denial of the mind'. Such a view passes for a feminism of sorts, elbowing itself in alongside the legitimate argument, found in works such as Caroline Criado Perez's *Invisible Women*, that our current social, economic and political structures prioritise a male-bodied default. It is all too easy to slip from noting the world is made for male bodies to deciding female bodies are not made for the world.

In this account, Mother Nature is indeed a massive bitch who's out to ruin your disembodied fun. 'Feminism,' wrote Camille Paglia in 1992's *Sex, Art, and American Culture*, 'was always wrong to pretend that women could have it all. It is not male society but mother nature who lays the heaviest burden on women.' In her 2015 essay 'Maternal Instincts', Laura Kipnis proposes that 'if it were up to nature, women would devote themselves to propagating the species, compliantly serving as life's passive instruments, and pipe down on the social demands. It's only modern technology's role in overriding nature [. . .] that's offered women some modicum of self-determination.' There is of course nothing wrong with the kind of progress that enables women to understand hormonal shifts, control their fertility, manage pain, or avoid death in childbirth. Nonetheless, we are not always clear about the distinction between this and the belief that progress – kindly driven by men – is there to help women deal with their tragic failure to have been born the right sex in the first place.

Growing up, I felt embarrassed by femaleness. It was the thing that made women weaker, slower, less human, more animal. It made us easier to hit, easier to rape, easier to destroy. I didn't want to think about the opinions of women such as Camille Paglia because I was terrified they might be right. Instead, I retreated into shame. 'To feel shame,' writes Eimear McBride, 'suggests becoming conscious of an innate flaw, an inappropriate, unacceptable element of the self, which cannot be simply apologised for and moved on from. It must be concealed and denied at all costs and, because of this, shame becomes the weapon within.' For me, this 'element of the self' was the fact of being female. I knew that if I ever let it slip that I was 'one of them' – one of those women like my mother, who invested so much in the story of her difference – I would be done for.

'Feminists,' writes Julie Bindel in 2021's *Feminism for Women*, 'have long avoided putting too much emphasis on the biological differences between men and women, knowing that these will be used against us to classify us as inferior.' In doing so, we have painted ourselves into a corner, accepting a politics which continues to regard male-bodied people as the default humans while downplaying the equally important experiences of female-bodied people. We have fallen victim to a patriarchal protection racket, which promised us the right to be considered as something more than walking wombs in exchange for the denial of our existence as a sex class, in much the same way we were promised sexual autonomy and reproductive choice in exchange for waiving any objections to hardcore pornography and the growth of the sex trade. In both instances, men have got what they wanted without delivering their side of the bargain, but still we wait. We don't want to make a fuss, because to do so would only draw attention to the fact that we remain female, after all. This is gender equality conceived of as a polite lie: men agree to overlook our quite obvious female inferiority, in return for which we ease up on the demands relating to actual sex differences. As the protagonist of Elisa Albert's 2015 novel *After Birth* puts it, 'Heaven forbid it might be true that female bodies are different [...] Because, what? We might lose the vote? Because we might get veiled, imprisoned? Best deny it, deny it, make it to the Oval Office, win, win, win.' And yet, as we know from 2016, we don't make it to the Oval Office anyhow.

The promotion of stigma surrounding biological femaleness is an essential tool for those who wish to control women. It achieves several things at once: it alienates us from our bodies and from other women; it transfers blame for the exploitation of women from men onto women themselves; it recasts specifically female capacities as liabilities; it robs us of a coherent analysis of why female people are oppressed; it cuts the threads that connect generations of women; it prevents us from organising politically on the basis of sex; it tells us that our body stories – the narratives that connect individual experiences of femaleness, placing them in meaningful personal and political contexts across a lifetime – are irrelevant. In all of this, the figure of the older woman, Mother Nature who must be outsmarted, looms large. Younger women can play the denial game, but know that with each passing year they are increasingly at risk of being exposed. Meanwhile, older mothers, menopausal women, those with longer back stories, are less willing to pretend sex differences don't matter, and are terrible at keeping quiet about it. The longer you live in a female body, the harder it is to deny its impact on your position in the world. We are encouraged to believe that any serious acknowledgement of sex difference and why it matters – and particularly any recognition of qualities which female people possess which male people lack – will lead to backlash, but once we examine what female bodies do over the course of female lifecycles, the difference between their socially constructed low status and their actual worth could not be clearer. Ageing can mean the shift from 'I will be treated badly if I am overly identified with what my (shameful) female body can do' to 'My (brilliant) female body did all this, and still I get treated this way?'

Take the fact that there is not a single person on the planet who does not exist because some female person, somewhere, went through all the stages of conception, gestation and birth. 'Motherhood,' writes Susan Maushart, 'is fearsome because it is so intensely powerful, entailing acts of creation before which all other human endeavour withers into shadow. In the creation stakes, motherhood is the big league, and everything else – art, science, technology – is a farm team.' And yet it is considered both unseemly and regressive for the female sex to blow its own reproductive trumpet. Because gestation is a natural process. Because women have been bearing children since the dawn of time. Because not all women can and/or wish to bear children. Because drawing attention to your uterus will only get you fired or denied an abortion. Because, because, because, but above all, because the sperm producers, the mighty impregnators, cannot do it.

Patriarchal cultures both ancient and modern adore creation myths in which male deities form the world, the creatures and all human life. Athena pops out of Zeus' head; God creates Adam and, as an afterthought, Eve; Mary dutifully carries the fully formed godhead implanted inside her. Scientists and philosophers throughout the ages have sought to make the male seed, eighty thousand times smaller than the ovum, central to the reproductive process. Aristotle argued that females merely provided the matter that the active male principle formed into a human being; seventeenth-century scientists swore they could see a miniature man in human sperm, just waiting to unfold himself within the passive female vessel. Freud argued – and people actually believed him – that little girls envied little boys their penises, not that men envied women their reproductive powers (which they have, nevertheless, sought to control through marriage, compulsory heterosexuality, forced sterilisation, the outlawing of abortion, rape, limited access to contraception etc.). A recent shift towards gender-neutral language to describe pregnancy and birth may be branded inclusive, but has the effect of once again refusing to name exactly who does the work of making new human beings. *It is foreign to me, therefore it is irrelevant.* So says the patriarch when confronted with any indication that female people might have world-defining experiences which remain inaccessible to him.

I understand the risk that comes with breaking the 'don't mention the womb' taboo. The conservative right will come in the night and steal away my reproductive rights, on the basis that taking any degree of pride in being a member of the sex class who makes all the humans is tantamount to declaring oneself and all of womankind brood mares. Nonetheless, it is not the fact that I am unlikely to get pregnant again that makes me more willing to speak out. By the time they get to my age (over forty-five), most women (81 per cent) have had children, but those who have not are similarly encouraged to see themselves as flawed because of the nature of human reproduction and how men have chosen to respond to it. The reason why I am prepared to look like one of those ridiculous women who wangs on about reproduction as though it matters – to risk being called 'fifties throwback, maternal revivalist, elitist, ethnocentrist. And worst of all, essentialist' – is that I am beyond shame. I can no longer be embarrassed into thinking that having been born female is something to be downplayed or for which I must atone, lest someone mistake me for someone like my mother, or her mother, or some random fifties housewives, or whichever women a woman like me is supposed to be fleeing at this point in time. I am too old, and too compromised, and I want my story, a story that connects with the stories of others just as flawed and compromised as me.

Teaching young women not to trust their own bodies goes hand in hand with teaching them not to trust older women.

As a young woman in the nineties and early noughties, I never came into contact with second-wave feminist ideas regarding maternity, reproduction or sex difference, but half-assumed I knew them anyway. Second-wavers, I magnanimously decreed, had been good on some things but were over-invested in the female body and childcare because so many of them were bored housewives. I thought of them in the same way many young women think of women on Mumsnet today: women who focused on the female body because their potential to transcend it had fallen by the wayside. These were women who'd had their shot at outsmarting Mother Nature and failed, and were now attempting to drag the rest of us down with them. The spectacle of female domestic exploitation – the lives of women my mother's age, which I saw right in front of me – stood not for a shared oppression, accumulating over a female lifecycle, but for what happens when you allow yourself to be all too female, investing too much in the female body, not the neutral (male) mind.

'Biology is not destiny' used to mean that your sex should not dictate your position in a social hierarchy. Now it is twisted to mean that 'any acknowledgement of reproductive biology destines you to remain subordinate'. Denial of the biological thread connecting you to older women can thus look like liberation. The sharp rise in recent years of sex difference denialism – seen, for instance, in mainstream articles decrying 'The Myth of Biological Sex' – and in young people disidentifying from femaleness but not maleness, as witnessed in changes in referrals to gender identity clinics, feels progressive because it appears to offer a literal version of the 'radical surgery' described by Rich half a century ago:

Thousands of daughters see their mothers as having taught
a compromise and self-hatred they are struggling to win

free of, the one through whom the restrictions and degra-
dations of a female existence were perforce transmitted [...]
The mother stands for the victim in ourselves, the unfree
woman, the martyr. Our personalities seem to dangerously
blur and overlap with our mothers'; and, in a desperate
attempt to know where mother ends and daughter begins,
we perform radical surgery.

But surgery, whether real or metaphorical, does not work,
because femaleness itself was never the problem. The problem
is, as Rich herself and later feminists such as Criado Perez
have identified, a world that is built around meeting the needs
of male bodies, which makes women ashamed of the bodies
they are, and girls ashamed of the bodies they might one
day become.

Fear of change

I'm sitting in a presentation on pensions (such is the exciting
life I lead). At one point it is mentioned, as an aside, that
female employees tend to have smaller pots because we are
more liable to 'take time out'. No one raises any objections
to this; it is true, is it not? We women interrupt the important work of being employees to be breeders and carers,
out there in the wilderness beyond what we think of as 'the
economy'. The older we are, the more interruptions we are
likely to have accumulated. The gap between what we and
our male peers are deemed to be worth widens with each
passing decade because we, the non-default humans, just
don't stay on course.

It is easier to believe biological sex is irrelevant if your own
sex is treated as the default one. Easier, too, to dismiss the

connection between bodies, life stages and social positioning
if your own life has not been presented to you as a series of
inconvenient stops and starts, interludes and interruptions:
monthly warnings, biological clocks, maternity leave, hot
flushes, commercial inconvenience versus reproductive obsolescence. When female bodies deviate from the paths set by
male ones, this is still treated as a design flaw pertaining to
non-males, not as an indication that we need different ways
of organising education, work and relationships to accommodate specifically female needs. Workplace accommodations
are 'special treatment'; the front-loading of education and
career progression into the life stage during which one might
also get pregnant cannot be questioned. If your pension pot
is paltry, that's your bad luck for having been born into the
category marked 'other'. A female employee, writes Katrine
Marçal, 'is encouraged to see her body not as part of what
it means to be human but as a ticking fertility bomb set to
explode at the same time she's going up for a promotion. Then
she will be exposed for what she is: a woman.'

The risk and reality of pregnancy is one thing, but the
female body's final act of treachery comes later, when
menopause is seen to expel a woman from the very mar-
kets – fertility, femininity, fuckability – built around it. This
is because the issue is not just one of patriarchal practicalities
but patriarchal psychology. Unlike a male body, a female one
is inconsistent, untrustworthy, unless you can find ways to
fix it in place. 'A man remains male as long as he lives,' wrote
Robert Wilson in *Feminine Forever*, '[...] No abrupt crisis
has to be faced. A man's life proceeds in smooth continuity.
His feeling of self remains unbroken.' Alas, this is not the case
for a woman: 'Though modern diets, cosmetics, and fashions
make her outwardly look even younger than her husband,
her body ultimately betrays her. It destroys her womanhood

during her prime. At the very moment when she is most able and eager to enjoy her achievements, her femininity – the very basis of her selfhood – crumbles in ruins.' Funny, that.

While few men today would be as openly sexist as Wilson, our continued acceptance of mounting inequality across female lifecycles rests on the assumption that female life paths are aberrant. Women fall further and further behind men in terms of status and access to material resources because our lives fail to proceed 'in smooth continuity'. The inescapable fact of menopause is used to bolster the impression that women are not so much deliberately excluded from the world of Economic Man as hardwired to short-circuit on a regular basis. The fact that, unlike men, we 'fail' to stay the same – or at least fail to maintain the illusion of doing so – is used to suggest we're just not fit for purpose.

Today's middle-aged women spent the nineties being routinely confronted by their own bespoke, 'post-feminist' version of Wilson's 'menopause as female body betrayal' myth. It doesn't matter if you never watched *Ally McBeal* or read *Bridget Jones's Diary*; you will have absorbed their message – or a cheapened, exaggerated version thereof – by osmosis. Those of us who came of age after feminism's second wave were taught that all those feminist gains might be well and good, but that our female bodies would catch us out in the end, just when we might be 'most able and eager to enjoy [feminism's] achievements'. We'd 'forget' to have a baby; our fertility would 'fall off a cliff' the moment we hit the age of thirty-five; we'd probably end up alone in a really expensive flat in London or New York, sort-of doing a job that didn't seem to require much work, but we wouldn't be happy, what with the very basis of our selfhood crumbling in ruins.

Constant warnings about the ticking of the biological clock function as a means of social control at a time when it is no longer considered good etiquette to say 'younger women shouldn't have access to the same career paths as men, and older women are useless'. It is obviously true that female fertility declines with age, before coming to a halt in midlife, but the 'warning' model is a poor substitute for reframing our understanding of the default lifecycle in order to work with, rather than against, natural stages of transition. Biological-clock panic imposes a sell-by date on all women, regardless of personal choices, and encourages us to see ourselves as fundamentally less productive than our male counterparts (high-flying women freeze their eggs because they cannot freeze themselves). It is a form of shaming, and it doesn't matter what you might want for yourself, or even if you have children already. In any case, the onset of menopause promises to make you someone who embodies the absence of choice. The clock was always ticking and look, now the alarm has sounded, just as you're entering your fifties, when the gender pay gap is at its widest, caring responsibilities mount and workplace discrimination increases. How convenient that it is now, when you are at your most exploited, that others should see you as someone who foolishly ran out of time in which to be properly productive.

Here, as elsewhere, practical justifications for the erasure of female labour dovetail with a kind of visceral disgust for female difference. This is the push-pull on which misogyny depends; it might seem strange to treat the female lifecycle, as opposed to man-made social and economic models, as fundamentally flawed, but it becomes less so when one considers this in relation to the psychological need to 'fix' womanhood in place. Menopause presents an existential challenge to male-default thinking, which sees bodies and minds reaching adulthood and simply remaining the same before slowly declining in very old age, and to a male-default understanding

of progress and change, one in which the loss of one's reproductive prowess is meant to signify a form of death.

In *Flash Count Diary*, Darcey Steinke compares the way
human society responds to menopause to the behaviour of orca
communities (orcas being our only fellow creatures known to
experience menopause): 'No one calls the female whales roadkill or dried-up cunts [...] In the matriarchy they've created,
children stay with their mothers for life, menopausal females
move into leadership roles, and the older post-reproductive
females train the adolescent males in sexual technique [...]
They demonstrate to me what no human woman could: that
it is not menopause itself that is the problem but menopause as
it's experienced under patriarchy.' Tempted as I am to wonder
whether young orcas are in fact swearing at Grandma and
we just don't know it, I think it's true that menopause, like
motherhood as described by Rich, exists both as experience
and as social construct. The narrative imposed on it is a
chosen one. That the interruptions which characterise female
embodied experience are viewed in negative terms and come
at a significant social and financial cost is not inevitable.
Indeed, if we were to be truly imaginative and open-minded
in approaching the relationship between biological sex and
socially constructed gender, we might be more willing to
embrace metaphors of change, interruption, transformation
and evolution in relation to menopause, instead of situating
all women on the wrong side of forty outside the sphere of
creativity and disruption (with a request that they pop back
and clean up afterwards, once everyone else has finished the
day's gender-binary-smashing activities).

You cannot enact serious change unless you also engage
with what cannot be changed. Ironically, one of the rigid
contemporary beliefs menopause blows apart is that which
says rejecting 'old' ideas about biological reality is in and of

itself progressive. If, as Janice Turner writes, 'increasingly feminists are told that biological sex is boring, outdated and reductive, while "gender identity" is modern and progressive', then of course menopause itself can be superficially constructed as anti-progress. Aren't bodies whatever we make of them? If so, then what the hell are older women *doing*? It is easy to picture everyone else partaking of an identity free-for-all while the dried-up, post-fertile hags lurk in the corner, death at the feast. But unless we grapple with the relationship between desire, the flesh and movement through time – unless we let go of a trivial, fixed view of ourselves as one unique person at one point in time – then all we are doing is writing a new version of Wilson's normative, male-default understanding of human experience as static, 'no abrupt crisis', only 'smooth continuity'. Because that's easier. Because it makes us feel safe.

As Martha Nussbaum wrote over two decades ago, with regard to Judith Butler, 'what feminism needs, and sometimes gets, is a subtle study of the interplay of bodily difference and cultural construction', not the glib insistence that difference denial has the power to undermine or reframe cultural construction in and of itself. I think when menopausal women talk about this, though – or even when we just exist in/as our menopausal bodies – it looks as though we are denying others the right to greater flexibility because we didn't have it or never wanted it. I come back to my younger self, scrutinising the body of the self I would one day become, unwilling to believe this could have been anything other than a very bad decision. That I once felt freezing myself in time, as though the body I had at twelve, fourteen, sixteen, would capture the unique self I would always be, now strikes me as a very strange way to understand freedom. I thought I would never change, and that those suggesting otherwise were the rigid ones, refusing to validate my essential self. Somewhere, I suspect, lurked a horror at the prospect of being a more unstable entity, someone who didn't actually know how she would feel twenty, thirty years down the line.

Because this is what menopause says: you aren't fixed in one place. You don't know. Whatever experiments you wish to undertake, whatever quest for true selfhood you embark upon, you are constantly moving, incapable of ever capturing that perfect, true, eternal self. Male bodies, however they present themselves, might threaten violence, and might genuinely scare us, but they don't challenge norms. Female ones do, especially older ones.

'Older women are not what we're supposed to be,' says my friend Marina. 'We do not fit the higher metaphysical conception that our society has based on what a woman is. It's like a car that won't start. You hit the menopause, or you get to forty-five and you've not had children, and it's like the car has started talking instead. The object no longer serves its purpose, but the software is still running. It's completely uncanny. That's why we seem to become invisible. It's a defence mechanism.' I think this is important. As discussed in the introduction, older women are not actually invisible; we are ignored and one reason for this is that people cannot cope with things which upset the patterns their brains have already formed, some of which are based around what women are and what they're for. To carry on living beyond menopause – to live half one's life beyond menopause – is categorised as a malfunction. In response to this, one can either revise one's assumptions and admit that female people are fully human and fully female at every stage of their lives, regardless of how this might fit in (or not) with the services male people might want from them, or one can panic at the very idea of such a fundamental overturning of gender norms. Most people panic, so much so that the aberrant older female body cannot even be acknowledged.

When we think of uncanny bodies, bodies that disrupt the social order, bodies that transgress the arbitrary bounds of normativity, we don't tend to think of menopausal ladies who lunch, or middle-aged Janet in HR, or some fifty-something shopper buying Tena Lady in Tesco. We think of glittery, fabulous bodies, bodies playing dress-up, surgically altered bodies, bodies that are telling us exactly what we want to hear: 'You're not like everyone else. The dirt and dependency – that old-style drudgery – isn't for you. Your body is what you make it.' Yet these are very normative delusions of grandeur, the continuation of millennia of patriarchal pretensions to exceptionality. We don't appreciate the way in which middle-aged female bodies, by their very reimposition of the primacy of the flesh and the inevitability of decline, disturb us. We should do, though, and if we took time to consider our own reactions to older women at every stage of our own lives, maybe we would.

Fear of death

Like many middle-aged people, I am intermittently in the throes of a major crisis about the fact I'm going to die. It's not that I haven't always known it, but there's something about the way time speeds up in your mid-forties which makes the mortality panics come thick and fast. Gripped by terror and outrage at the thought of no longer existing, I'm at a complete loss for what to do with myself. Some people respond by reminding themselves of their utter insignificance in the grand scheme of things; I tend to retreat to a fantasy in which I'm actually alive all the time at all stages of my life due to something to do with quantum physics which I haven't worked out yet but find comforting all the same.

Being a body is horrifying if you think about it too hard. Your future and mine involve sickness, dependency, pain, then nothingness, and in between, if we're not suffering ourselves, we'll be complicit in the suffering of others. There's a need to find ways to offload the horror of this onto other, lesser creatures, or else to find ways of overriding the truth of our physical state. Traditional ways of doing this have included becoming religious, blaming women or, in a classic belt-and-braces approach, combining the two. Modern times require a more sophisticated approach.

In *How to Be Animal*, Melanie Challenger describes how we respond to the threat and the embarrassment of our embodiment by clinging to a belief in our own human exceptionality. Where once religion comforted us with the idea that we were more than base, decaying matter, today 'technological and industrial advances have distanced us from and, increasingly, medicalised our animal nature such that some of us treat our bodies as a malfunctioning part of us'. The delusion that we are pure spirit, our bodies mere 'meat suits', is fuelled by an exaggerated faith in the power of science to overcome the ageing process and the inconveniences of human reproduction, and by social lives led increasingly online. 'An understanding of the bodies we inhabit as biological organisms with limits is no longer enough,' writes Susie Orbach. 'We are coached towards a dematerialised existence where almost everything we understand about living [...] will occur in the realm of thought, not in the physical, worldly body.' Online gaming makes it possible to spend the majority of one's waking hours experiencing the world as an avatar interacting with other avatars, moving through space and time in ways which the basic human form does not permit. It is possible to live this way and feel highly politically engaged, perhaps even more so than those who are mired in the reactionary world of the body. Yet, as Challenger notes, the most significant problems we face – hunger, disease, environmental collapse – remain grounded in the physical world. Denial is comforting, but it is not sustainable. Something has to give. Someone else has to be body so you don't have to. It's usually your mum.

I mean this quite seriously. Perhaps not your actual mum, but that sort of person – that tranche of older women you're aware of in your teens and early adulthood who represent the tasks you'd never really want to take on, the places you'd never really want to end up, the jobs you'd like to see done but would never actually want to do yourself. Those women who remind you of your own vulnerability and dependency, and of the horror and humiliation of corporeal limitation. One minute you can be pondering a future in which you download your true self onto a supercomputer in order to live out eternity, the next she's there, bringing you a cup of tea and a biscuit, picking up your pants and giving you a look that says, no, you're not on the cusp of transhumanist immortality. She's literally denying your right to exist on your own transcendent terms. I think this is part of why older women manage to be perceived as simultaneously threatening and pathetically submissive, menopausal harpies screeching in the grocery aisle. The most horrific things humans ever face – our own bodily needs and limits – seem so ridiculously un-progressive, domestic and mundane.

'To be human,' writes Marçal, 'is to subordinate the body to the intellect [. . .] Woman became "body" so man could be "soul". She was bound more and more tightly to corporeal reality so he could be freed from it.' The relationship between fear of mortality and fear of women is rooted in the conviction that women are body in a way that men are not, a conviction reinforced every minute of every day in a male-default world that pretends to be sex-neutral. In *Misconceptions*, Naomi Wolf describes taking an aqua-aerobics class while pregnant and noticing all the women around her are 'elderly or middle-aged':

I felt as if I had slipped. I had fallen into a primordial soup of femaleness, of undifferentiated post-fecundity [...] I, a woman, was also experiencing for the first time the feeling of misogyny, and understanding why the fear of women is grounded in the fear of death.

Responses to ageing female bodies combine a type of highbrow moral panic at corporeal limitation, and mundane irritation at bad old mummy for being so boring and unimaginative.

This is particularly noticeable at a time when, to quote the journalist Mary Harrington, progressive politics has embraced an overcoming of the body as 'a civil rights and social justice issue'. 'Emerging digital and biological technologies,' argues Harrington, 'from egg-freezing and commercial surrogacy through online sex work to the aggressively expansionary medical field of transgender medicine, are all fiercely championed by progressives today – because they advance the cause of individual freedom.' Anyone who stands in the way of this is anti-progress, the existential equivalent of the controlling parent who won't let you be yourself. Yet here we women are, still getting periods, still gestating humans, still experiencing menopause, still existing as humans with distinct, linear lifecycles, as though we never got the liberation memo.

'Women,' writes Challenger, 'because of their visceral

role in reproduction, serve as potent reminders that we are animals':

> After repeated studies on attitudes towards women, psychologist Christina Roylance has concluded that believing humans to be a unique and superior species might offer the benefit of existential confidence, but such beliefs may come at the cost of derogating women [...] In making sense of our times, it's worth remembering that – consciously and subconsciously – many people don't like to be reminded that we are animals, so much so that we may unconsciously rebel against anything that seems to place us in this category.

Older women told they must 'update' their understanding of biology because it is 'stuck in the past' are really being told something else: don't tell your body story, because it undermines the delusion that we have put all that messy stuff behind us.

What is particularly disturbing about this thinking, beyond the fact that it replicates a religious model it purports to quash, is that it furthers exploitation while preaching liberation. Fantasies of disembodiment are a luxury for the young, the healthy, the wealthy and the male. Death, as Zadie Smith so aptly put it, is 'so anti-aspirational'. The mind-body, human-animal hierarchy is overlaid with male-female, rich-poor, young-old and healthy-sick. If, like most people, you do not want to engage in 'lowly' work, this overlaying can be psychologically useful, at least until you, too, get poor, ill, old and/or are forced to remind the world of your own femaleness. In the meantime, you will need a scapegoat for all those times when reality intrudes, when you become conscious of the degree to which social and economic inequality depends on the fact that a minority of people, most of them female, spend their time clearing up the shit, piss, blood, vomit and detritus of the rest.

The economic oppression of postmenopausal women, argues Jacquelyn N. Zita, is 'enhanced by an ideology of sexist ageism that views the older female body as a surface for the metaphors of disease, disability, and medical dependency, calling into question, with increasing age, female entitlement to state-sanctioned public power'. The practice of dumping 'the more odious meanings of ageism [...] on the female body' is connected to the maintenance of a patriarchal status quo: demonise the middle-aged women who perform the majority of unpaid care work so that you don't have to value them; classify the elderly women who need the majority of care as 'not having worked', hence not having earned a functioning social care system; alienate younger women from both groups by tapping into their own fears about ageing and exploitation, convincing them that rejection of the body constitutes rejection of a similar fate. Like the beauty myth, body denialism alienates women from one another, preventing them from understanding what is done to them because of – and in spite of – their bodies.

Middle-aged women's bodies, and their work in dealing with the mess of other people's bodies, are devalued and degraded because they remind us what we are and what we will become. They also remind us that Mummy, Mother Nature, whatever we want to call her, cannot save us, despite her own sacrifices. 'That's one of the fundamental dynamics,' says Lucy, an academic in her fifties who relates the ageist misogyny of younger colleages and students to existential panic, particularly in the face of climate change. 'It's blaming older women for the difficulties with ensuring life itself. It's this "we hate you, but you're not looking after us". No one expects that of the blokes.'

Old age, infirmity and death are everyone's future, but older women are being scapegoated for the human condition. We're all going to die but first, blame your mum.

Nothing in common? Why body stories matter

'Woman has ovaries, a uterus,' wrote Simone de Beauvoir:

> ... these peculiarities imprison her in her subjectivity, circumscribe her within the limits of her own nature [...] Man superbly ignores the fact that his anatomy also includes glands, such as the testicles, and that they secrete hormones. He thinks of his body as a direct and normal connection with the world, which he believes he apprehends objectively, whereas he regards the body of woman as a hindrance, a prison, weighed down by everything peculiar to it.

You may have noticed that people rarely quote that section of *The Second Sex* these days. They're much keener on the bit at the start of Book Two where Beauvoir declares 'one is not born, but rather becomes, a woman'. This is because if you squint a bit and don't take the trouble to read the sentence directly after it, you can pretend Beauvoir was suggesting biological sex is irrelevant, not that 'the figure that the human female presents in society' is the product of 'civilisation as a whole'. She understood that the positioning of man as One, woman as Other, denies women a body story which is permitted to stand alone. Men's perceptions of themselves as, alternately, the default bodies, the only bodies that matter, or not bodies at all, remain untouchable, while women must constantly flit between flight, denial and apology, until it gets too much.

'You know it's not possible to reach your forties as a woman and not have come against some pretty physical realities,' says the journalist Helen Joyce. 'It's hard to maintain a sort of ghost in the machine idea when you know you've been made such an animal.' Men age, too, but the twin illusions of self-sufficiency and 'smooth continuity' – facilitated by offloading the social, economic and psychological costs of embodiment onto women – enable the sex that remains One, not Other, to treat the idea that one might need a body story as self-limiting, fetishistic, perhaps even a ploy to make others uncomfortable. Men might, at a push, be able to empathise with women at specific points in the female lifecycle, but it is harder to convey the need for a bigger picture, one that links past and present.

If puberty is a shock that certain young women have sought to resist using whatever narratives their era has on offer – desperately seeking ways 'of shrinking back, of reserving, preserving the self, fighting free of sexual and emotional entanglements' – then the shock of menopause is of a different order. By this point, you tend to know that the fault is not yours. You have worked out that the game is rigged, pushing you first to deny your difference, as though acknowledgement itself is the thing that brings it into being, then judging you for this difference, having robbed you of the linguistic and analytical tools with which to defend yourself.

Language matters, because the shift towards gender-neutral language to describe female embodied experiences – reducing female people to gestators, menstruators, birthers, chestfeeders and the like – has a particular impact on older women. When you are younger, it is easier to conceive of discrimination as a series of isolated events to which the label 'something that happens to women' may be applied. For many of us, it is only when we are older that connections become clearer.

Sex-based discrimination is the story of a body, multiple stories of multiple bodies, each one different, but each one gaining weight and consistency as each year passes. It is not just about what someone is doing to your body at this very moment. It is not about whether you are a menstruator or a birther or a pregnant person. Indeed, the impact of where your body is situated because it is female – regardless of what it is doing, has done or will go on to do – increases over time, even as fertility wanes. Postmenopausal women are not pregnant, not fertile, not rated fuckable, do not fall into any of the official 'feminine bodies at risk' categories most frequently highlighted by liberal feminism, yet they pay the price for having potentially been all of these things and more. They will still be paying this price into very old age, no matter how 'defeminised' their bodies are deemed to have become. 'All that sexes the body is the here and now' is the luxury belief of someone who doesn't have a postpartum prolapse and a decimated pension plan. 'All we have is what we did,' says one interviewee. 'We have no potentiality in the patriarchal marketplace. All older women have left is their fucking womanhood.' That womanhood is not a series of arbitrary snippets, but continuous.

'The thing I keep coming back to,' writes Suzanne Moore, 'is the relationship between biology and the way women are treated. I too would love a drug that could disconnect me from that. Who wouldn't?' Perhaps to some it appears that menopause is the drug that disconnects women of Moore's age and mine from the multiple traumas inflicted on female bodies. We don't experience the drama of reproductive control, so what do we have to complain about? Only the dull, obvious things that have built up over the years, drop by drop: trauma, poverty, increasing domestic responsibilities, walls closing in. These are the things that require the most dramatic, far-reaching transformations to resolve, but they are boring. You don't see them happening in real time. It is hard to explain why and how a rape or an abortion at the age of twenty will still be changing your life when you are in your fifties, or how it connects to all the other ways in which your body has been sidelined over the years. A common argument as to why transgenderism differs from transracialism is that racial inequality accumulates across generations whereas sex inequality does not. This is correct. Sex inequality accumulates across lifecycles. This is what makes disidentification from older women such a great draw. You think you can get in fast and disinherit yourself.

When younger women do not identify a common thread across the generations – because they have been told this is 'essentialist' – this naturally benefits the class of people who do not want sex inequality to be understood as a cumulative process. There is no shortage of men, many of whom call themselves feminists, who are more than eager to support younger women in their efforts to cut ties with the middle-aged hags. The enthusiasm such men show in decrying 'biological essentialism' (rather than, say, pensions inequality, the unequal distribution of domestic labour or the motherhood penalty) is a thing to behold. Simply for naming our bodies we can be accused of being cruel, exclusionary, colonialist, traditionalist, racist, misogynist, and of engaging in commentary akin to 'discussions of women, gays and black people in the magazines of the fifties'. It is not the fault of middle-aged women that we do not live in 'a world in which we all have the autonomy to make our own bodies', but just as we have been blamed for crop failures, sour milk, being cast out from Paradise and death itself, we are now being blamed for this. There is something quite comical about the way in which denial of the salience of sex marries up with disgust for women at the point at which biology means they fail to fall into the categories 'fuckable' or 'reproductively useful'. Regardless of whether they plant their ideological roots in religion or postmodern theory, men who don't want you to share knowledge about the politics of a sexed lifecycle are hyper-aware of the biological stages of women's lives. The trouble is, one cannot simply present this as something these men are doing alone. There are women who cheer them on. I think I would once have been one of them.

Embodied life stages are all that any of us have; they're what being a person is. The linguistic and political dismissal of the female body is the dismissal of the cultural, social, economic, racial and class-based histories of women. It denies women any recognition of the differences between us precisely because it prevents us from identifying the one thing that connects us. It says 'there is nothing – absolutely nothing – that you have in common'. No reason for the annihilations of the past, no sense of why you find yourself where you are now, and certainly no link to older women, who are not, can never be, your future.

Knowing only what I didn't want to be, I once thought I could edit my story before it was written, scripting it in such a way as not to end up with loss, interruption, grief. I didn't want a body story because, being female, I saw that as the genre in which I'd end up playing the loser. It is terrible to live this way, with every sensation reminding you of the trap you have made of your own self. I wanted to be 'a pure mind, a walking brain', but the irony is, it is not rejection of the flesh that gets you there. I am as much mind/brain now as I ever was, not in the sense of being a starving genius, but in the sense that my 'purest' thoughts arise from the tangled threads of my body story. It is all one, and it is impoverished thought, a limited vision, that cannot cope with flesh, time, legacy, and must instead slice all away.

Feminism is not an escape hatch. If you want that, there is religion, and there's the path of the women I knew who never got beyond thirty-five. And anyhow, as Ursula K. Le Guin wrote with regard to menopause, 'it seems a pity to have a built-in rite of passage and to dodge it, evade it, and pretend nothing has changed. That is to dodge and evade one's womanhood, to pretend one's like a man. Men, once initiated, never get the second chance. They never change again. That's their loss, not ours. Why borrow poverty?'

3

DIRTY HAG

There would, in fact, be no youth culture without the powerless older woman. There can be no leisure elite consuming class unless it is off the back of someone. The older woman is who the younger women are better than – who they are more powerful than and who is compelled to serve them.

Barbara Macdonald, *Look Me in the Eye*

#JustBeKind

Anon

When people ask me what I am writing about, I am eager to avoid embarrassment, for them and for me.

'Oh, just middle-aged women,' I say, panicking, somewhat ridiculously, at the thought that I've suddenly exposed myself as one.

'What about middle-aged women?' enquire the more foolhardy among them.

'Oh, you know,' I say, waving a suddenly very obviously middle-aged hand.

'Go on.'

What to say? I don't want to mention beauty. Or menopause. Definitely not sex and violence, and gender is out of the question.

'Housework,' I announce. 'Unpaid labour. The care crisis. Pensions inequality. The impact of Brexit and Covid-19 on the gender pay gap as it relates to women in the cohort that first experienced—'

Obviously by this point the eyes of my interlocutor have glazed over, which is a shame, because these are actually fascinating and important topics. They sound very boring, though. They're issues belonging to yesterday's feminism, unresolved; we've moved onto brighter, shinier things, controversial themes, the kind of stuff that might get you a death threat on social media. The most online drama you're likely to get with matters domestic is some performative privilege jostling over who's allowed to pay for a cleaner. Other than that, we're all quietly watching the dust mount, hoping no one notices when it's our turn to get down on our knees.

Yet it seems to me the subject of women and unpaid work is everything. It's deeply entwined with questions surrounding life stages, generational difference and identity. It's about political ideology, gender stereotypes, 'natural' roles and the multiple ways in which exploitation can be recast as virtue. It's about motherhood, regardless of whether or not you are a mother yourself. Above all, though, it's about who does the jobs nobody else wants to do, and what we believe about these people and these jobs as a consequence.

Like many women of my generation, I didn't think housework, or child- and eldercare would be disproportionately loaded onto women by the time I reached middle age. The injustice of this had already been pointed out back in 1963, when Betty Friedan identified 'the problem that has no name'. Resistance to a more equal distribution of domestic labour was, I was quite convinced, cohort-specific. Media representations of the so-called 'mummy wars' made it look like a battle between ageing traditionalists, who wanted women barefoot and pregnant, and young progressives, who believed we should be able to make the same choices as men. It didn't cross my mind that men my age would end up wanting a housewife in all but name, too. I thought that the problem that had no name had been vanquished by the naming.

To me, a Generation Xer, the politics of mess – dirt, dust, bodily effluvia – was itself a form of mess that a previous generation of women were supposed to have dealt with, saving me and my sisters the bother. I didn't realise that feminism is like housework, like all women's work, requiring routine goings-over, constant maintenance, year after year. I couldn't see how much my own prejudices about older women – the Universal Mummy class – informed my unrealistic expectations regarding my own future. I simply thought these older women would have sorted matters, quietly, invisibly, domestic equality materialising like freshly washed pants appearing in an underwear drawer. I wouldn't say thank you, obviously. I'd just notice if something wasn't quite as it should be.

And so I notice it now, like the boorish husband lying on the couch while his wife sweeps up, occasionally informing her she's 'missed a bit there'. Oi! Friedan! I think. This isn't the utopia you hoped for! Only Betty's no longer around, and it's my generation's turn to be both victim and emblem of 'that' problem. We've become the women who weren't supposed to exist by the time we got to be them, fairy-tale heroines outliving our virtue.

The moment we picked up the broomstick, we became the witch.

The drip-drip effect

According to Ada Calhoun, author of *Why We Can't Sleep: Women's New Midlife Crisis*, the 'sandwich generation' 'feels far too tame' as a way of describing the experiences of middle-aged women caring for young and old: 'I prefer to think of it as being on a rack, wrists and ankles tied to opposite ends, with two pulls ever strengthening.' It shouldn't be this way.

Over half a century since the publication of *The Feminine Mystique* and four decades after the Wages for Housework campaign, no one ought to be able to plead ignorance regarding the impact of domestic inequality on women's lives. It is a form of theft, transferring leisure time, opportunities and material resources from one sex class to another. Its impact builds over a lifetime, culminating in headlines such as 'Women could face £100,000 pension pot shortfall compared to men – and need to work longer' and 'Women will be poorer than men in retirement for another 140 years due to pandemic'. Women are penalised towards the end of life for having been progressively exploited at earlier life stages. That's *penalised*, not compensated. Why do we continue to tolerate such a massive, obvious con?

'On average, women carry out 60 per cent more unpaid work than men,' states the Women's Budget Group's 2020 report, 'Spirals of Inequality'. 'Women spend around twice as much time on unpaid cooking, childcare and housework than men, with transport being the only area where men do more unpaid work than women.' The disparity increases around the time most women have their first child, and is further impacted by lifecycle events, with women aged forty-five to fifty-four being 'more than twice as likely as men to have given up work to care and over four times more likely to have reduced working hours due to caring responsibilities'. As Linda Scott notes in *The Double X Economy*, 'it is virtually always the woman who quits or shifts to part time work when children come [...] Women's "responsibilities" in the home gradually result in lower pay and less advancement at work.'

It is important to understand this not just in terms of 'traditionalism' or isolated incidents of explicit sexism, but as a story playing out across life stages, often invisibly. In the words of the UN Development Programme's 'Tackling Social Norms' report, 'older women's challenges accumulate through the life course [...] Along the way, social norms and path dependence – how outcomes today affect outcomes tomorrow – interact to form a highly complex system of structural gender gaps.' The inequality is cumulative and it is also latent, meaning women who are not yet or only marginally affected remain more vulnerable to exploitation than men.

We are a free resource in reserve, placed on standby for when disaster strikes, something which has become more obvious in recent years due to the impact of Conservative austerity policies, Brexit and Covid-19. Each has contributed to a drip-drip effect which sees women pushed further and further to the peripheries of economic life. In *Invisible Women*, Caroline Criado Perez points out that UK cuts to public services following the 2008 financial crash 'are not so much savings as a shifting of costs from the public sector onto women because [care work] still needs to be done'. Looking at mixed-sex couples, the Institute for Fiscal Studies has found that during the 2020 lockdowns women's home work involved far more interruptions for domestic and care work, 'irrespective of [the couples'] pre-lockdown relative pay', while

Department of Health warnings that 'women will be forced to quit their jobs to look after ill or ageing relatives if the supply of EU care workers is severed after Brexit' look set to become a reality.

Looking at the impact of Tory welfare changes on women, Philip Alston, the UN's Special Rapporteur on extreme poverty, remarked that 'if you got a group of misogynists in a room, and said guys, how can we make this system work for men and not for women, they wouldn't have come up with too many other ideas than what's already in place'. Such a meeting might never have been held, but still we get a series of choices which, however casually and unthinkingly they are made, take resources from women and give them to men. The more this happens, the more important it becomes to shift the blame onto women.

There are multiple ways in which this can be achieved. From an historical perspective, the sheer effort that men have put in to persuading women that we are morally and/or biologically pre-programmed to undertake dull, repetitive work behind closed doors for no pay whatsoever is staggering (it would have been less effort for them to just do the dishes themselves). *It's your Christian duty! ... No, wait, it's just a moral duty to your lord and master! ... Wait, hang on, it's all to do with science, which has found absent mothers destroy their children's mental health ... Sorry, news just in: you're needed at home because the destruction of the nuclear family is causing drug addiction and a major crime wave ... Breaking: masculinity in crisis! You need to get behind the hob before your husband loses his sense of self and takes to the woods, Iron John-style! ... No, we're back to science now. Turns out MRI scans show you're hardwired to take on all the unpaid domestic shitwork, even if you don't feel thus hardwired (objecting to the science here being evidence of your lack of male, science-y hardwiring)* ... Debunking this is a never-ending game of whack-a-mole: yet another thing on the to-do list that women don't need.

The nineties and early noughties saw a fashion for books with titles such as *Men Are from Mars, Women Are from Venus, The Essential Difference, Why Men Can't Iron and Women Can't Read Maps,* and *Women Are Hardwired to Wash Underpants, Men Are Born to Rule.** The work of academics such as Cordelia Fine and Deborah Cameron might have since debunked the idea (again) that women love cleaning but are just too unscientific to know it, but something else had to come in its place. The fact that labour exploitation increases over time, reaching a peak when women are in midlife and the pay gap is at its widest, makes the demonisation of older women a particularly attractive option.

Today's sandwich generation women find ourselves caught, not just between responsibilities towards those who are younger and older than us, but between old-style, if now unvoiced, expectations of servitude and a more 'enlightened' rejection of 'the domestic woman' as identity. In this sense, no matter how much we talk about the care crisis or the pay gap, the problem *still* has no name. Several trends in contemporary politics – the alignment of domesticity with conservatism; a 'reinvention' of the family that ignores the intractability of sexism; the insistence that the majority of female people identify with the socially constructed gender assigned to them; plus the prioritisation of identity over class, and cohort over lifecycle, in analyses of inequality – combine to make unpaid labour a political issue in theory, but those who are most affected political outcasts. No one can claim that older women are not being exploited; they can, however, position

---

* I may have invented the last title, but am sure someone, somewhere, will have considered it.

the figure of 'exploited older woman' in such a way that she becomes undeserving of sympathy.

Doing it all differently – or not

Second-wave feminism deconstructed the housewife, but didn't get rid of the housework. If, as Judith Butler claims, 'gender is an identity tenuously constructed in time, instituted in an exterior space through a stylised repetition of acts', what does that say about the ageing hag who still does the unpaid domestic work, day after day? Untethered from a power analysis that accommodates wiping arses and cleaning the toilet, contemporary gender politics might well look upon such a woman and see just a throwback, someone who ended up *there* because *there* is a daily enaction of what she is.

'When I was pregnant with my oldest,' recalls Mary-Ann Stephenson of the Women's Budget Group, 'my own mother said to me, "What you've got to realise is that nobody makes a decision to end up where they are. They make a series of individual decisions, all of which seem right at the time."' Where a woman finds herself at forty, fifty, sixty, is not a direct expression of her politics, desires or inner self. It's the result of a series of twists and turns: the jobs, the relationships, the pregnancies, the sick relatives, the dishes, the dust. It's the result of chance, of compromise, and of coercion. It's a messy story, and not one that appeals to a feminism that prizes self-definition, autonomy and freedom. Becoming the woman who's torn between stressed teenagers, ailing parents and managing the menopause is not aspirational. Before you've become her yourself, it is easier to look at such a woman and think, as Stephenson puts it, 'I'd never let myself get into that situation. There's that sense, isn't there, that somehow you won't be as foolish.'

Adrienne Rich wrote of looking at her own mother and thinking, 'I too shall marry, have children – but *not like her. I shall find a way of doing it all differently.*' Yet such revolutionary intentions can fall by the wayside as the jobs mount and you find yourself occupying that sleep-deprived zone in which the distinction between obligation and natural inclination is blurred. 'You know,' says Esther Parry, forty-nine, 'your children have to be picked up from school, they have to be fed, a house has to be cleaned. Women aren't doing it because they're into it. They're not, like, orgasm, orgasm, orgasm in the frozen aisle of Tesco because they love it so much. They're doing it because it has to be done.' Yet the more that needs doing, the more you are visibly caught in a network of demands that ties you to identities and roles you might once have sought to reject.

A polarised political landscape that divides people into goodies and baddies – those on the right side of history, and those who must languish in eternal shame – plus a gender politics which prioritises superficial transgressions over labour redistribution simply cannot comprehend how one might end up a fifty-something housewife ranting on Mumsnet – at least if that wasn't who one was to begin with. It cannot allow itself the wiggle room to understand the subtleties of complicity and coercion, or that ageing is not just a process of loss but of accumulation. Women lose time, status and economic power in relation to men as we age, but accumulate relationships, social obligations and, crucially, compromises. Viewed only through the lens of identity politics, this can be written off as acquiescence to 'traditional' values, as though one's true self – someone who never really wanted to 'do it all differently' – is finally being revealed. This creates a new, pseudo-progressive way of essentialising the relationship between femaleness and domestic servitude. If what middle-aged women do is an endlessly repeated, re-negotiated expression of what we are, then who are we to complain about it? Indeed, given that what we do harks back to a less progressive era of pipe-and-slippers traditionalism, doesn't that make us the enemy?

The generation of women who came of age in the wake of the second wave are hamstrung due to the contrast between what feminism says about women in terms of our potential and what has happened to us over the course of our lives. Younger women can tell themselves it is not the fault of older women that we cannot see beyond the kitchen sink – our brains are dulled by repetitive, thankless tasks, making whatever analysis they might offer of our plight of no use whatsoever – whereas they, with their bright, sharp minds, will never end up where we are. I have lost count of the number of times I have seen older women told that they are stupid for having failed to 'train' those around them to take on an 'equal share' of unpaid work. The 'equal share' message was already out there in the nineties, was it not? How did they miss the memo? The fact that these women's choices have been progressively limited, both directly (through social and familial pressure, violence, economic necessity, gender stereotyping) and indirectly (through social and economic structures which favour male lifecycles), is utterly discounted. We are, as Stephenson says, regarded as having been 'foolish'. We are not structurally oppressed in the way that earlier women were, just hopeless at delegation.

While a failure to redistribute unpaid work is our fault (for some reason, redistribution, like remembering birthdays, is 'our' job), those whose hands are unsullied by the compromises of domesticity are able to appoint themselves judge and jury regarding our feminist missteps. In a 2016 *Guardian* piece entitled 'Yes, there is one great contribution men can make to feminism: pick up a mop', Helen Lewis describes her experiences of attending feminist events and being asked by men what they can do to help the cause. So she tells them: 'The washing-up. Or the laundry, I'm easy. Or going part-time while the kids are small':

> At this point, the light in their eyes tends to die. It turns out that when they said they wanted men to be involved in feminism, what they actually meant was 'have someone listen to their ideas about what feminists are currently doing wrong'. Not do a load of boring unpaid work in return for absolutely zero praise.

Dull domestic labour is of little interest to those who want to 'smash the gender binary', presumably because those currently engaged in dull domestic labour are already written off as enforcers rather than victims of gender norms. As Gia Milinovich tweeted in response to pop singer Harry Styles's rather bold assertion that he wished to 'dispel the myth of a binary existence' – unlike, say, every woman who's so much as expressed an opinion without male permission – 'You know what men could do that would "dispel the myth of a binary existence"? Do the laundry. Wash the dishes. Do the cooking [...] Do some of their family's emotional labour.... Now THAT would be revolutionary.'

Only a woman who refuses to do the laundry, or who demands that *you* pick up the kids for once, is rarely perceived to be bravely queering gender. On the contrary, she's just some Hausfrau going off on one about domestic matters, which only proves how obsessed she is with such trivia rather than with something of genuine importance. Meanwhile, a woman who gets to work without complaint can be dismissed as having the privilege of being totally attuned to her position in life. What is missing is any acknowledgement of a relationship between gender and power, which develops over time and across life stages. Such an acknowledgement risks undermining the assumptions about older women, conservatism and domesticity we use to avoid feeling guilty about exploiting Mummy, and to avoid addressing the fact that we might be next in line. The belief that we can 'do it all differently' depends on seeing the woman we don't want to become as someone without an inner life or a story that could have turned out differently, too.

Domesticity as complicity

Many contemporary criticisms of middle-aged women and their alleged 'reactionary' or 'harmful' politics call on tropes evoking domesticity. It's not so much that older women have no place in politics because their place is in the home, so much as those women who *are* in the home – in this day and age! – represent a politics that is by definition out of date. In articles mocking idiotic 'White Facebook Aunts' and wholesale dismissals of 'the lost cause of suburban wine moms', it's implied that to end up fussing over the petty details of relational, embodied human life – who drives Grandma to her colonoscopy, when the next PTA meeting is, who tackles that odour behind the fridge – is to fail to realise that it's a brave new fluid world out there. Sexist archetypes such as the soccer mom and the frumpy, middle-aged antivaxxer link older women's role in the family to regression and fear of progress. The trans activist Grace Lavery has associated an old, exclusionary, pleasure-phobic feminism with 'leaky boobs and the school run'. It's a form of victim-blaming, one

which ensures the critic can float above such lowly, reactionary beliefs as 'middle-aged women exist to serve me' while
never actually being denied service. The unpaid carer, the
middle-aged woman sandwiched between older and younger
dependants, isn't actually a person; she's an emblem. She's the
creature the rest of us evolve out of being.

And yet ... Much as I would like to claim there is no truth
in stereotypes about middle-aged, middle-class housewives
and their regressive views, the relationship between domesticity, feminism, conservatism and privilege is a complex
one. The unpaid labour undertaken by women entrenches
divisions between women, with some groups enacting subtle
pay-offs between short-term personal gain and long-term
global inequality. To deal with the politics of mess we must
acknowledge just how tremendously messy it is.

Women's unpaid work is an intersectional issue, by which
I do not mean it is 'an issue which provides yet another
excuse to tell white, middle-aged, middle-class women how
privileged they are so they can shut the hell up about having
to do a bit of cleaning now and then'. I mean that while it is
essentially true that men are progressively stealing time and
money from women, it matters to identify which men, which
women. If I refer to pension poverty, or falling behind in the
workplace, am I referring to losses that are absolute or relative? As a white, middle-class woman in a white, middle-class
family, my knee-jerk response is to compare myself to white,
middle-class men, ignoring all the ways in which I steal from
less privileged men and women in order to live as I do. I don't
write this – on a laptop built under conditions about which I
know far too little – in order to indulge in some self-serving
declaration of privilege. It's just true. As the Women's Budget
Group reports, white women are least likely to be classified as 'economically inactive', while women of Pakistani,

Bangladeshi and Black African origin experience the biggest
gender pay gap relative to white British men.

When discussing the sex inequality that builds over a lifetime, it is difficult to claim 'they', the men, are doing this to
'us', the women, without also recognising how deeply inter-
twined our personal lives are with those of the men around
us. Domesticity, particularly in a heterosexual context,
demands a level of complicity that impacts on matters of race
and socio-economic class. Depending on where one is located
on three axes of privilege – race, sex, class – the unpaid work
one performs can be an act of submission, reinscribing one's
own disadvantage within one's immediate circle, but also a
deal brokered in order to preserve advantages over outsiders.
That it is not just one thing or the other can be profoundly
discomfiting, conferring on a certain type of woman a high/
low status that denies her the position of 'true' victim.

In *Jews Don't Count*, David Baddiel describes how anti-
semitism plays on a 'high-low duality': 'the image of Jews [. . .]
is always weak and contemptible but never victimised. In the
double-sided hate, the low-ness of Jews is that they are hide-
ous and irritating and repugnant, but this is just a condition of
being Jewish, it is not forced upon them.' While these are different forms of oppression, each deserving of consideration in
its own right, there are similarities here to responses to 'privileged' women deemed to be so deeply embedded in the family
structures of dominant groups that issues of exploitation and
coercion are no longer deemed to apply. A white, heterosexual, middle-class woman who is marginalised within her own
home isn't so much a victim as a failure. This is a problem
not just for her, but for women for whom domesticity offers a
form of respite from intersecting oppressions in public space.

In their rush to avoid being tainted by the compromises
of Mumsnetters, Facebook Aunts and suburban wine moms,

young white (and largely middle-class) feminists risk repeating a longstanding white feminist failure to identify positive aspects to domesticity. 'Historically, black women,' wrote bell hooks in 'Revolutionary Parenting', 'have identified work in the context of family as humanizing labor, work that affirms their identity as women, as human beings showing care and love, the very gestures of humanity white supremacist ideology claimed black people were incapable of expressing.' This is very much in contrast not just to Friedan's tunnel-vision rejection of white fifties housewifery, but also to current third-wave feminist obsessions with family abolition.

Whether or not the family is a source of humanisation or privilege consolidation depends very much on one's position in the world beyond it. Second-wave white feminists such as Sara Ruddick and Adrienne Rich wrote about the way in which (white, middle-class) motherhood imposed conditions of compromise on (white, middle-class) women, for which they were then blamed (as the average Mumsnetter is today). 'A mother,' argued Ruddick, 'typically takes as the criterion of her success the production of a young adult acceptable to her group [...] She is the person principally responsible for training her children in the ways and desires of obedience. This may mean training her daughters for powerlessness, her sons for war, and both for crippling work in dehumanizing factories, businesses, and professions.' I often sense this is the context in which many idealistic, privileged young women rage against middle-class mummies one generation above them. 'Patriarchy,' wrote Rich, 'depends on the [white, privileged] mother to act as a conservative influence, imprinting future adults with patriarchal values.' She may do so because she believes in them; or she may do so because she thinks it the only way to protect her child. She might not be able to distinguish between the two. Part of the anger felt by more privileged younger women towards their older counterparts comes, I think, from this unspoken awareness: that their relative safety might come from their mother's 'badness'. That their hands are dirty, too, and offering Mummy as a sacrifice to the social justice gods will not be enough to make them clean.

'Feminist theory,' wrote Maureen Freely, 'has a hard time with motherhood because it has a hard time with legacy':

> because it has a hard time acknowledging that it has benefited from this legacy, and that it reflects this legacy even when it doesn't want to, and perpetuates this legacy even as it is struggling to do the opposite. If you are unwilling to accept the cruel truths about the cultural heritage that has made you what you are, if you are unwilling to accept that, like it or not, the version you will be passing on to the next generation will, at best, be only slightly better, then you cannot help but think of mothers as beyond redemption. You cannot even look at a mother without seeing the ideological problem monstrously illustrated.

Freely was writing in 1995, but I suspect this is more relevant than ever today, when motherhood is, for younger middle-class women, increasingly deferred and associated with generational privilege as well as more 'traditional' views. The belief that one will 'do it all differently' is applied not just to parenting practices and labour redistribution, but to the passing on of race- and class-based privileges. If one decides one can, through sheer force of will, avoid reproducing white supremacist capitalist patriarchy when one eventually reproduces, then those who have already reproduced must indeed have been 'beyond redemption'.

A tidy discussion of mess is not an honest one. The neglect of the middle-aged, unpaid carer is rendered more palatable by the caricature of the privileged, middle-aged mummy – but it is a caricature based on the reality of privilege, how it is embedded and how it is transmitted within a social group. We can make this all Mummy's fault – her mess to deal with – as though no one else has a body and no one else is wrecking the joint, but this only perpetuates the problem. Personal disidentification is an ego trip, not a solution. For a solution, we need to recognise the importance of dependency as much as that of freedom.

I hate you, Mummy: the older woman as scapegoat for dependency panic

In 2019 *UnHerd* published a column by Giles Fraser, in which he recounted the experience of a male GP friend receiving a call from a desperate woman in her fifties:

> Her elderly and confused father had soiled himself and she wanted to know if the surgery could send someone round to clean him up. 'Did you have children?' my friend asked her. She did. He went on: 'When they were babies did you ever contact the state to see if it would come round to change their nappies?' She went quiet. Ouch, what a question.

What a question indeed. Thankfully, Fraser reached the conclusion that Britain's departure from the EU would force such shirkers to take more responsibility for their loved ones, since no one else would be around to do it. Dependency is a good thing, providing it's on middle-aged women and not paid help or the state or other countries, or indeed anything that involves money or formal recognition. Then dependency is a bad thing. It's funny that way.

Fraser's argument isn't explicitly gendered, but it doesn't have to be. The GP's retort calls on a principle of continuity. The person who took time off work to look after babies will be the person more likely to do the same to look after older relatives, not least because her earlier career breaks and/or recourse to part-time work will mean she is earning less than a male partner or male siblings. Indirect discrimination begets further indirect discrimination. And anyway, if a woman who's already spent years providing such services suddenly says no, isn't she just being mean?

On the surface, this is a right-wing/traditionalist position on gender being used to bolster a right-wing/traditionalist position on international politics. Except it's not that straightforward. Just as the result of the 2016 referendum cannot be understood in terms of a pure split between left/right or Labour/Tory, 'traditionalism' is something of a red herring when it comes to explaining the expectation that care work is performed by individual women on an informal, unpaid basis. People often want the same things – self-determination, sovereignty, relief from the terrifying knowledge that we are all defined by and reliant on other humans – while using different political framings to justify and meet their desires. Traditional heterosexual marriage provides a package deal for men wishing to access female reproductive, sexual and domestic labour; those who prefer a more bespoke arrangement, paying one woman for gestational services, another for cleaning, still others for sex, can declare themselves anti-traditionalist, perhaps even feminist in their calls for surrogacy reform and sex workers' rights, but the difference is superficial. Often, the 'traditionalist' is merely the man who is still using the previous generation's marketing message to get what he wants out of women, as opposed to the latest, most fashionable one.

What underpins Fraser's argument isn't a belief about

middle-aged women per se; it's the assumption that some forms of exchange – say, arranging to pay a care worker from an EU country – are socially constructed and politically charged, whereas others – middle-aged women providing care to older relatives – are just 'natural'. One thing comes at a cost which can be deemed too high, whereas the other is provided by love and hence cost-free. In this model, the creation of a better, kinder society involves directing people towards the cost-free option, which exists beyond the realm of moral and political compromise. If dependency on an imperfect institution or social set-up can be eliminated and replaced with a system reliant on virtue, then it is as though one's personal debts have been written off. The work itself hasn't gone anywhere, but its reclassification eases the consciences of the beneficiaries (who are, at one stage or another, every human being who has ever lived).

What's ironic, and particularly damning for women already stuck on the unpaid labour treadmill, is that there are strands of feminism which reinforce such a view while claiming to do the opposite. A new-found enthusiasm for family abolition led by texts such as Sophie Lewis's *Full Surrogacy Now!* offers up the same reclassification of female-coded labour masquerading as redistribution. Here, the imperfect institution is not the EU or the nanny state but the family itself, and there is the same expectation that virtue – in this case, a less stuffy version, with a trendier haircut – will save the day. It's all about squaring the self-determination circle, pretending that if we find the right set-up – the family? Not the family? The anti-family? – we can outwit the human condition. But this is impossible; our vulnerability and dependency on others, their vulnerability and dependency on us, and the compromises we have to make as a result of this, cannot ever be eliminated. But who is going to tell people this? Who will be the one telling Giles Fraser 'no, family ties are not enough to stop me reaching breaking point'? Who will be the one telling Sophie Lewis 'no, the anti-family revolution won't liberate me from the need to wipe noses and arses'?

Mummy, obviously. Probably in some crappy Mumsnet thread where she ought to be sticking to moaning about school catchment areas and her neighbour's leylandii.

Reminding others of the inevitability of human dependency always ends up being 'women's work', another thankless, boring job upon which everyone else's far more interesting leisure activities – watching *Love Island*, ripping up human rights treaties, pretending you're an actual cyborg – rely. I used to think it was analogous to domestic drudgery; now I'm convinced the two things blend into one. The woman who does the drudgework implicitly reminds you that the drudgework exists and that you are not, in fact, someone who gets to define themselves in isolation without imposing unreasonable demands on others. 'There would, in fact, be no youth culture,' wrote Barbara Macdonald in 1984, 'without the powerless older woman [...] The older woman is who the younger women are better than.' This is the real kicker: the dull, sell-out 'sandwich' woman doesn't just engage in activities which create the space for others (the conservative men, the revolutionary youth) to engage in idealism. She is deemed inferior for making them aware of that which is non-idealistic and lowly, for not getting on with things more quietly, for reminding people that their 'cost-free' politics does in fact come at a cost.

Mary-Ann Stephenson locates some of the misogyny experienced by older women in deflected guilt:

Because although people ignore [the exploitation], they also know it. And to admit it would be to admit you're complicit in inequality and particularly if you're someone who's got a

vested interest in being one of the good guys, then finding a
reason that these women are actually evil witches and therefore you don't have to listen to them is incredibly convenient.
Because it never forces you to challenge your behaviour.

It's one of those patriarchal catch-22s, which even the most
ardent feminist would have to applaud. You'd support the
cohort of women tied to the domestic sphere but for the fact
they're baddies, and they're baddies because of their ties to
the domestic sphere.

'Being human,' writes Katrine Marçal, 'is experienced
precisely through a gender, a body, a social position, and
the backgrounds and experiences that we have. There is no
other way. But we suppose that it's precisely this that we must
deny.' Being whoever you want to be is an impossibility which
patriarchal thinking – transcending any superficial divisions
between left and right – has recast as a human necessity. To
some, it is all about self-sufficiency, individualism, liberation
from the welfare state; to others, it is about self-identification,
autonomy, liberation from conservative (fixed) norms.
Different buzzwords, same objectives. It's that desire to 'take
back control', as though by sheer force of will we can shed our
uncomfortable reliance on other people and their unreliable
bodies. Were it possible to do this, then we would be safe
(lonely, less human, but safe).

I think this explains some of the rage that rises to the
surface in debates on both gender and Brexit, especially on
social media; people feel genuinely, very personally under
attack when they imagine themselves reaching some longed-
for point of self-realisation and some reality-bound, Project
Fear naysayer intervenes. It's hard to believe those insisting
on the fact of your dependency – that a 'no deal' relationship
with reality is no relationship at all – aren't just doing it to be

malicious. It's like Mummy yelling at you to tidy your room. No, scrap that: it *is* Mummy yelling at you to tidy your room, oblivious to the fact that you don't even see dirt, what with it being an arbitrarily defined social construct created only to reinforce a fascist distinction between the pure and the impure, which almost certainly didn't exist before European colonisers invented it. Take that, Mummy.

Dependency panic, and its deflection onto older women, is a response to the offloading of the 'invisible' work of dependency onto women as they age. It's also a response to the female reproductive role. The realities of pregnancy destroy people's perception of themselves as self-contained and self-defining; as Marçal notes, regardless of what an ultrasound image might show, the foetus is not 'an independent astronaut, with only an umbilical cord connecting it to the world around'. We can live in denial of our dependency, even our femaleness, but we all come from someone, someone who is, when we are in early adulthood and finding our political feet, already in middle age. You may love her, but also despise what that cohort of women represents. The mother, wrote Martha Albertson Fineman, 'embodies dependency at the same time she is trapped by the dependency of others [...] she is marred by her burdens of obligation and intimacy in an era where personal liberation and individual autonomy are viewed as both mature and essential'. Alas, she cannot expect any sympathy from her daughter's feminism; on the contrary, true to gender-normative form, all she can do is give, give, give.

The kindness trap

In a quote attributed to the novelist Henry James, three things in human life are important: 'The first is to be kind. The second is to be kind. And the third is to be kind.' Who, you might ask, would object to that? Only an evil hag.

Right now, advertising one's kindness is very much in vogue. The slogan 'Be kind' has been slapped onto T-shirts, bags, even girls' underwear. On social media we are experiencing, in the words of Suzanne Moore, 'an epidemic of #bekind'. At first glance, this is great.

Kindness culture transcends the mess of human bodies and dependencies. It is simple and superficially gender neutral. Moreover, when people – perhaps women, perhaps older women, perhaps (urgh!) mums – suggest life is complex and that the very nature of human dependency sets rights and values in competition, they can be told 'just be kind!' For those not tied down by anything so passé as actual responsibilities, ordering others to be kind can be a highly effective way of outsourcing compassion.

The trouble is, while kindness is a human value, 'being kind' remains a female-coded duty. In a world where, as Jane Caro writes, we still face 'the entrenched belief that women exist primarily for the convenience of other people', men can show their appreciation for kindness by lecturing women deemed to fall short. 'Telling other people to be kind,' writes Sarah Ditum, 'qualifies as an act of kindness in itself, which a cynical person might point out is convenient, because otherwise being kind seems a lot of work':

> Women are the ones who are supposed to be kind, to give of themselves, to play the universal mother and make other people happy. People find it particularly shocking when a woman refuses to be kind: there's something unnatural, offensive about a female mouth declaring that the limits of her care are here and she will not be giving any more.

In 1973's *Beyond God the Father*, the radical feminist philosopher Mary Daly proposed that 'much of traditional morality in our society appears to be reactions on the part of men – perhaps guilty reactions – to the behavioural excesses of the stereotypic male':

There has been a theoretical one-sided emphasis upon charity, meekness, obedience, humility, self-abnegation, sacrifice, service. Part of the problem with this moral ideology is that it became accepted not by men but by women, who hardly have been helped by an ethic which reinforces the abject female situation [...] Basically, then, the traditional morality of our culture has been 'feminine' in the sense of hypocritically idealizing some of the qualities imposed upon the oppressed.

Men create a world that is hard, aggressive, destructive, then use the fact that it should be otherwise to police female behaviour – *the world is unkind, so you must compensate on behalf of us both*. The worse the world gets, the more women are deemed to owe others. #BeKind is not gender neutral, but it is unkind – and therefore unfeminine – to point it out. This may be why it is left to the hags to do so.

When J. K. Rowling wrote about the need for less privileged female victims of male violence to access sex-segregated spaces, the actor Rupert Grint (famed for playing one of Rowling's creations) justified his decision to join those attacking her by saying 'I wanted to get some kindness out there'. The implication is that Rowling, in seeing complexity when it comes to the provision of resources, is being unkind. Nowhere is it suggested that the class of people who create the need for domestic violence refuges, sex-segregated or otherwise, are the ones who need to work on being kinder (or rather, radical feminists might suggest this, but this is cast as man-hating, which again is 'unkind').

Performing kindness is not like doing care work, which involves accumulating compromise, getting your hands dirty, offending others by reminding them of their vulnerability and dependency on everyone else. Being caring involves the risk of losing status in the eyes of others; performing kindness only elevates status. In the demonisation of the 'unkind' middle-aged woman, we see a perfect symbiotic relationship: the more she loses status, the more opportunity you have to boost yours. The dirtier her hands are, the purer you get to look alongside her. To place your own neck on the line is to be caring; to dismiss the very idea that necks ever have to go on lines is to be kind.

When David Cameron's Conservative Party proposed the Big Society to create a climate that 'empowered' people and communities to take control of their lives, many saw this as a cynical attempt to facilitate government cuts by pushing small-statism. Today's #BeKind culture has echoes of this – those with power outsource abstract values of kindness, charity, generosity and care to others while pretending this is the same thing as embodying those values themselves – but it is smarter and smoother. The work of kindness has always been something the privileged assign to the little people while preaching its virtues, but the targeting of eternal mummies by those who wish to appear progressive is a particular stroke of genius. Lip-service kindness is prized over the caring that takes time, costs money and might, if we all got behind it, require a significant degree of social reorganisation and wealth redistribution. We know that it is easier to criticise others than it is to clean up vomit, lug around failing bodies and face up to the realities of suffering, materiality and death. We can even tell ourselves that in adopting the role of critic we are, in a very real sense, the very real carers, sitting there with our very kind thoughts, whereas frumpy old Mummy, resentfully rushing around after a husband (so heteronormative!), children (so biologically essentialist!) and ageing parents (so traditional!), is not only reinforcing oppressive norms but is too stupid to even notice she is doing so.

Woman, wrote Barbara Ehrenreich and Deirdre English, has long been seen as 'a more primitive version of man – not because there is prima facie evidence of her lower intelligence, but because of her loving and giving nature, which is itself taken as evidence of lower intelligence'. The social conditioning inflicted on girls from babyhood requires them to be complicit in a performance of natural servitude: don't be too clever, don't complain, always smile. The problem with this is twofold: any woman who does this perfectly is judged an inferior being, but no woman can do this perfectly anyhow. It's a situation in which failure is baked in. Even when women who have become progressively embroiled in domestic exploitation assert themselves, this is not taken as proof that no woman is an evil-yet-bovine, norm-enforcing Stepford wife. On the contrary, pushing back against the alleged gender normativity that is one's first sin then becomes one's second.

There is in fact evidence that women in their fifties are more empathetic than men of the same age and younger or older people of either sex. Put together with the amount of unpaid labour this cohort takes on, it seems absurd that these women are so often characterised as less caring, less inclusive, less conscious of need and difference than younger women. 'The thing about being a middle-aged woman,' says Mary-Ann Stephenson, 'is that your default role is to be the person who is kind and puts everyone else ahead of you and worries more about everybody else's needs than your own.'

And so when you're doing that people don't even notice
it. They only notice it when you stop doing it. There are
still some pressures on younger women but there isn't that
same message. For them it's 'this is your time to go out
in the world and have fun and have adventures and all
of those sorts of things'. It isn't yet 'you need to sacrifice
everything'.

A further layer of difficulty is added when older women
want care for themselves. 'As little girls in our society grow
into the role of nurturer,' writes Susan Maushart, 'they inter-
nalize the lesson that, for them, the wish to be nurtured is
"inappropriate". By extension, the needs of other females for
nurture will come to be regarded with suspicion also.' Baba
Copper proposes that this dynamic is worse for older women,
the only humans from whom it remains legitimate for younger
women to expect care: 'the old woman is one whose labor/
energy can be assimilated by everyone else. We are someone
to listen to others' troubles without telling ours. We are the
dump where others are free to unload [. . .] We are subject to
a different code of honor than other women.'

In *More Than a Woman*, Caitlin Moran likens older womanhood to being 'Janet', the 'middle-aged Scottish woman'
in customer services who's always the one to sort out your
problems when everyone else has been fobbing you off:

You're Janet, now. You're the Janet in everyone's lives. If
anything's going to get sorted out, you're the one who's
going to have to do it. No more messy nights out, or voy-
ages of self-discovery. You are about to be required to hold
the fabric of society together. For no pay. That's what being
a middle-aged woman is.

It is sort-of edifying to be that person – apart from when you have needs of your own. There's a scene in Marilyn French's 1977 novel *The Women's Room* in which her protagonist Mira muses on the difference between men and women in middle age:

> But think about this: none of the men is wrecked [...] I'll leave their pain to those who know and understand it, to Phillip Roth and Saul Bellow and John Updike and poor wombless Norman Mailer. I only know the women who are all middle-aged and poor as shit and struggling [...] I remember Valerie saying once, 'Ah, don't you see that's why we're so great. We know what matters. We don't get caught up in their games!' but it seems an awfully high price to me.

I think it is interesting, and not altogether hopeful, to see the way in which the seventies rage narrative has morphed into something wry, resigned, even amused, in the intervening years. I'm still with Mira: 'knowing what matters' is all well and good, but exploitation is exploitation. #BeKind seems to function as a re-conditioning programme for older women, a booster jab administered once you've reached midlife and the effects of childhood socialisation have started to wear off.

Kate Manne suggests misogyny is used to police the woman who 'asks for or tries to take what's meant to be *hers* to give to *him*', by which she means 'feminine-coded goods', such as empathy and moral attention. Such a woman has not understood the terms of her role as an employee of Patriarchy, Inc. Men look at middle-aged women, the Eternal Mummy division, while shaking their heads and muttering about not being able to get the staff. Still, at least the younger trainees are showing great promise; once our lot have been pushed into early retirement, things will really be up and running.

For now we're continually castigated for underperformance at our regular #BeKind reviews, while our managers – the Mr Frasers and Mr Grints – are showered with plaudits for merely restating their subordinates' key performance objectives. Later these men will muse on how strange it is that female employees never quite fulfil their potential. Is it the mummy track? The impact of menopause? Training, they'll conclude. They just need more training (*methods of delivery: GP mockery; social media threats; a fist in the face if my tea isn't on the table at 6 p.m. prompt; ??print-out certificates of achievement?? Make note to ask Janet.*)

Rousseau believed that 'the whole education of women ought to be relative to men. To please them, to be useful to them, to make themselves loved and honoured by them, to educate them when young, to care for them when grown ... these are the duties of women at all times, and what should be taught them from their infancy'. The veneration of performative kindness is a restatement of demands for female-coded labour and as such it is profoundly conservative. It functions not just to extract work from women in the immediate term, but to rein them in as political and social beings. It's the gender politics equivalent to corporate woke-washing.

Patriarchy, Inc. loves shaming older women for their alleged failure to be more inclusive, empathetic and caring, because this is a substitute for men embodying these values, and a means of preserving and justifying the ongoing appropriation of women's time and labour. What's more, Patriarchy, Inc. will continue to do this to the next generation of women. The demands of the body, of age and of other people are not going to ease up. On the contrary, they may be about to get worse.

Who cooked Judith Butler's dinner?

As noted in the previous chapter, we are all going to die. First, though, we are going to have to deal with a ton of shit. There will be no great disembodied future running on AI, cyborgs and BeKind hashtags. Neither environmental collapse nor multiplying cancer cells care about your big ideals.

But enough of the cheery stuff I like to tell my kids at bedtime. What are we going to do about it? In February 2021 the cross-party think tank Demos produced its Care Commitment report. This presented 'a new model of social care funding and delivery', reflecting 'the great change that is underway across society'. Such change was characterised in terms not of wealth redistribution or a shift in responsibilities between the sexes, but 'a growing focus on social and environmental concerns; a recognition of the value of home, family and neighbourhood; a retreat from the purely material questions of economic growth and individual wealth'.

Hmm.

For all the vaunting of its 'newness', there's something about the tone of the report that smacks of eighties-style 'materialistic career women are now seeing the error of their ways' moralising. Once again, it seems we're being invited to throw away our shoulder pads and consider our future pension poverty proof that we refused to be mere cogs in the capitalist machine.

To their credit, Demos predicted cynicism from the likes of me. While the report concedes that 'it may be argued that the effect of supporting and therefore increasing unpaid care work will be to drive women out of the workforce and back into the domestic sphere', it suggests this would be 'to mischaracterise the world of work in the twenty-first century':

Human beings are increasingly being edged out of manual
and clerical jobs by automation and globalisation. What
remains as uniquely human responsibilities are the
functions of creativity – all the activities of innovation,
exploration and artistic endeavour – and of care – looking
after each other, whether as children or adults with care
needs. Choosing to do this for one's own dependant, rather
than being paid to do it for a stranger, is increasingly a
preferred option for many people; it should not be assumed
that the only valid career for a man or woman is a paid role
far from home.

In other words, the world of paid work isn't up to much,
either (if you overlook the 'paid' bit), and wiping arses is a
bit like painting a great work of art, only with shit as your
medium. And let's just gloss over the sex imbalance regarding
who does what. If one group of humans ends up being viewed
as our innovators, explorers and artists, and another our
carers, well, they're all 'uniquely human responsibilities'. If
we're all doing general human stuff, isn't it just petty to gripe
about who does which stuff in particular?

In his introduction to the report, the Conservative MP
Danny Kruger is at pains to reassure anyone concerned that
too much outside help is being proposed that the degree of
support recommended remains 'consistent with the traditional
conservative concern with personal responsibility'. There is
a delicate balance to be struck between idealising the concept of selfless care enough to sugar-coat the exploitation of
carers, and not so much that the concept starts to seep into
other areas of life (the 'uniquely human responsibilities' of
the higher-rate taxpayer must remain to himself). The care
crisis may be a social and economic reality born of existential
anxiety, but it is not one to be faced head-on. Instead we get

a combination of peripheral economic tinkering, thinly veiled guilt-tripping and word games.

The only way to eradicate the inequalities associated with care work – work that is essentially human, that cannot be outsourced to AI or done remotely, that gets to the core of who we are – would be through a serious redistribution of resources, rewards and expectations across the three axes of sex, race and socio-economic class. We should not underestimate the will *not* to do this on the part of all those who picture themselves residing on the more 'creative' side of the innovation/arse-wiping divide. Antipathy towards the redistribution of 'women's work' transcends other political differences: first, because everyone thinks they're too special and unique for drudgework until they're actually doing it, and second, because different groups use different semantic tricks in order to pretend they're doing more than moving the same mess from one side of the room to another.

Writing in the *Guardian*, Judith Butler complains that 'the vanishing of social services under neoliberalism has put pressure on the traditional family to provide care work, as many feminists have rightly argued':

In turn, the fortification of patriarchal norms within the family and the state has become, for some, imperative in the face of decimated social services, unpayable debt, and lost income. It is against this background of anxiety and fear that 'gender' is portrayed as a destructive force, a foreign influence infiltrating the body politic and destabilizing the traditional family.

A skim-read of this might suggest Butler is saying the exact opposite of Kruger by rejecting 'the family' as the primary solution to the care crisis. Only the problem is not, and has never been, 'pressure on the traditional family'. It has been pressure on female members within it, particularly older ones, with gender being the means through which this pressure is applied (and it is that which many feminists have 'rightly argued'). By attacking 'the traditional family' (vaguely, without differentiating between members) and defending 'gender' (equally vaguely) Butler, just like Kruger, indulges in hands-clean moralising without acknowledging who is exploiting whom. And just like Kruger, Butler proposes nothing more than a rebranding exercise, recasting a location on a social hierarchy (gender) as a free choice (gender identity), while doing absolutely nothing to challenge a fundamental belief: that biologically female people, whatever you call them, are 'naturally' predisposed to serve others for free.

In *Who Cooked Adam Smith's Dinner?*, Katrine Marçal argues that 'in the same way that there is a "second sex", there is a "second economy"':

> The work that is traditionally carried out by men is what counts. It defines the economic world view. Women's work is 'the other'. Everything that he doesn't do but that he is dependent on so he can do what he does.

Adam Smith, notes Marçal, might have thought about the self-interest of the butcher and the baker when it came to getting his dinner onto the table, but not about the mother who cooked for him. In a similar way, both traditional conservatism and the academic theories which play-fight it continue to treat the unpaid work of female people as 'the other'. No one gets to play at 'asserting sovereignty' or 'smashing norms' without relying on someone – Mummy – being on hand to clear up afterwards. Judith Butler has the privilege to muse on the (glaringly obvious) limitations of 'the patriarchal family'

without ever having to consider the relationship between
biological sex, power and who ends up doing the cooking.
Because in Butler's world, as in Smith's, dinner will always be
on the table, and the ivory towers will always be kept clean
and sparkling by some disappointingly non-radical female
person on minimum wage.

In 2020 the impact of Covid-19 demonstrated that what
progress actually has been made in labour redistribution can
swiftly be put in reverse. In the UK and beyond, the closing of
schools and nurseries led women, not men, to lose time, jobs
and promotions. As Anna Ziggy Melamed writes, 'it turns
out, however women identify – as empowered, as a career
woman, maybe not even as a woman anymore but as a non-
binary person – when things are stripped back, it's you with
your toddler or teenager and the washing-up'. Unless we are
able to name what is happening, we cannot prevent things
from getting worse.

Today's middle-aged woman will become an old woman
whose own needs for care may be resented (as the pandemic
showed, the belief that old people are merely a drag on the rest
of us still thrives in our kinder, more caring society). Today's
young woman will take her place in the middle of the sandwich
(or on the rack). We cannot change course until we abandon
our expectation that change will happen naturally, as though
time itself will make us better, fitter, more efficient people,
better women, who don't make foolish decisions, who don't
allow themselves to become complicit in the darker aspects of
social reproduction, who manage to perform that longed-for
magic trick of combining total self-determination with 'being
kind' (because, on some level, self-determination for women is
no different from an embrace of self-sacrifice. The angel in the
house will reinvent herself, again, as an eternal truth.)

The exploitation of older women's unpaid work, and

women's subsequent poverty in old age, ought to be a significant source of shame, yet a combination of wilful ignorance,
dependency panic and carefully constructed narratives about
older women's prejudice and meanness enable us to look
away. The final blow comes when, approaching the end of
a life of caring for others, women are officially judged to
have contributed less to the system to men, and hence be
less deserving of care themselves. As far as capitalism is concerned, women transition from parasite to outright burden,
whereas men put in money – measurable, neat, clean – and
ought to be paid their due.

In fairy tales, older women – widows, stepmothers,
witches – seek to maintain power in cultures where those
without sexual or reproductive resources are thrown on the
mercy of men. The nudge-wink nature of the genre, as much
warning and critique as it is justification of the status quo,
reminds us how long women have been aware of the intrinsic
inequity of an economic system built around meeting men's
needs, but also of the long-standing relationship between
the construction of the hag and guilt around unpaid work.
Shame becomes anger and denial, which then becomes outright demonisation. After all, what might the witches do if a
sufficient level of organisation could be achieved? What might
they be owed? If we radically transformed our understanding
of progress, change and dependency, who would find themselves holding the broom?

4

WRONG SIDE OF HISTORY HAG

That perhaps there has been no progress for women
when it comes to the recognition that women exist
creatively and intellectually in their own right is a
concept difficult to formulate in a patriarchal culture, partly because the belief in progress is so deeply
entrenched. It is a belief bolstered by the premises
of growth and expansion which underlie capitalism,
by the justification of evolutionary theory, and the
construction of history as a steady march of human
improvement. It is almost beyond our comprehension
to question the notion of progress.

Dale Spender, *Women of Ideas*

I can't believe I still have to protest this fucking shit.

Meme from Polish pro-choice protests, October 2016

If you're reading this, the chances are that you're a loser. You
may not have realised this yet, but don't worry. 'The truth,'

as Gloria Steinem famously put it, 'will set you free, but first it will piss you off.' (To be fair, it may continue pissing you off long after setting you free, but losers can't be choosers.)

I first noticed I was a loser when I was in my late thirties, around the same time I noticed I was becoming a hag. Before then, I'd clung to this quaint idea that my generation of women was special. We were living at just the right point in history: one generation earlier, and we'd have missed our chance to fulfil our potential as fully formed human beings. To be born eight years after the passing of the 1967 Abortion Act, and a mere five months before the 1975 Sex Discrimination Act, felt randomly, absurdly lucky. What were the chances that, after millennia of women being oppressed and hence unable to achieve anything much, I should arrive on the scene just as we were about to come into our own?

Naturally I felt bad for the women who'd been born at the wrong time – that is, all women who'd ever lived prior to this unique moment. I felt particularly bad for those feminists who'd come of age around the time I was born, to whom my generation owed so much, but who were obviously too past it to capitalise on their own gains. The sexism they had fought was still around, but it was residual, a hangover from the past that would die with them. Men who genuinely hated women were throwbacks, furious at us because they knew they had lost. The women who'd had to take them on had not had the freedom to engage with gender on a more sophisticated, playful level. That would be the task of women like me. What better way to honour the achievements of our foremothers than to be the trusting, non-combative, open-minded women they could never afford to be?

In my defence, these were not unreasonable assumptions for someone growing up with no knowledge of women's history. Most of what I learned about feminism came from popular culture, which told me, a teenager of the nineties, that the era I was living in was not just feminist, but maybe even postfeminist. As a concept, postfeminism – like most 'post-' plus abstract noun combinations – sounded incredibly complex and certainly not anything for the likes of me to question. I presumed that someone, somewhere, had undertaken extensive academic research which demonstrated we'd reached the point of being so damn feminist we'd come right out the other side. It wasn't as though anyone would make this stuff up, right? Any time I felt drawn towards a more radical reading of the situation – when I caught myself worrying about male violence rather than my postfeminist future as the lonely, childless, Michael Douglas-harassing CEO of a FTSE 100 company – I'd rebuke myself for being petty and unsophisticated. When you are told you have won the long game, noticing that you remain disadvantaged for the time being feels just plain churlish.

What's more, early nineties men really did seem to think they'd lost the mortifyingly titled Battle of the Sexes. We'd see books with titles such as *No More Sex War* and *Not Guilty: In Defence of the Modern Man* and hear complaints about 'masculinity in crisis' and 'the pendulum' having 'swung too far'. Starting university in 1993, I remember sitting in the common room of my male-dominated college, noticing a spate of articles in the right-wing press complaining of male students having their lives ruined by false rape accusations. Such articles unnerved me, but also made me doubt myself for feeling unnerved. These men really did feel under attack, didn't they? Wasn't that a sign that we were on the verge of assuming the upper hand? Even news reports focused on discrediting rape complainants carried with them the message that this wasn't your father's sexism; such things were on their way out. 'Yes,' they said, 'we still don't believe you, but look:

we *almost* did. Give it time and you'll soon be getting men locked up with a click of your manicured fingers.' Rampant misogyny was recontextualised as a preventative measure, a way of battening down the hatches in preparation for the coming deluge of female entitlements.

Teenage me couldn't have known that, three decades later, headlines warning of the virtual decriminalisation of rape due to low conviction rates would be the norm. Nonetheless, had I had a better understanding of feminist history, I could have guessed this. I'd have understood that masculinity is always 'in crisis', the pendulum always deemed to have swung 'too far', and that it is through such paranoid narratives that male power is shored up; that the evolution of women to where you stand now, fully human, unlike the half-formed creatures who went before you, is itself a misogynist trope; and that the woman who is good enough to be free – intellectually, morally, physically – is always tomorrow's woman, never you. That you might genuinely believe yours is the golden generation (more intelligent, more inclusive, more worthy) is part of the trick. It's the false reassurance that alienates you from dead women, older women, and the things they knew. They were victims, yes, but more crucially, they were losers.

You may need to witness several false dawns fully to understand that all women are, in patriarchal terms, the losers. That is our role; it is baked into patriarchal understandings of history, progress, success, failure, creativity, genius, what really matters, what doesn't. Insisting yours is the cohort of women who will finally smash the patriarchy, whereas the one that preceded it represents its last stand, is itself patriarchal.

I know what you may be thinking: *you would say that, what with you being a loser yourself.* Well, yes. I'm a woman past her 'prime', go-to repository for all projections of female loserdom: potential wasted, trajectory interrupted, politics

outdated. For younger women, the belief that you are destined for greatness – whether this finds its expression in
career success or moral purity – relies on the conviction that
older women were never really worth it, and that you will
never be them.

I'm here to tell you this is all a massive con. Join me in losers'
corner. Admit it: you never liked this stupid game anyway.

Mother-in-law 3.0

It is hard to think honestly about the entire history of female
oppression without feeling a little hopeless. As I write, I have
before me a mug of coffee. Printed on this mug are 'women
who changed the world'. There are thirty-five in total. Woo-
hoo! Much as I appreciate their work, I despair at the thought
that this is really it. Yet if you start to think that maybe there
were more remarkable women, you then have to deal with the
fact that being remarkable obviously isn't enough, otherwise
we wouldn't still be fighting for such basic rights as reproductive choice, equal pay and respect for our physical and mental
boundaries. If you want equality in your own lifetime, then
you need a reason to believe women like you are fundamentally different from your predecessors.

One way of constructing a narrative which serves this
purpose is via the portrayal of older women – and by extension, all previous women – as bigoted and ignorant. It's a
characterisation which absolves you of responsibility for
caring too much about *their* oppression as opposed to your
own, while reassuring you that your own advanced education and more complex moral vision will enable you to avoid
their fate. This maps neatly onto a simplistic right-side-of-
history, steady-march-of-progress view of the world, which

suggests that however bleak things might seem right now, you needn't worry too much. Just sit it out, don't say anything that could be construed as phobic, and all good things will come your way. An additional bonus is that it appeases actual misogynists by offering them a woman whom it's still okay – feminist, in fact – to denigrate, because she's genuinely unworthy of anything more. Hag hate truly is the gift that keeps on giving.

The older female figure who has best served this purpose in my own lifetime and social milieu is the mother-in-law. 'The mother-in-law figure of my youth was a gorgon, a dragon and a grotesque,' writes Jane Caro. 'She was ugly, loud, interfering, fat, badly dressed and – yet – powerful.' As any older woman will recall, the seventies and eighties were the heyday of the mother-in-law joke. We'd watch male comedians launch into extended spiels about these vicious, intolerant harridans, then witness male relatives repeating the quips, striking fear into the hearts of wives and daughters. *Dear God, don't let me become one of those.* It wasn't sexism, because the mother-in-law, tyrant of the domestic sphere, could not be oppressed. She was the oppressor.

Later, when such comedy was deemed politically incorrect, a revised, noughties version replaced it. The television sketch show *Little Britain*, which ran between 2003 and 2007, featured the characters Maggie Blackamoor and Judy Pike, middle-aged white ladies from the Women's Institute. The two would judge food at charitable events and whenever it transpired that an item had been prepared by someone who was not white and/or heterosexual, Maggie would vomit copiously. It was, ostensibly, a joke about bigotry, embedded in a series now notorious for its transphobia, ableism, classism and use of blackface.

It's a perfect example of the older woman as scapegoat.

Laughing at Maggie's bigotry proved to the viewer – who may, seconds earlier, have been giggling at Matt Lucas blacking up, or David Walliams ridiculing trans women – that he wasn't a bigot himself. On the contrary, he could tell himself it took a particular level of refinement to distinguish between the ironic bigotry of the privately educated white male comedian (which, in knowing itself to be bigotry, cancels itself out) and the actual bigotry of the middle-aged white woman (who, with her housework-addled brain, wouldn't know irony if it smacked her in the face with a dishcloth). For those who bought the argument that good comedy relied on punching up, not down (fans of punching, in other words), this was punching down masquerading as punching up. When you punched a middle-aged white woman, you could tell yourself you were punching The Man, who just happened to look like a cross between Hyacinth Bucket and Ann Widdecombe.

Lucas and Walliams have since apologised for certain aspects of the show, with Lucas saying 'society has moved on a lot since then'. Yet the noughties were not a wasteland in which no one knew that prejudice was bad, or who might be a target; the *Little Britain* sketches in which responsibility for prejudice is loaded onto the shoulders of middle-aged women already demonstrate this.* The problem Lucas and Walliams face today is context: remove a sketch from the broader, gaslighting framework and you find yourself without any scapegoat, wholly exposed.

It is incredibly convenient for men to portray aggression and intolerance as qualities specific to older women. It makes a virtue of the latter's marginalisation while reassuring younger women that the same thing won't happen to them.

---

* I have my own vivid memories of angry discussions of the 'bitty' sketches at the breastfeeding support groups I attended in the late noughties. But what would we, uncool breastfeeding mummies, know about prejudice?

Once this particular cohort of shrews has died out, so it is implied, women may assume their rightful place alongside men, finally standing with poise and dignity as opposed to lurking, purse-lipped, rolling pin in hand, ready to strike. Yet time and again, the next batch fails to live up to expectations. Generation X women, who may once have joined in with what Germaine Greer calls 'the never-ending jibes against menopausal women, against mothers-in-law, against crones in general', now find themselves on the wrong side of history, too.

The latest iteration of the mother-in-law joke continues what Lucas and Walliams started by implying that if you are offended, you're on the side of the bigots. A typical example is found in the 2020 Pixar film *Soul*, which tells the story of Joe, who falls down a hole and finds himself in the Great Before, where souls are prepared for life with the help of mentors. Mistaken for a mentor himself, he's assigned to train the difficult, persistently negative Soul 22, voiced by Tina Fey. Joe asks Soul 22 why she, as yet unborn, sounds 'like a middle-aged white woman'. 'I just use this voice because it annoys people,' is the response. Joe confirms this is 'very effective'. It's a throwaway comment, a passing quip, the mention of race even lending it a progressive sheen. You'd need to be old enough to have lived through several iterations of the mother-in-law joke to realise just how tired and reactionary it actually is.

Writing on *Soul*, the *Guardian*'s Hadley Freeman asks, 'What, exactly, [do] the directors (two men) and the writers (three men) of *Soul* think the little girls watching this film – who may have a middle-aged white woman for a mother, who may themselves one day be middle-aged white women – should make of the implication that this is the most annoying voice in the world?' She concludes that children are being taught 'that middle-aged women are the worst. Even their souls are bad!' Only it is not simply 'middle-aged women'; it's middle-aged white women. Here the sinister power of the middle-aged woman in comedy has shifted from the mother-in-law's rolling pin (visible marker of aggression) to Maggie Blackamoor's vomit (explicit expression of prejudice) to Soul 22's whiteness (immutable privilege and dominance). The space in which to call out ageism and misogyny has narrowed because the binding together of privileged and marginalised status makes the identification of one look like the denial of the other. It becomes incumbent on the viewer not to see misogyny or ageism in order to demonstrate his or her anti-racist credentials.

Social media responses to Freeman's piece, which referenced the mother-in-law trope, inevitably called the writer a Karen, an entitled white woman who responds to accusations of bigotry (or in this case just annoyingness) by playing the victim. There was little engagement with the fact that, in using anti-racism as a cover for revisiting age-old stereotypes about the shrill, whiny voices of women, you do nothing to counter racism, just as in sniggering at Maggie Blackamoor, you do nothing to counter the very racism and transphobia you were sniggering at moments earlier. Middle-aged white women become both a projection for everyone else's bigotry and an excuse to do nothing about it. As such, they are necessary props for people whose unwavering belief in the march of progress and their own innate compatibility with it transcend the need for any serious self-analysis.

Being the symbolic mother-in-law is yet another messy, necessary role assigned to older women because no one else wants to do it. Like dealing with housework; like performing eldercare; like admitting you have a sexed body; like setting boundaries on sexual liberation; like recognising you're going to die. Everyone needs a repository for bad, harmful, outdated beliefs, in order to clear the way for a prejudice-free future. Why should you, a good person, a younger person, or a man, possessor of a complex inner life, have to engage in the type of deep self-examination which might necessitate changing your day-to-day activities when you can simply impose the moral equivalent of cleaning the toilet on someone else?

I understand this impulse. A misplaced belief in our own generational exceptionality, combined with a sprinkling of hope, can lead to strange perceptions of time, progress and the speed of change. The past is another country; they were massive bigots there. We like to convince ourselves that harmful, deeply ingrained beliefs – beliefs which undergird our thinking and social interactions as much as our public institutions – can be resolved within one or two generations. Now is the time! Evil can be eradicated. Just burn the witch.

Only this time, pick the right witch – a real one – and do it for virtuous reasons. Turns out the historical witch-burners were massive bigots, too.

Woman: new, morally pure upgrade available soon

'Do you think,' Kirsty Wark asked Suzanne Moore on *Newsnight* in November 2020, 'that sometimes you just have to put your hands up and say, "I'm representing something that's going to very soon be in the past and actually the incoming generation has a more enlightened attitude"?' Moore had recently left her post as a columnist for the *Guardian*, after months of pressure resulting from a piece she had written in defence of women's right to organise as a sex class. Tense meetings had been held, and an open letter (which did not name Moore) had been circulated, protesting trans-phobia and garnering more than three hundred signatures. In a piece for *UnHerd* describing the nature of her departure, Moore recalled an earlier instance of a young male colleague telling her she was just 'insecure because a new generation of leftists have caught the public mood'. In asking her question, Wark seemed to be pushing Moore towards admitting said colleague was right.

It's a familiar question, one that is asked many times of older women who cling to the belief that biological sex is politically salient: aren't you just behind the times? One could counter that since the flesh has always been considered passé (and female), the mind, cutting edge (and male), the times haven't changed much at all. The trouble is, the message has been pitched in a novel way, making it easy to cast the likes of Moore in a Boomer-bashing Simpsons meme: she's the old man yelling at a cloud, or Principal Skinner asking himself 'Am I out of touch?' before concluding, 'No, it's the children who are wrong.' Whatever you believe, it's embarrassing to be viewed this way. 'Aren't you just uncool?' Wark might as well have said. It's a stupid, trivialising way of dealing with a complex discussion relating to competing rights. And yet. 'Change, youth, and novelty are ironically traditional values,' wrote Elissa Melamed in 1983. 'We all still want to be "with it", whatever "it" is.' We probably wouldn't use the term 'with it' today but we're still drawn to the same dumb narrative.

It's a narrative in which history is always marching in the right direction, with 'more enlightened' youth leading the way. One that assumes a person's politics, like their fashion sense, gets fixed in place at a particular age, unable to develop further, waiting to be picked up and improved upon by who-ever comes next. One that sees knowledge and experience as encumbrances, needlessly weighing down idealism. Older

people – as one privileged, environment-destroying, wealth-
and property-hogging mass, undifferentiated by race, sex or
class – are expected to stand aside, conceding that their time
to contribute to political thought has come to an end. It is,
ironically, the only cool thing left to do.

The problem with this way of thinking is not just that it
suggests, as Oliver Burkeman points out, 'we can expect a
progression toward betterness thanks simply to the passage
of time'. 'The past,' notes Burkeman, 'is full of periods when
people endorsed ridiculous or horrifying views, but they evi-
dently didn't think so at the time.' The insistence that younger
equals 'more enlightened' also jettisons any intersectional
analysis of why views differ between and within generations.
'Young people are new and clean,' says Kiri Tunks, veteran
trade unionist and founder of the activist group Woman's
Place UK, 'it's tabula rasa, you know, the idea that they've
been born enlightened and that the rest of us are jaded and
damaged. They know what's what and you think, well, yeah,
but they haven't had any of the experiences that people my age
have, so who knows where they'll be in thirty years' time?'

In his 2021 book *Generations*, the social scientist Bobby
Duffy presents three explanations for how 'all attitudes,
beliefs and behaviours change over time: period effects; lifecycle effects; and cohort effects':

> Every change in societal attitudes, beliefs and behaviours
> can be explained by one – or, more often, a combination –
> of these three effects. This, therefore, highlights the basic
> problem with the generational 'analysis' in most commen-
> tary: assuming that when a person is born explains all their
> attitudes and behaviours relies solely on identifying cohort
> effects – and misses out on two-thirds of the power of this
> fuller understanding of societal change.

I would argue that this has particular significance for women, given the way in which sex-specific lifecycle events – real or potential – such as pregnancy, childbirth and menopause shape a woman's life course and transform her social and economic status in relation to that of her male peers. 'The importance of lifecycle effects,' writes Duffy, 'is easy to miss among the generational narratives we're fed, but they exert an extraordinarily powerful force over attitudes and behaviours.' Women who began their adult life assuming their sex didn't matter can be shocked to find that, actually, it matters a great deal. Duffy describes 'cohorts that start off by moving in a very different direction from previous generations [being] pulled back towards a well-worn life course'. This does not mean the same thing for women as it does for men, though it can be to the advantage of men to pretend otherwise.

For instance, in March 2021, the *Times*'s Andrew Billen wrote an article explaining 'Why It's Time to Join Generation Woke', in which he pitched the politics of J. K. Rowling – 'his' generation – against those of his teenage daughter:

> Until last June ... there was no greater lover of the Harry Potter books than my teenage daughter. Suddenly, however, their author ceased to be her hero. J. K. Rowling had criticised the phrase 'people who menstruate'. 'If sex isn't real,' she tweeted, 'the lived reality of women globally is erased.' Surely, I said, Rowling had a point, but her ardent former fan, my girl, could not understand why I was defending her. 'Why,' she asked puzzled, 'would you want to be mean to trans people?'

The daughter's response is a strange one, the equivalent of asking 'why would you want to be mean to oranges?' in response to the statement 'apples exist'. Yet it's enough to make Billen conclude that he would 'never win an argument with [his daughter] again', opting instead to concede the point on behalf of his entire generation and – though he doesn't acknowledge it – the entire female sex. He goes on to explain his epiphany, shared with other men his age. 'Those groups who today ask us to feel their pain are precisely those whose pain, until recently, was ignored and their voices unheard,' he writes. 'Their feelings howl for attention because for the first time society is willing to give it.' These groups do not include middle-aged women such as Rowling, who – experiences of domestic abuse notwithstanding – he seems to believe occupy the same privileged position as him.

Older women cannot dictate to younger ones what their politics should be, or vice versa. A younger woman's perspective on the political salience of biological sex might differ from that of an older woman because the former has been exposed to 'newer' ideas, but it could also be the case that a younger woman's perspective is rooted in a more limited range of embodied experiences, at a stage in life when the drip-drip accumulation of sex-based inequality has only just started to build. There's something amiss with men breezing in – as many do – to decree that this group of women are right, that group wrong, using age as the only experiential axis that matters, discarding its intersection with sex. It highlights the way in which viewing youth as inherently progressive favours a male-default life narrative.

If you are a white, middle-class, middle-aged man who wants to feel virtuous and progressive, there's a lot to be said for adopting an 'all in this together' attitude towards generational transfers of power. It allows you to set aside the balance sheet of losses and gains that operates within your generation, writing off your own debts in an instant. You get to hand over the proverbial baton to the next generation, having never permitted your less privileged contemporaries to lay a finger on it. In the case of debates relating to sex and gender, it's particularly galling. All the middle-aged women who watched as, year after year, their male counterparts capitalised on women falling behind due to economic structures which continue to treat the female body as an inconvenience – these women are now expected to join the men in confirming the irrelevance of biological sex, as opposed to, say, warning younger women that it still matters.

It is easy to announce that you have had your time when 'having your time' has involved taking sufficient resources from others to provide for the rest of your life. While J. K. Rowling may not face a future of pension poverty, many older women do, not least because of a universal failure to account for reproductive and domestic labour, work pertaining to bodies, not identities. How nice to be able to write off such concerns as old hat. Middle-aged women are expected to get with the programme, not by finding someone else to wipe noses and make sandwiches, but by abandoning any political analysis of why they're the ones relegated to the 'traditional' role. The attraction for older men of 'going woke' is that it never involves rolling up their sleeves and taking on some of the work they've heaped on the shoulders of their female contemporaries; instead, they can condemn the unequal distribution of unpaid labour and trust – generously – that the next generation will deal with it. *Sorry, wife; can't help you with organising the care home visits. Our generation just doesn't have the complex, binary-smashing gender politics – what are 'we' like?*

That our narratives of progress and revolution prioritise male life stages is not a new observation. In 1979 Gloria Steinem wrote 'Why Young Women Are More Conservative' for *Ms* magazine (originally titled, less confrontationally, 'The Good News Is: These Are Not the Best Years of Your Life'). In it, she argues against the perception that 'student-age women, like student-age men, were much more likely to be activists and open to change than their parents', proposing instead that 'women may be the one group that grows more radical with age'. She describes having been 'conned into believing the masculine stereotype of youth as the "natural" time for freedom and rebellion, a time of "sowing wild oats" that is made possible by the assurance of power and security, later on'. Rebellious, inclusive males rebel and include on the basis that none of this will cost them their status and boundaries further down the line; their female counterparts, already on an unequal footing, have no such assurances. Younger women are pressed to prioritise generational solidarity over solidarity with those of their own sex, with no allowance for an approach which recognises the ways in which one's generational experience is shaped by one's sex. Steinem suggests that 'a young woman's most radical act toward her mother (that is, connecting as women in order to help each other get some power) doesn't look much like a young man's most radical act toward his father (that is, breaking the father-son connection in order to separate identities or take over existing power)':

It's those father-son conflicts at a generational, national level that have often provided the conventional definition of revolution; yet they've gone on for centuries without basically changing the role of the female half of the world.

When Billen writes of 'half the world', meaning the 'unwoke' old set against the 'woke' young, he really means a quarter of it. His narrative is another rehashing of the father-son conflict, roping in female voices as and when they provide the correct echoes. Of course it feels kind and compassionate to give up things that were never yours in the first place, the benefits of which you have already extracted. He talks to the comedian Frank Skinner, who discusses retiring some of his sexist gags 'for the greater good':

'I will not,' he told me, 'be part of a movement that thinks political correctness is anything other than one of the great social movements of the late twentieth, early twenty-first century – because it is so kind. At heart it is so kind and so compassionate.'

Yet, as with Lucas and Walliams's apologies regarding *Little Britain*, it's hardly the case that no one noticed the problem with sexist gags twenty or thirty years ago. It is women of my generation (and older) who have paid the highest price for the culture perpetuated by male peers who now declare themselves on the side of the angels; we didn't have the privilege of not yet existing back when their now-unfashionable brand of humour was 'acceptable'. No one apologises to us, let alone defers to our extensive knowledge of how sexism functions in relation to sex, since the point isn't really 'being less sexist'; it's older men repositioning themselves in relation to youth culture. Far from being acknowledged as the generation who suffered most and longest from the sexism of their male contemporaries, women such as Suzanne Moore and J. K. Rowling are castigated for failing to retire their own hard-won understanding of sexism, built over decades of life experience, and replace it with something less inconveniently experience-laden.

In addition to this, despite the assumption that the younger a person is, the more open-minded their beliefs about sex and gender, the evidence doesn't stack up. Recent research into younger men's attitudes towards women and feminism indicate there is no natural evolution away from misogyny and entitlement. As Andrea S. Kramer and Alton B. Harris reported in the *Harvard Business Review* in 2016, Millennial men, despite their reputation for 'ushering in a new era of enlightened interpersonal relations', aren't so progressive after all. Examples they cite include a 2016 National Institutes of Health study in which male biology students consistently underestimated the intelligence of their female peers, a 2014 Harris poll showing younger men to be 'less open to accepting women as leaders than older men were', and a 2013 Pew survey in which Millennial men are the group most likely to say 'all necessary changes have been made' to achieve gender parity (while their female peers are the least). This trend is not confined to the US, or Millennials. Research in 2020 by the UK Hope Not Hate charitable trust showed half of Generation Z men agreeing with the statement 'feminism has gone too far and made it harder for men to succeed'. The 2020 UN Human Development report, 'Tackling Social Norms', showed 'bias against gender equality increasing in some countries', with some surveys showing 'that younger men may be even less committed to equality than their elders'. 'Painting all young people as battling for "social justice",' writes Duffy, 'misses the fact that less "progressive" values persist in significant minorities of them. Generational analysis is to some extent part of the problem, as it can give the impression of an unstoppable march towards greater liberalism.' My own view is that this distorted narrative benefits younger men who are not openly anti-feminist in addition to those who are. Rather than work to offer new, genuinely progressive models of male behaviour, the former can sit back and rely on the presumption that their youth automatically makes them better than their fathers, not to mention their uneducated, gender-ignorant mothers.

Once you make the oppression of women into a 'regressive' activity embedded in a network of other 'regressive' activities which will die out once your 'side' triumphs, then you don't have to do much about it other than tell women to wait their turn. This has been a longstanding issue in supposedly 'progressive' circles. Indeed, one of the catalysts for second-wave feminism was left-wing women's frustration at their marginalisation within left-wing politics, and at lazy assurances that their own liberation would be a 'natural' consequence of men's. As Robin Morgan put it in 1970's 'Goodbye to All That', her blistering rejection of a male-dominated revolution, 'To hell with the simplistic notion that automatic freedom for women – or nonwhite people – will come about zap! with the advent of a socialist revolution. Bullshit.' Or, as Adrienne Rich expressed it more carefully, 'There is no guarantee, under socialism or "liberal" capitalism, Protestantism, "humanism", or any existing ethics, that a liberal policy will not become an oppressive one, as long as women do not have absolute decision-power over the use of our bodies'. 'Progress', even in its shiniest, newest guise, does not necessarily carry women along with it. Today we see supposed anti-capitalists remarkably unmoved by the commoditisation of female bodies via the growth of the global sex trade and commercial surrogacy. Unmoved, too, by the suggestion that the unrewarded, invisibilised labour of older women might give these women greater insight into inequality as opposed to rendering them passive, unthinking representatives of the status quo. As long as any woman past the prime of youth can be used as a dumping ground for other people's anxieties over the body and dependency, older women can be written off as reactionary. We lose out because 'progress' can't be sexist, and because ageing and female embodiment can't be 'progressive'. It's not that they aren't; they simply *can't* be. To make matters worse, it is not just male-default 'progressive' politics that behaves this way; much of post-second-wave feminism, now welcomed back into the mainstream fold, does this, too.

In *Agewise*, Margaret Morganroth Gullette associates a rise in ageism with ageing being positioned as a narrative of inevitable decline, set in opposition to moral and political progress narratives. I think there is a similar decline narrative tagged to femaleness, as female people are considered more worthless – sexually, reproductively and economically – than their male peers as they age (remember Wilson's distinction between manhood's 'smooth continuity' versus womanhood's crumbling 'in ruins'?) Mainstream feminism is, by contrast, a progress narrative. The movement that represents women goes forwards while actual women go backwards, moving ever further from the liberated, evolved ideal the older they get. Hence the bizarre chronological fudges and definitional revisions which characterise modern feminism. What is often described as a tension between younger, liberal feminism and older, radical feminism often comes down to something else: the movement is deemed more worthy than those it represents. Feminism is an idea, not a body; it's not dragged down by the accumulation of flesh, relationships and compromise. The end point of this thinking sees femaleness in its entirety being treated as outdated. In a sketch for his Netflix special *SuperNature*, Ricky Gervais parodied tensions between trans activists and feminists by playing off 'the old-fashioned women, the ones with wombs, those fucking dinosaurs' against 'the new women'. Many found the sketch crass, but I think it captured a manifestation of misogyny that is real and has been emerging for quite some time (explored, for instance, in Tania Modleski's 1991 book of film criticism, *Feminism Without Women*).

'*Do you think that sometimes you just have to put your*

hands up and say, "I'm representing something that's going to very soon be in the past"?' When Wark asks this of Moore on *Newsnight*, she suggests old ideas must make way for new ones, when what is really happening is compromised, used female meat gets cast aside, to be replaced with fresh, untouched flesh. The inevitabilities of ageing become ideological liabilities; there is no way around it. The implication that knowledge from an older female perspective is worth less, not more – that the baggage you have acquired makes you less 'enlightened' – sets a trap into which all women must eventually fall.

Moore's original *Guardian* piece, with its focus on the materiality of the female body – 'female oppression,' she wrote, 'is innately connected to our ability to reproduce' – was ripe for dubious accusations of biological essentialism. It marked her as out of step with 'young' thinking, considered open to change. Yet those who claim to be on the side of change often don't seem to like it very much, or rather, they only like change in terms of younger women replacing crones who might have seen a little too much. The change that happens as women progress through different life stages is less appealing. To have shifting perspectives depending on where one is in life and what one has experienced is inevitable but it is also disconcerting, especially if you are passionate about your politics in the here and now. Just like admitting that you depend on others, admitting that your perspective is limited, provisional and contingent is deeply unsettling. It means you might not be correct in what you think right now; it means you might never know at what stage of your life your beliefs were the most 'correct' ones.* Far easier to carve up the generations into a succession of goodies and baddies,

---

* I write this now; I might think it's rubbish in ten years' time, which creates its own paradox.

people whose thought is shaped not by a complex combination of personal experiences coloured by specific structural
privileges and disadvantages at a particular point in time,
but by whatever they were reading in the news at the age of
twenty. The *Guardian* columnist Owen Jones once tweeted
that 'when you boil down a lot of UK political discourse, it's
fear and loathing of millennials and Generation Z by right
wing boomers and centrist Generation Xers who collectively
dominate the media'. It is, when you think about it, a bizarre
way of viewing the world. Does everyone become a centrist
once they reach middle age, right wing once they draw their
pension? Or will Gen Z and Millennials stay pure?

The fate of Generation X feminists might provide a clue.
If you study the way in which feminism is described using
the wave metaphor, you will notice a curious thing has happened. Despite occasional rumblings about a fourth, or even
a fifth, there hasn't really been another wave after the third;
instead, women once deemed to be third wave progress along
a conveyor belt toward the past, whereupon they are granted
second-wave status. In strictly chronological terms, the
second wave of activism originated in the sixties, the third
in the nineties (with Rebecca Walker publishing 'Becoming
the Third Wave' in 1992), which would make me and other
women approaching their fifties third-wavers. However, as
Astrid Henry notes in her 2004 book, *Not My Mother's
Sister*, 'while Generation X ages, the third wave remains
young, unhinging the relationship between the two terms. It
would appear, then, that "third wave" suggests a particular
politics is the province of the young.'

Whether or not it is an honour to age into second-wave
status depends on your perspective. Having done none of the
work, I'm rather taken with the idea of being able to shove
my Girl Power T-shirt into the back of a drawer and claim

responsibility for legislation that had nothing whatsoever to do with me. To others, such as the (at time of writing) eighty-seven thousand people favouriting a tweet which declares both feminism and Covid-19 to have 'problematic second waves', it might appear less than flattering. It's often the case that what's meant as an insult for older women isn't taken that way (I treasure one rather well-known writer on gender identity politics denouncing me as a 'batshit Mumsnet thread made flesh'). Either way, I'm not a second-wave feminist. I'm just someone who isn't allowed to be a third wave one any more because of what experience has done to my body and my perspective.

'Do you think,' Kirsty Wark could have asked Suzanne Moore, 'that sometimes you just have to put your hands up and say I'm representing something that may or may not be approved of by history, and which I may or may not agree with in twenty years' time, and upon which, furthermore, I may never receive a final, definitive verdict?' If being on the right side of history is your ultimate goal, that's a more relevant question. It's too messy, though; to keep your politics neat and tidy, you must scrub actual people – including your future self – out of the picture.

Why female history matters (and women of the past did not achieve 'fuck all')

November 2020, the month in which Wark invited Moore to admit to her own obsolescence, also saw the live-streamed unveiling of Maggi Hambling's statue for Mary Wollstonecraft in the latter's former home of Newington Green. After ten years of campaigning by the group Mary on the Green, the author of *A Vindication of the Rights of*

Woman was finally getting the recognition she deserved. Only the statue looked nothing like Wollstonecraft. What was revealed was a tiny naked form, all pert breasts and tight abs, atop a pile of unformed matter. In the words of Marina Strinkovsky, it 'brought to mind a Bratz doll emerging out of a mountain of spunk'. But that's okay, we were told. It wasn't meant to look like Wollstonecraft the flesh-and-blood human. This was Everywoman, in honour of the fact that Wollstonecraft agitated on behalf of all women. That Everywoman just so happened to be represented as a naked Barbie didn't mean anything.

Or rather, in Hambling's own defence of her work, it was absolutely necessary that her figure had no clothes: 'She has to be naked because clothes define people. We all know that clothes are limiting.' As for her thinness, 'she's more or less the shape we'd all like to be'. And the mass below her? According to Mary on the Green, this 'combines female forms which commingle and rise together as if one, culminating in the figure of a woman standing free'. She's the perfect warrior woman, rising from – or paying homage to, depending on how you want to spin it – the sludge of all the messy, fleshy females who went before her. She doesn't look like someone from the bad old days of yore, someone specific, someone you'd have to pin down. She doesn't look like someone in her late thirties who could ever end up dying that most female of deaths, infection following childbirth. Unlike Wollstonecraft herself, let down by her imperfect, non-male body, Everywoman is pristine.

It's funny how woman emerging in her full, emancipated glory looks like woman with all the experience stripped away: no wrinkles, no sagging, no scars. Neither physical decay nor political compromise have sullied her. Providing you don't think too hard about it, it's possible to see in this, and the formlessness which 'commingles and rises' beneath her, an alternative to a male-default view of history. Women aren't in thrall to rigid figures of the past. Rather than standing on the shoulders of giants, we're standing on sod all, and you could be fooled into believing there's a freedom in that. Feminism has long been drawn to the notion of giving birth to oneself, even if that means killing the mother we'll one day become. Mary Wollstonecraft isn't good enough to represent the Everywoman for whom she wrote. She was too real, and too mortal (she might have died giving birth to another female genius, Mary Shelley, but she died all the same). Instead the spotlight turns on a woman who is not yet there, in the act of becoming, birthed by 'forms' rather than anything so flawed as an actual body.*

There is shame driving this urge to portray women as always on the verge of becoming better, harder, shinier, with all the dirt sloughed away. It confuses the experience of being a member of an oppressed class, restricted in terms of choices and opportunities, with genuinely being inferior. A striking example of this is found in Caitlin Moran's *How to Be a Woman*, which is generally excellent at cheerleading for womankind yet also contains the claim that 'women have basically done fuck all for the last 100,000 years':

> Come on – let's admit it. Let's stop exhaustingly pretending that there is a parallel history of women being victorious and creative, on an equal with men, that's just been comprehensively covered up by The Man. There isn't [...] I don't think that women being seen as inferior is a prejudice based on male hatred of women. When you look at history, it's a prejudice based on simple fact.

---

* If only someone – ideally someone not too distant from Wollstonecraft – could have taken apart that patriarchal, matricidal, egotistical impulse to give birth without the female, perhaps using the medium of a gothic novel.

This argument is Maggi Hambling's statue on speed and it's easy to see the attraction. If we admit that 'nearly everything so far has been the creation of men', we can set about changing the world, rising from the sludge at the statue's feet. Otherwise, Moran argues, 'women are over, without having even begun. When the truth is that we haven't begun *at all*.'

Loser's shame is agonising. In the short term it can be relieved by shoving the pitiful loser status of woman into a box marked The Past. Bind it together with all those other sources of shame: her servitude, her complicity, her flawed, mortal, female flesh. Hide it away, forget about it. Henceforth, it's nothing to do with you. If women have barely got started with the complex business of being fully formed human beings, then you don't even have to try rehabilitating those who've failed to come up to standard. You have nothing to learn from them. Indeed, it's best to distance yourself from them, lest anyone should think that you're a loser, too.

It's not difficult to see how this impulse to flee the past plays out closer to home, in our attitude towards the generation that immediately precedes us. 'Women,' declared the UN Women's Twitter account on International Women's Day 2021, 'are no longer taking a back seat, waiting for equality.' Good for us! Given the millennia we've had to come up with this plan, it's amazing no one thought of it sooner! The same month, in a piece announcing the launch of the Noon website for middle-aged women, journalist Eleanor Mills heaped praise on the generation of women that came of age in the nineties: 'We raved, we broke down barriers and confronted sexism, racism and workplace prejudice, and ploughed our own furrows. We don't want our mothers' midlife and menopause; we refuse to fade politely away.' Great though this is, I'm pretty sure our mothers weren't all that keen on fading politely away either. There comes a point at which it becomes difficult to keep representing this batch of women, here, now, as inherently more equality-worthy than the last without getting the creeping sense that it's all a matter of role play. One day it will be your turn to play the role of the woman who took the back seat, waiting for equality, politely fading away while achieving fuck all. You might know that isn't your truth, but the imagined future successes of womankind depend on you playing the patsy. You're basically the 'before' photo in the great woman makeover, having previously been told you'd one day get to pose as the 'after'. (The 'after' photo is Maggi Hambling's skinny Everywoman; how could you, a mere mortal, ever have thought you could compete with that?)

As long as women's loser status is equated with inferiority, you are left with two equally unpalatable options: either you mine the past for examples which 'prove' that 'we' didn't lose at all, or you are left with a shame that can only be countered by out-and-out disidentification from earlier women. In *How to Be a Woman*, efforts to take women's history as seriously as men's are treated as a kind of special pleading, as though feminist historians have been demanding an extended VAR review of the past in the vain hope that, actually, *that* was a foul, *this* should have been a red card and if it had gone to penalties, Women vs Men would have been a draw. This is not how we should be thinking about it. What a true appreciation of women's history does is embed a class consciousness. This counters the political and psychological hobbling – the deeply embodied discomfort – that occurs when we feel so ashamed of our female heritage we'd rather deny we have any heritage at all.

'We need to know how patriarchy works,' wrote Dale Spender in 1982's *Women of Ideas*. 'We need to know how women disappear, why we are initiated into a culture where women have no visible past, and what will happen if we make that past visible and real.' When I first picked up a copy of Spender's book, I was bothered by the length of it: eight hundred pages, too long to be just a summary of *why* women need a history. I worried it was therefore attempting to tell the stories of all the women who'd ever done anything of significance, in which case eight hundred pages is very short indeed. Happily, this isn't its intention. Spender uses the detailed life stories of particular women as examples for her broader thesis (it's as though individual women are important enough to be representatives of greater human truths, like men). One such example is the American suffragist, Native American rights activist and slavery abolitionist Matilda Josyln Gage. I found her story particularly arresting, because it's clear how well she, a woman living in the nineteenth century, saw the pattern: women's history will always belong to the women of tomorrow – and hence never really exist at all – until you grant it to the women of the past.

In 1852, Gage gave a speech at the Syracuse National Convention in which she listed women whom she deemed 'beacon lights of what may be attained by genius, labor, energy, and perseverance combined'. In doing so she was not just cherry-picking from history in order to make women seem more significant than they actually were (something Moran likens, in a nineties context, to constantly putting Echobelly on the cover of *Melody Maker*); she was, writes Spender, challenging the belief 'that history was a process of gradual improvement, an evolution towards a higher and more civilised goal, and that the time had now arisen for women to take their steps and to become full members of the civilised community'. In other words, Gage was challenging the myth of Everywoman only just arising from the swirly, indistinguishable 'female forms' beneath her:

To women who believed that the barriers against them in a male-dominated society had to be broken *before* women could begin to participate in the organisation and cultural activities of society – and there are still such women who accept that women are 'under-achieving' and that this will pass once the last discriminatory barriers are removed – Gage's documentation came as a revelation [...] Her speech served as a source of strength, of pride, of confidence; it repudiated the 'inferiority' of woman, and introduced the issue of how women came to know and believe what they did – who had told them?

Upon first reading this, I did not find it a source of strength, pride and confidence; on the contrary, it saddened me to think that Gage had been speaking out 123 years before I was born, and Spender writing about it when I was seven. If women's time is not some magic 'now', then maybe it is 'never'. Yet once you get over the initial shock, the overall message is reassuring. Women have not been waiting to evolve. There is no pressure on us, right now, to be better than the women who went before us, including our own mothers. There is no need to feel shame at the female body, that terrible burden that has been claimed to exclude us from the world of the mind. We are and always were good enough. We do not need to be made small, recast in silver. The ultimate combination of misogyny and ageism is the one that says the best women, the only good women, are the ones yet to be born.

'Many women resist feminism,' claimed Andrea Dworkin, 'because it is an agony to be fully conscious of the brutal misogyny which permeates culture, society, and all personal relationships.' I think this is also a reason why many women embrace a feminism which disregards its own, wrong-sided history. It is painful to know that your loser status isn't down to anything other women were, or did or didn't do. Without this pain, though, we are in constant flight from the self-acceptance – which must include an acceptance of our female bodies and our future, older selves – upon which the knowledge that we are not inferior to men depends. Most women will say they do not see themselves as inferior to men, but I'm not sure they mean it. To really, truly feel it, you must feel no shame at the thought of sharing a connection with older women, and women long dead.

5

FRIGID HAG

But surely, we do not want the new world to be built up only by women who have long ago forgotten what sex means, or who have never experienced strong sexual emotions, and regard them as a sign of grossness or decadence.

Stella Browne, 'The Sexual Variety and
Variability among Women'

Women know too much. I'm all for girls that don't know too much.

Jimmy Savile

Imagine we lived in a time in which there was no Pornhub. No OnlyFans, no revenge porn, no mega brothels, no normalisation of prostitution as a way for female students to fund university courses. No choking and hitting as 'standard' sex, no 'rough sex' defences, no child sex dolls on Amazon, no exponential rise in sexual assaults in schools. No redefining of femaleness as 'an open mouth, an expectant asshole, blank, blank eyes'. Imagine none of that was happening now, but it had been happening in the nineties.

Would you look back and think, wow, that was a golden age for sexual liberation! It's a pity the prudes went and ruined it! Or would you think, wow, that sounds like a heteropatriarchal capitalist hellhole! It's a pity women back then didn't know how to stand up for themselves! When sexual exploitation is normalised – and the only thing that changes is the form it takes – it's impossible to know what you'd only notice after the fact.

The nineties were hardly a feminist utopia, but the era had its plus points. Female pubic hair was still legal. The clitoris was still mentionable, even if only as a punchline in *South Park: The Movie*. Lesbianism was merely dismissed as a sexy girl-on-girl performance, as opposed to being dismissed as an exclusionary genital fetish. The sexual double standard was alive and well, but men had the decency to pretend they were being ironic when they called you a slag. Being strangled to death during sex was not yet considered a lifestyle choice.

The sexual landscape was far from perfect, but to many of us it genuinely seemed things could only get better. Liberalisation felt unstoppable and only for the good. The 'sex wars' of the eighties – clashes between pro- and anti-porn second-wave feminists – were over, and porn, or sex (depending on how you looked at it), had been declared the winner.

Like most women coming of age at that time, I was not well-versed in the political or philosophical intricacies of arguments for and against pornography and prostitution. I only knew that if feminism was the future, both politically and morally, this made it inconceivable that the wrong side might have won this particular battle. I casually positioned anti-porn feminists, the sex wars losers, alongside conservative housewives, moral majority pearl-clutchers and no-sex-before-marriage fundamentalists – people who just didn't understand that the only way to end the sexual objectification of women was to elevate their status as sexual agents, and that the only way to elevate one's status as a sexual agent was to get one's tits out for the lads in an act of ironic, knowing self-objectification. This totally made sense at the time.

Thirty years later, I'm not so sure (and it's not just because my tits have become less lad-friendly). There is more than one way to deny a woman sexual freedom. One might be to tell her that she has no sexual identity, that her desires are shameful and that the only role for her in sex is a passive reproductive one. Another might be to persuade her to define herself not as a sexual being in her own right but as the negative image of another folk demon, the frigid, castrating prude. No one wants to be a sexless harridan, 'the frump at the back of the room, the ghost of women past', as Ariel Levy put it in 2005's *Female Chauvinist Pigs*. Instead you embrace a sexual identity based not on what you desire but on what you've been told other women don't want you to have, do or become. That this might overlap with precisely what men have always demanded of you is, well, pure coincidence.

A key theme of this book is the way in which women are encouraged to create themselves in opposition to the older women we will eventually become, and the ways in which this hurts us personally and politically, facilitating and perpetuating the exploitation of women as a class. Perhaps nowhere is this more obvious than in discussions of male sexual entitlement and female sexual desire. The spectre of the undesiring, undesirable older woman, uncomprehending, envious or disgusted in the face of a free, untethered sexuality, dovetails with the myth that all the ugliness and hate of rape culture and sexual abuse could vanish in an instant were men to

understand that women experience desire positively, that we
are not simply voids (or, if we are voids, all expectant assholes
and blank, blank eyes, it is because we positively desire to be
such). All too often, those standing in the way of this understanding are not deemed to be men themselves (which would
be terrifying), but women of our mothers' generation (which
is decidedly less so). Men do not need to change; women need
to present themselves differently, so that men may desire us
differently. That this has not happened thus far is the fault,
yet again, of the women who went before us.

In 1985's *The Spinster and Her Enemies*, Sheila Jeffreys
describes the way in which 'sex reform activists' of the
twenties were able to defeat 'the threat [. . .] posed to male
pleasure by the criticism of male sexual behaviour': 'The
much vaunted change in sexual mores was not a change in
the expected behaviour of men, but a change in the expectations made of women through a massive campaign to
conscript women into enthusiastic participation in sexual
intercourse with men.' As a young woman in the nineties,
I was unaware of Jeffreys's writing. Had it been presented
to me, I would have argued I had no need to read anything
coming from feminism's sex-negative losing side. Books I
was prepared to read included Natasha Walter's 1999 third-
wave clarion call, *The New Feminism*, in which it is asked
'Can a woman dress like a mannequin and be a feminist?
Can she have rape fantasies and be a feminist? Can she
have a white wedding and be a feminist? Can she buy pornography and be a feminist? Can she be a prostitute and a
feminist? Can she be a Conservative voter and a feminist?
Can she be a millionaire and a feminist?' The answer to
all these questions was, of course, yes. Always yes, always
enthusiastically. Yes, yes, yes. Because as long as you change
your expectations – and as long as you never say no – who

can possibly hurt you? Only the woman whose own past might shine a light on the lie of your present.

Great reckonings vs small revolutions

Every generation likes to believe it invented sex and no one likes to think of their parents doing it. These are boring, obvious truths which nevertheless have a particular resonance for older women. If there was a time before women were considered sexual beings, and an age at which they cease to be considered sexual beings all over again, it can make sense to conflate the two. 'As a woman, I don't feel I can own up to loving sex' declares one 2021 *Guardian* piece on 'the taboos that still need breaking', as though no woman ever confessed to wanking until this very moment in time. It's the sexual equivalent of the 'finally, women are on the right side of history' myth discussed in Chapter Four. It's as though Anne Koedt's *The Myth of the Vaginal Orgasm* and Judy Blume's *Forever* never happened.

Misrepresenting history, women, or both at once in order to make the present seem more revolutionary is easier than effecting permanent changes in the behaviour of men and/or withdrawing male 'entitlements' to porn and bodies. I write this in what is, apparently, 'the age of #MeToo' or even 'the post-#MeToo era'. This refers to the movement started in 2006 by African American activist Tarana Burke to raise awareness of sexual abuse, based on her own experiences as a child and the lack of support she'd been given. In 2017, it was picked up by high-profile female celebrities, who invited women to share their own experiences of sexual assault and harassment using the hashtag #MeToo. It's important that women can talk about abuse without shame. However, there is something unsettling in the transition from Burke's actual work to the 'era' model we have now. As Julie Bindel points out, 'As the #MeToo stories of Hollywood actors and powerful men shifted from social media to mainstream media, women's control of their own stories became limited and depoliticised [...] The #MeToo movement, like all hashtag campaigns, is no substitute for action.'

When I see headlines such as '#MeToo – you will remember this as a revolution!' and 'The #MeToo Movement Changed Everything' there's a part of me that baulks at the thought of yet another great reckoning with male sexual entitlement. Every few years women and girls witness one of these – Steubenville, Rotherham, Operation Yewtree, #TimesUp – after which, so we are told, nothing will be the same. The veil has been lifted and henceforth no one shall deny the ubiquity of rape culture and child sexual abuse! It is only when you have witnessed several such Great Reckonings that you start to get suspicious. There is a pattern: everyone chants the slogans and uses the hashtags; a few ritual sacrifices are made; certain voices start to worry things are going too far; in one or two very well publicised instances, things do indeed go too far; the 'going too far' incidents are considered far greater tragedies than all the instances in which women have never seen justice at all; people start to talk about things being 'post-#MeToo' or 'after Rotherham', as though we have witnessed an irreversible cultural shift; everyone will shake their heads at the fact that 'no one' ever noticed the problem before. In practice, very little changes. The men still have their rape porn; everybody hates Ghislaine Maxwell but only a prude would suggest sex trafficking might be a fundamental part of the sex trade itself.

It's not that attitudes never improve, but most change in sexual mores happens slowly and incrementally, with the need for constant vigilance to ensure things don't start to go in reverse. The Great Reckoning way of understanding challenges to male sexual entitlement is risky for several reasons: by offering up a few instances of big game (the Saviles, the Weinsteins, the Epsteins) it prioritises the quality of those held accountable over the quantity; like the 'arc of progress' take on feminism, it creates a false sense of security (and if one does not feel sufficiently secure, one is deemed to be 'against' what progress has been made); above all, it feeds the myth that men in the past – both as perpetrators and as bystanders – couldn't have fully understood the impact of their behaviour on the basis that nobody ever knew or said that it was problematic before.

Misremembering the past is a way to cope with the present. You can tell yourself everyone was more sexist, victims more compliant; what happened to them wouldn't happen to us; predatory men are no longer hiding in plain sight – if they were, we'd spot them. In much the same way that the 'women's time is now!' message is double-edged – on the one hand relieving women of the shame of being female, on the other, denying them a heritage and priming them for future obsolescence – the Great Reckoning claim that we're only just coming to terms with the reality of predatory male sexual behaviour offers a superficially positive narrative at the expense of earlier women's truths.

From the vantage point of the 2020s, it is possible to identify the sexual exploitation and objectification that was prevalent in public life and popular culture twenty or thirty years ago in a way that would have been difficult at the time. The culprits are less powerful, less popular, or even deceased; their victims may be safer, more confident and – as a consequence of the waning power of those they accuse – more credible. Particular expressions or manifestations of sexist behaviour will have become unfashionable. This is a natural process which doesn't necessarily tell us anything about whether previous cultural moments were objectively more sexist. A failure to recognise this risks miscasting the behaviour of other women as rooted in passivity or ignorance rather than a cost-benefit analysis.

Articles which look back on the nineties and early noughties as a period that feminism forgot recognise, correctly, that the sexual exploitation of women and girls was often downplayed or ignored. At the same time, they risk misrepresenting the present as less misogynistic and more sympathetic to victims than it actually is. 'The 2000s were a very long time ago,' writes Sirin Kale in a *Guardian* piece asking why the decade was so toxic for women. 'That past was a different country. I hope we never go back.' As evidence for how far we've come, Kale points out that 'two-thirds of young women now identify as feminists; to say so when I was a teen would have been unthinkable'. I can, however, think of plenty of feminist things I could have said as a teen or as a young woman, which a young woman might not find it safe to say now, for fear of being called phobic or bigoted. The space has been cleared for young women to identify as feminists because the women who identify with what 'feminist' used to mean now get called far worse names.

As Rich wrote in 1976, 'Many daughters live in rage at their mothers for having accepted, too readily and passively, "whatever comes".' I can understand why the average Zoomer might feel this, looking at the past of Generation X (why didn't we notice Ross from *Friends* was a sexist arsehole? Why did we allow the Spice Girls to be presented as the best feminism had to offer? WTF was 'ladette culture' anyway?) This can lead to the assumption that today's middle-aged women have a naivety that makes us ill-equipped to contribute to feminist debate today. That younger people might be able to pick apart earlier cultural artefacts and trends from a position of greater safety rather than one of greater nuance or political wisdom tends to be overlooked. So, too, is the possibility that many of the women who spent a good part of the nineties laughing at bad jokes and toeing the liberal feminist line might now know a thing or two about self-censorship, false consciousness and the similarities as well as the differences between sexisms old and new.

When we think only in terms of Great Reckonings, we once again prioritise a simplistic cohort narrative (the generation that hasn't done any hard thinking about consent) over a narrative which takes lifecycle into account (how does your changing status on the patriarchal meat market influence your response to male behaviour? What will keep you safe? What thoughts must you delay thinking until later?) We underestimate what makes sexual assault, rape and child sexual abuse such intractable problems, as though passing trends in language and self-expression are more significant than the enormous cultural and economic institutions that prop up male sexual entitlement, institutions that adapt to fashion while keeping their key principles intact. Finally, we overlook the smaller, more personal reckonings taking place over individual lifetimes, ones which, added together, can be more dangerous to the status quo than the occasional felling of disposable heroes.

The revolution that takes place within a woman when she reaches the age of taking no more prisoners – when she is no longer willing to talk around risk, or pretend it belongs to another time and place – is much more threatening than the faux revolution that insists 'we', as a culture, are better at dealing with predatory behaviour than those who went before us. It's the difference between using the past to absolve the present and using the past to inform our understanding of where the present is going wrong.

What did you do in the sex wars?

If the emergence of a feminist utopia had been dependent on women opening their legs and putting their agency on show, the young women of the nineties would have had that achievement unlocked. We were once the vanguard of third-wave, 'sex-positive', anti-prude activism. We'd been sold the line that stigma and phobias – abstract, free-floating, knee-jerk responses, unconnected to any materialist politics – fuelled the abuse and control of women as sexual subjects, and that those responsible were not men who took pleasure in female pain but older feminists hawking a victim narrative. Not all of us bought this line, but many did, including me; it might not have been the most convincing argument, but it was the most attractive one, and as long as you had currency in the sexual marketplace, it put you on the winning side. Sex-positive feminism, raunch feminism, power feminism – whatever you wanted to call it (there were plenty of options), what we had was essentially an 'as if' feminism. Behave as if you are already free, as if the power imbalances between women and men become mere play-acting the moment orgasms are involved, and that pretend freedom will become a reality. Fake it to make it, and always be sure to look as though you're having fun.

It is hard to overestimate the degree to which nineties conceptions of a liberated feminist sexuality were fixated on the caricature of a recent, far more repressed feminist past. That there had been fierce disagreements between second-wave feminists regarding pornography and the sex trade – that these disagreements were what the term 'sex wars' was supposed to describe – had quickly been forgotten. The past and the women who made it became whatever we needed them to be, just as we would one day become the timeless prudes upon which contemporary 'sex-positive' feminism now relies to (sort of) make its case.

In *Not My Mother's Sister*, Astrid Henry describes the way in which the nineties response to the sex wars eventually recast it not as an intragenerational conflict but an inter-generational one. 'I can think of no feminist who describes herself as anti-sex,' writes Henry. 'When Generation X does the sex wars, however, it seems to want to have a war of its own, recreating a battle to fight. In order to have such a battle, some third-wavers ascribe the anti-sex position to the second wave in order to grant themselves an unrivalled claim to pro-sex feminism.' The result of this is that 'rather than seeing themselves as part of an ongoing debate within feminism – one that can be traced back to the first wave – about the meaning of sexuality for women's liberation, some third-wavers describe as a generational perspective what is more accurately a particular feminist philosophy of sex'. Henry was writing in 2004; when she refers to 'third-wavers', she means women like me, who might well have thought ourselves the new dawn. That the model we were buying was not one of revolution but repetition, in which the work of earlier and/or older women was simplified, misrepresented or even erased, was easy to overlook in the search for an identity which felt liberating without posing any actual challenges to the men around us.

A 1994 *Esquire* article, featuring prominent feminists such as Rebecca Walker, Naomi Wolf, bell hooks and Katie Roiphe, proclaimed the arrival of 'do-me' feminism, in which women were shifting the discussion 'from the failures of men to the failures of feminism, from the paradigm of sexual abuse to the paradigm of sexual pleasure'. Writers such as Roiphe and Rene Denfield decried the notion that women needed to prioritise self-protection, as though this in itself made us weaker. Roiphe's

1993 book *The Morning After*, a polemic against 'take back the night' marches and the concept of rape culture, insisted that 'proclaiming victimhood doesn't help project strength'. Denfield's 1996 book *The New Victorians* was subtitled 'a young woman's challenge to the old feminist order', characterising an obsession with sexual repression and powerlessness as the province of feminists past their prime. In this, one might see a foreshadowing of contemporary warnings against 'weaponising trauma' and 'calling the manager' in response to sexual assault. Alternatively, one might detect echoes of age-old prejudice against women who play the victim and 'set a trap with tears'. Stigmatising victimhood is easier than challenging those who make victims of women, yet each generation somehow believes itself the first to try the former tactic.

There is a German verb – verschlimmbessern – which means 'to make something worse in an effort to improve it'. I cannot think of a better term to describe the 'progress' of so-called 'sex positive' feminism over the past forty years. That women's sexual autonomy could ever be contingent on compliance with male demands is absurd, but the liberal feminist focus on making compliance look like choice has not only pandered to these demands, but given scope for them to become more extreme in advance of any actual autonomy being granted. In the mid-eighties Andrea Dworkin noted the way in which the male-dominated left used abortion as a bargaining chip, implying female sexual compliance ('accessibility') went hand in hand with the right to a termination. Today one sees the left use similar arguments to suggest women who wish to organise politically as a sex class are jeopardising their own reproductive rights. Yet abortion has not become more freely available the more the sex trade has expanded and the less willing women have become to name which class of people actually gets pregnant. In many instances, progress has gone into reverse. Similarly, as Julie Bindel documents, there has been a reversal of progress in terms of abuse of women during sex, rape conviction rates, widespread access to violent porn and disbelief of female victims of assault.

Heterosexual Generation X women who return to the dating market in their forties and fifties discover a world in which male expectations have become harsher, colder, less respectful of female desire and pleasure. 'When I was a teenager,' one woman tells *Independent* reporter Victoria Richards, 'girls who wouldn't willingly have sex were labelled "frigid". The new "frigid" is "vanilla". Girls who don't want porn-inspired sex – anal, hair-pulling and choking – are shamed for their "inhibitions".' 'I've been sexually active since 1987,' says another, 'and spitting, slapping and choking were simply not a thing until very recently [...] Porn is eroticising violence against women.' Hardcore porn is shaping the defences men offer for violence against women, providing variations on the old 'crime of passion' defence. Child abuse expert Michael Sheath claims mainstream pornography sites are 'changing what is normal': 'Before the internet there was a ceiling on how much porn you could consume [...] For the younger men who had their adolescence after about 2000, men up to forty, they will have watched a huge amount of online pornography before they have sex with a human being.' Sheath suggests extreme porn has become a gateway drug, not just into violence against women but child abuse.

If the removal of 'stigma' was working as promised, things would be getting better, not worse. I personally think we have to reach one of three possible conclusions:

- one, Generation X women have been middle-aged prudes since the day they were born and everything

that's happening now is because they're in league with
conservative, stigmatising, anti-sex forces;
- two, there was such a thing as 'sex-positive' feminism
in the nineties and early noughties but, rather like
communism, it wasn't being done *properly*;
- three, 'sex-positive' feminism is a massive, exploitative,
male entitlement-pandering, female pleasure-denying
con.

The first two options might be unlikely, but the latter is
untenable for institutions, feminist organisations and individual activists who have invested a great deal in associating
any criticism of unbridled sexual liberalism with conservatism, prudishness and the promotion of stigma. It's untenable
for men who want to be 'nice guys' without giving up their
Pornhub habits. More importantly, it's untenable for women
who do not have the physical or emotional security to start
questioning the conditions of acts to which they have only
nominally consented. You'd have to be the woman who has
exited the fertility-fuckability-femininity market, is taking
stock of her own past exploitation and frankly has nothing
left to lose – essentially, middle-aged woman reprising her
regular role as the child in The Emperor's New Clothes – to
plump for option three. As far as everyone else is concerned,
it's so much easier to blame the hag.

If you can, for one moment, ignore the physical injuries,
psychological trauma and death caused by the global sex
trade, the state of sex-positive feminism today is darkly hilarious. It's the tragedy of the unhappy winner, who expected so
much more from the prize and is now convinced that someone,
somewhere, has robbed them. How can it possibly be that you
put in all this service to the pro-sex cause, yet the men that
you sleep with hate you as much as ever? It can't be that the

two things were never related to begin with! There has to be a ridiculous, constant goalpost shifting: *you know when we said more threesomes would be liberating? Well, turns out we meant threesomes in which you're spat on, and possibly also slapped in the face.* No argument is too ridiculous, providing it facilitates the avoidance of ever having to set limits on male sexual entitlement. It's funny, providing you don't think too hard about words, bodies and the reality of pain.

Today's older women undermine a narrative which is needed more than ever by those cheering on the breaking down of boundaries in the name of liberation – and by those who, seeing there is little they can do to stop said breaking down of boundaries, are desperately seeking a way to convince themselves that what threatens them is not a culture in which female pain is sold as pleasure, but the older women who dare to point this out. It's essential our personal histories are misrepresented to protect a feminism that has taken a wrong turn (which is entirely in keeping with what we did to others). The greatest irony of all is that, as older women who now say no, we pose far more of a threat to conservative sexual norms than ever before.

Prudes: An old-new moral panic

'You know,' says Cathy, fifty-two, 'it's true that once women are past childbearing age, everything changes and they're no longer part of the sexual economy. And that's really, really hard to deal with as a woman, for lots of reasons. But one thing that's worth talking about in this context is, how do you deal with the fact that you participated in the sexual economy at all? The economy which, you now see, is total bullshit? It's heartrending when you reach that point, when you realise that all you've really done is enabled it to continue, participated in it, gatekept it, looked the other way, smoothed things over ... How do you deal with that fact?'

When older women 'become prudish' – when we ask too many questions about the power hierarchies that underpin 'liberated' sex – this tends to be understood not as a life-cycle effect in the way described by Cathy but as a cohort one. It's not that the change in perspective that comes with age provides us with an insight we didn't have before; it's that we were born at the wrong time, destined to age out of fuckability long before anyone imagined that sex need not be the vanilla, missionary-position, reproductive-purposes-only kind. Like right-side-of-history politics, sex-positive feminism is a progress narrative that moves ever forwards, leaving behind actual female bodies and the trauma imprinted upon them. There is no scope for revisiting the past once your time is up.

I always considered myself too modern, too clever, too damn open-minded to become one of those creatures who can be dismissed, as Jeffreys puts it, 'as anti-sex, prudish, puritan-ical and as potential allies of the moral majority'. Their truths seemed so crass, so lacking in nuance. 'Things are,' I'd tell myself, 'a bit more complicated than that. These women don't get it because they're from the olden, sexist, sexless days, and just don't know any better.' Years later I find myself feeling somewhat affronted that my promiscuous past hasn't bought me a magic ticket out of what Dworkin called 'the Puritan camp, that hallucinated place of exile where women with complaints are dumped, after which we can be abandoned'. Like an overlooked celebrity, I occasionally get the urge to ask younger women, 'Don't you know who I am? Have you any idea how much of the nineties I spent on my knees, only to later be dismissed for the sins of "critical thought" and "deep feeling", just as Dworkin said I would be?' It can be hard not to think that if you expose your own past a little more – show the world just how up for it you really were – then your present, older woman's perspective might be granted a little more credibility. Sadly this is not how the prude construct works.

In her essay 'Aging While Female is Not Your Worst Nightmare', Lori Day wryly observes that 'if I condemn pornography as systematically damaging to women, it is my age that provokes my labelling as a prude and a pearl-clutcher':

> It cannot be that I base my opinion on studies and statistics and the understanding that feminism is a movement – one that supports the liberation of all women, not to be confused with individual women who choose to reduce their identities to the sexual uses and abuses of their bodies, calling that empowerment. [...] The wisdom that comes with age has little value to anyone but those possessing it, because wisdom is another word for old, and old is what no one wants to be.

This is one half of the problem in re-evaluating one's liberated past: the fact that you are an older woman undermines your critique. The other is that the critique itself is coded as belonging to an older woman, one who has not kept up with the times (because simply ageing while female is to be falling behind in terms of 'what matters' as far as women and sex are concerned).

Calling an older woman a prude or a pearl-clutcher is not merely irritating or offensive; it is, as Day suggests, deeply political, a way of defending sexual exploitation by demonising those who seek to define its causes rather than tackling their arguments head-on. As the negative impact of a male-default sexual liberalism becomes more and more apparent, it becomes ever more important for those championing it to make caricatures of their critics. In a 2021 lecture for the Scottish PEN Women Writers Committee, the poet Jenny Lindsay described her fears that 'our sexual liberation has, like our social and cultural liberation, been co-opted and repackaged and sold back to us as faux-autonomy by those for whom our bodies, our pleasure, our sex, is a mere marketable asset', and that those who dare to challenge 'this happy-go-lucky embrace of "non-consensual" porn are called the prudes and "anti-sex" caricatures of the past'. In *Feminism for Women*, Julie Bindel argues that '"progressives" have rewritten the [anti-porn feminist] narrative and been given carte blanche to smear those who campaign against it as sexless harridans'. Any criticism of sexual exploitation can be reframed in this way, associating criticisms of pornography and the sex trade with homophobia, anti-abortion politics and religious extremism. It is not that no links can ever be made, but they are not necessary ones. Moreover, there is a refusal to acknowledge that older women might have different motivations from men and younger women when it comes to setting boundaries and questioning social norms. The puritan can be blamed for everything, and since the puritan is sexless in more ways than one, no sex disaggregated analysis of his or her motivations is required.

The irony at the heart of the prude-shaming aimed at older women is that it positions itself as an activity in defence of progress, when it could equally be described as a traditional means of preserving and reinforcing social norms which favour men. Both Jeffreys and Susan Faludi, in her 2010 article 'American Electra', describe the same ritual shaming of first-wave feminists and early campaigners against child abuse and pornography, who found themselves recast as the 'real' enemies of women and girls. The figure of the agency-denying sexphobe – whether she's a cartoon character in the 2020s or one of the 'cold women [who] have a perfect mania for prohibition as a solution for all ills [and] have long ago forgotten what sex means' described in a 1917 academic paper on sex psychology – is incredibly useful to those who wish to draw attention away from male abuses and stigmatise women who set boundaries. By relying on a male-default understanding of progress in relation to personal experience, psychology and lifecycle, those seeking to make a virtue of extending male entitlement are able to lump together male and female opponents, intimating that both share the same 'conservatism'. The truth is far more complicated.

Describing the 'pro-purity' campaigning of Republican women during the nineteenth century, Faludi acknowledges 'the problematic aspects of Victorian maternal protectionism' – 'its cloying sentimentality; its consecration of "feminine" piety and sexual purity; [...] its "protective" rhetoric that often cast women as weak' – but points out that 'what gets overlooked is the degree to which this maternal campaign centred around an increasingly radical desire for mothers to arm their daughters, both literally and figuratively, against male control, especially male sexual control'. There is a form of gender essentialism in the activism Faludi describes, but its aim is also to undermine a male dominance perceived as 'natural'. On the one hand, campaigners play on regressive stereotypes of feminine innocence in order to make their case; on the other, to use such stereotypes to resist male control is profoundly subversive. A truly compliant, submissive woman would accept the sexual marketplace as it is.

In *The Spinster and Her Enemies*, Jeffreys describes the way in which nineteen-twenties debates on 'sexual purity' and 'sex reform' allowed for only two positions on sexuality:

The pro-sex camp, which included the sexologists and the sex reformers, characterised the feminists as 'anti-sex', as prudes and puritans [...] Instead of being credited with having a worked-out theory around sexuality, these feminists have been dismissed as having an old-maid, prudish attitude of mind.

Jeffreys compares this to the treatment of feminists at the time she was writing, the eighties. In both cases she points out that campaigns for 'social purity' come from different places, and mean different things, depending on the sex of the person doing the campaigning and whose interests they represent:

Women and girls are the objects of prostitution and sexual abuse, and men are the exploiters. It cannot therefore be expected that one form of explanation could describe why both men and women were involved in campaigning against a form of sexual behaviour to which men and women bore such a very different relationship.

This line of thinking can be connected to Gloria Steinem's argument about the different relationship men and women have to radicalism (as discussed in Chapter Four), and to the way in which 'conservatism' and complicity, for older women and mothers in particular, can be associated with female self-defence rather than male entitlement (as discussed in Chapter Three). Male-default political narratives erase the specificity of female perspectives, leaving space only for a battle over what kind of property women and girls should be: private (the conservative view) or public (the 'progressive' one).

One contemporary illustration of the refusal to see any difference between male and female critiques of sexual liberalism is found in the *Simpsons* character Helen Lovejoy. A vicar's wife, Lovejoy regularly appears in memes along with her catchphrase 'Won't somebody please think of the children?' She stands for the bigoted prude who uses child safeguarding as an excuse to police other people's sex lives, with references to her being trotted out any time it is tentatively suggested that perhaps not every activity that is superficially consensual is without harm. While it is perfectly true that 'think of the children' can be a rhetorical device, appealing to emotion to deflect attention from the paucity of one's own arguments, the meme has itself become a way of avoiding scrutiny. It's a straw-man attack that mocks the idea of straw-man attacks. Criticising lad mags is 'a bit Helen Lovejoy'; placing limits on Pornhub is the province of 'a minority of moral crusaders mimicking Helen Lovejoy'; discussing gender on Mumsnet means adopting 'a Helen Lovejoy-style "think of the children!" tenor'; questioning whether sexualised drag should be in primary schools is a form of 'faux sincerity' that has been mocked by *The Simpsons* 'since the nineties'. These are all areas which can and should be open to discussion, but the Lovejoy meme places them out of bounds.

Through the meme, older women become, once again, the receptacles for the unacceptable beliefs that everyone else insists they have 'grown out of'. By this I mean not just illicit fantasies about having boundaries, but actual prejudices: racism, classism, homophobia (all of which are prevalent, and go unchallenged, on the average porn site menu – but to question this would itself be 'a bit Helen Lovejoy'). Lovejoy is another iteration of the mother-in-law or *Little Britain*'s WI women, offering right-thinking people the opportunity to cleanse their souls by projecting all their fears and hang-ups onto her.

This is not to say that older women never have sexual hang-ups and prejudices that need challenging. There is, however, a distinct imbalance in approach. For instance, in 2021's *It's a Sin*, Russell T. Davies's excellent drama on the eighties Aids crisis and the way in which it was exacerbated by extreme prejudice, there are two main female characters who stand in relation to Ritchie, a young gay man who dies of Aids. His best friend Jill is compassionate, selfless and seemingly lacking in any desires of her own; his mother Valerie, meanwhile, is bigoted, cold and utterly unwilling to respect her son's identity. In a showdown in the final episode, the young woman confronts the older one just after her son has died and tells her, 'All this is your fault. The wards are full of men who think they deserve it. They all die because of you.' It is striking that violent, bigoted fathers such as Richie's and that of his friend Roscoe are not targeted in this way, but instead are offered a tentative shot at redemption. There is, it seems, something human and forgivable in being a bigoted father, but not a bigoted mother. Valerie is one of TV and film's maternal monsters as described by the Acting Your Age campaign, 'entrenched in bigotry like unredeemed homophobia, or the apparent "cause" of her daughter's mental health issues'. Davies has said that had the series been longer, it may have shown that sexual abuse from her father explains 'how Valerie ended up like she did'. Personally I am not convinced that stigmatising female victims of childhood sexual abuse by using them to explain the origins of homophobia is entirely helpful here.

Accusing older women can be a safe substitute for the more difficult task of accepting one's own complicity in injustice. In 2015 I attended a feminist talk in which a young woman from the exclusive private school hosting the event stood up to declare that 'sex work is work' and denounce all regressive, older, non-intersectional feminists who thought otherwise. She didn't quote from the non-existent passage of Kimberlé

Crenshaw's 'Mapping the Margins' in which the right of
men to rent out the bodies of vulnerable women is justified,
nor did she mention her own plans to follow this particular
career path. What she did do was distinguish herself from the
bad women, making a grab for a catch-all, 'good girl' identity which didn't actually require any serious thinking about
the relationship between wealth, race, gender and sexual
exploitation. ('One of the favourite myths to be propagated
by sex reformers,' writes Jeffreys, 'was that "frigidity" was
a problem of the middle-class woman and that the working-
class woman was somehow more primitive, spontaneous and
sensual.' Prude-shaming provides a neat way for a middle-
class woman to divest herself of all charges of 'frigidity' while
justifying the exploitation of her less privileged but more
'sensual' sisters.)

It is true that female sexual agency has been demonised
by men wishing to control female bodies and appropriate
female reproductive labour. Hence it is not entirely irrational
to think that since those who abuse women do not respect
female agency, the questioning of anything going by the name
of agency must be suspect. This creates a loophole whereby
the embracing of mainstream objectification and hypersexu-
alisation can be misrepresented as a form of rebellion against
patriarchal norms. In *Witches, Sluts, Feminists: Conjuring
the Sex Positive*, Kristen J. Sollée correctly points out that
'from the spiteful old hag to the promiscuous young woman
to the man-hating shrew, the negative stereotypes about the
women we call witches, sluts, and feminists have filled vol-
umes'. However, I don't think it is correct that 'the "slut" is
in many ways the "witch" of the twenty-first century'. The
line of attack has shifted. To suggest a strip-club performance
might invoke the same moral response as intimations of dark
magic – 'Like the witches of legend who could summon a

sudden downpour, some witches of today can summon the forces to make it rain at the strip club [...] Whether conjuring the elements or crisp $100s, such acts require working with potent, unseen energies' – is frankly ludicrous. The fact that men still slut-shame should not be confused with there being a genuine moral panic about a version of female sexual expression that has already been co-opted by the dominant culture. No one is shocked by tits and ass any more; tits and ass are everywhere. The real moral panic surrounds those older women – whose tits and asses are now surplus to requirements – who object to it.

Even younger women who see the problems with today's pornified culture know they must engage in ritual acts of disidentification. In a 2021 article for the *New Statesman*, thirty-year-old Megan Nolan frets that objecting to the rise in violent sexual practices driven by porn puts her in the same camp as the 'dogmatic' and 'exclusionary' feminists whom her friends dislike. These women, it is suggested, make it harder for everyone else – presumably 'normal' people, of 'normal' ages – to criticise the potential for harm. That the reason why these women are cast as dogmatic and exclusionary might be down to them making the exact same argument Nolan is trying to make seems to pass her by. Older women are to blame when the bad things they predicted come to pass because they have made objecting to the bad things look like something only a mean, purse-lipped, sex-hating older woman would do. The work of feminism would be done and dusted if it wasn't for those pesky representatives of Millie Tant – the *Viz* comic feminist who sees all men as 'potential rapists' and all women as 'fellow lesbians' – making reasonable women look bad. 'I'm not a feminist, but ...' – the classic phrase used to preface any statement which demonstrates the speaker is, in fact, a feminist – has found new life in 'I'm not exclusionary/phobic/anti-porn, but ...' The trouble is, as Generation X women – many of whom spent most of the nineties trotting out the 'not a feminist, but' line – learned to our detriment, trying to sweeten the pill of feminism with a little casual misogyny just doesn't work. Feed the patriarchal monster as much older female flesh as you like, but you'll only be whetting its appetite for the bigger feast.

It is no good starting to think the same thoughts as the 'bad' women, then stopping halfway through. A feminist analysis that could recognise the degree to which male sexual violence is linked to both reproductive exploitation and social control ends up being jettisoned in favour of one which sees any form of restriction as hating sex and/or not wanting marginalised people to enjoy it. Crass, male-default definitions of left versus right, and liberalism versus conservatism, end up conflating the fight for abortion rights and same-sex marriage with a defence of rape porn and renting the bodies of prostituted women. This is offensive when you think about it, therefore many of us try not to. After all, what would you rather take on: the multi-billion-pound porn industry, seeping into every aspect of life in ways in which you (apparently) can't control? Or an unsexy cartoon woman, whether she takes the form of a pearl-clutching Christian in *The Simpsons* or a lesbian separatist in *Viz*? I'm not saying these characters are never funny; I'm suggesting their positioning as the enemies of sexual freedom is convenient, to say the least.

Thinking of the children

It's February 2020, one month prior to the UK's first lockdown, and I'm in a room called The Sinner's Enclosure; it says so on the door. The man and the woman to whom I am talking are mortified about this.

'We're very sorry,' they say. 'If we have to come down another time, we'll insist that they give us somewhere else, maybe even try another hotel.'

I tell them it's fine; part of me finds it vaguely, inappropriately amusing (though I don't say that).

'Oh, no,' says the woman. 'It could have been terrible. For some of the adults we talk to, the abuse took place in a religious institution. Can you imagine how they'd respond to seeing a name like that?'

I say that would indeed be terrible. I haven't been abused in a religious institution. Nothing that bad has happened to me. Nothing very bad at all, in fact. I say I'm sorry for those other people. Rather me in The Sinner's Enclosure than them, ha ha.

I'm trying to tread a very fine line. I don't want the woman and the man to think I'm wasting their time. They've travelled a long way to hear me make my statement, had to stay overnight, in a hotel so posh it has meeting rooms with ridiculous names on the door. This must be costing a lot of money. I don't want it to seem like I'm taking the piss. Then again, neither do I want it to look like I'm making too big a deal of something that happened a long time ago. It's just a memory, a memory about bodies. I don't want to be overthinking it, making it mean something it never meant at the time.

'I'm sorry, this is really nothing,' I keep saying.

'No, it's all very important,' they insist, but then they would. I'm trying not to keep second-guessing what I must look like to them.

The truth is this: I'm in several places at once. Young self, old self, whore, prude. My older children are approaching their teens, and I'm watching being twelve years old from the outside, thinking how young it is, hoping they know less than I did then. I contacted the child abuse inquiry telling myself I would play a part in fixing the future, though I now wonder if I am in fact attempting to revise the past. *Think nice thoughts.* That's what you tell yourself when you disassociate. I've become less good at this the older I've got.

The older I've got, the more I've found myself edging towards becoming that most grotesque of creatures, the middle-aged mummy who worries about *breaches in safeguarding* and *premature sexualisation* and *adults preying on minors.* All those Schrödinger's events which we know actually happen, which might even have happened to us, but which we simultaneously write off as conspiracy-theory-driven moral panics. All that made-up shit only family values conservatives and bored, Mumsnet-addled housewives pretend to care about in order to demonise outsiders. Since I hit my forties, I've started caring about them. I've lost the battle to keep thinking nice thoughts and instead a horrible *knowing* and *remembering* have descended on me. It's all such a terrible cliché.

Child sexual abuse is a 'right side of history' issue which invariably illustrates the uselessness of the 'right side of history' concept, dependent as it is on the idea that in ten, twenty, thirty years' time, your critics will know you were right and they were wrong. Child abuse whistle-blowers are almost always found to be on the 'wrong' side when abuse is taking place. Then in ten, twenty, thirty years, when it transpires that – gasp! – they were onto something, they are still pearl-clutching bigots on the wrong side of history, since it is only time itself, and the relative sophistication of the present day in relation to the past, that has revealed the truth, in true Great Reckoning style. When pearl-clutching hags are right, it is only in the way that stopped clocks are right twice a day, whereas when those on the right side of history are wrong, it is only because they were too busy being right in general – by avoiding 'moral panic' – to focus on the specifics.

Describing the relationship between 'moral panic' and generational differences, Bobby Duffy suggests that 'new generations are more proficient at adapting to innovation, which can create a perception among older generations that they are losing control of the culture they helped shape'. As an example, he refers to the fact that 'the US Surgeon General suggested that games like *Asteroids*, *Space Invaders* and *Centipede* were a leading cause of family violence. The reason that older examples of these panics sound more ridiculous to us than the latest ones is not that the world is getting worse – it's just that we're getting old.' I wonder, though, whether these examples actually sound ridiculous because Duffy has, using the benefit of hindsight, selected ridiculous examples. Few would refer to whisperings about Jimmy Savile or Rotherham or the impact of Page Three as 'moral panics' now; on the contrary, the moral panic that turns out to have been correct stops being classed as a moral panic and is magically transformed into yet more evidence that the past was another country and hence cannot be used as a framework with which to judge the present.

For many of my generation in the UK, the 2001 *Brass Eye* paedophilia TV special, 'a parody of the hysteria stoked by the British news media', fed the perception that caring about child sexual abuse was an unsophisticated, common thing to do, something you'd only engage in because you were too stupid or uneducated to question what the newspapers (or programme producers) told you. Like many young, liberal, middle-class graduates I went along with this. Over a decade before the Jimmy Savile scandal broke, I didn't think about the reality of children being abused in the here and now. I didn't think about my own past, or that of other people I knew. As Judith Herman writes in *Trauma and Recovery*, 'it is very tempting to take the side of the perpetrator. All the perpetrator asks is that the bystander do nothing. He appeals to the universal desire to see, hear, and speak no evil. The victim, on the contrary, asks the bystander to share the burden of pain.' The victim is demanding and uncool; the perpetrator has all the best jokes.

Added to this is rarity perception. 'We do not really want to know,' writes Bessel van der Kolk, 'how many children are being molested and abused in our own society [...] We want to think of families as safe havens in a heartless world and of our own country as populated by enlightened, civilised people.' Freud famously suggested that hysteria was caused by sexual abuse in the family, then backtracked purely on the basis that for this to be true, abuse would have to be extremely widespread. Thanks to the 'moral panic' narrative, child sexual abuse can feel a little like nuclear war: something people were incredibly panicked about in the past, but which has now gone away. It was all a bad dream. Except the weapons and potential for annihilation remain, and the abuse still happens.

When the Netflix film *Cuties* was released in 2020, exploring the experiences of an adolescent girl caught between her traditional culture and involvement in a highly sexualised dance crew, the *Telegraph* described it as a 'powder keg provocation in an age terrified of child sexuality', advising us to 'forget the moral panic' because 'Netflix's controversial French import is disturbing and risqué because that's exactly what it aims to be'. I don't think this is an age terrified of child sexuality; I think it's an age terrified of those who name the power imbalances between male and female, young and old, in relation to sex. It is trite to observe that very young people can be sexually curious, as though this is a groundbreaking revelation with the power to blow apart harmful social norms (if that were the case, it would have done so in the seventies or earlier). What would be truly challenging is to make the connections between a 'normal' culture that sexualises youth and demonises female ageing in particular, and a culture that we deem 'abnormal' or abusive.

'It is no coincidence,' argues the novelist Helen Walsh, 'that our society construes and vilifies the ageing female body with the same reckless generality that it celebrates and objectifies its pubescent incarnation':

> We're quick to express rage at Jimmy Savile's reign of abuse or the taxi drivers who targeted vulnerable girls from care homes in Rochdale, yet our culture is still casually at ease with its sexualising of young female bodies. Our lionisation of size zero, our aversion to pubic hair, even an increasing trend towards vaginaplasties are all symptomatic of a desire to take the female body back to its pre-pubescent state.

Rather than ask questions about how this facilitates the exploitation of the very young, we shoot the matronly messenger, who has marked herself out as anti-sex merely by having the temerity to age. The insidious conflation of the fact that very young people can and do feel sexual desire with the insistence that young people can consent to sexual acts in the same way that adults can is used to pathologise older women – those frigid prudes who somehow bypassed a normal stage in their youthful sexual development – rather than those who want to fuck children, who don't in any case exist, not really.

When, for instance, older women objected to the 2022 announcement of *The Family Sex Show*, a live show which aimed to encourage children as young as five to sing with adults about masturbation, they were characterised as right-wing bigots who were too past-it to get with the programme. 'Children aren't anxious about the idea of the show,' protested one of the organisers. 'It's older people who feel discomfort in something that's challenging their preconceptions.' As though as the mother of a six-year-old – and someone whose own boundaries are hard-won – I should defer to my child's 'lack of preconceptions', otherwise known as ignorance. When the very idea of experience is associated with closed-mindedness, the most vulnerable are easy prey.

'Women know too much,' said Jimmy Savile, in what was somehow not considered to be a raging red flag at the time. 'I'm all for girls that don't know too much.' A serial abuser in plain sight, Savile could nudge and wink at the wise old hag trope and trust his listeners not to take her side. After all, as Helen Joyce notes, 'the most despised and dispensable person in a sexist society is an older woman. She has no value or purpose to men. And she tries to stop the predators among them by protecting younger women and children.' 'When anyone stood up to Savile,' writes Louise Perry, 'it was older women: nurses, matrons, grandmothers – the sort of obstinate ladies who flocked to [Mary] Whitehouse's campaigns':

> Misogynists have always reserved a particular well of hatred for women like this – creatures with heavy ankles and sagging necklines who have nothing to offer in terms of nubile beauty, but an annoying habit of saying 'no' to male demands.

Their opposition to males preying on children is written off as hysteria; when, years later, it is acknowledged that what was happening then (but not now!) was indeed abuse, no one thanks them, let alone apologises. On the contrary, the fact that such things were 'allowed' to happen cements a perception of the past and its inhabitants as sexual hypocrites.

In a 1995 update to 'Why Young Women Are More Conservative', Steinem proposed that recovery from personal experiences of sexual abuse and the safety in which to reflect could be a significant factor driving older women's radicalism. As Karin Ward, a fifty-eight-year-old victim of Jimmy Savile put it, 'Now I know I'm a victim but back then I didn't know I was a victim.' This is one of the reasons why I end up in the Sinner's Enclosure. Because I remember the past from a position of greater power, and don't think the problem of male sexual entitlement, predatory behaviour and female silencing has gone away. My understanding of my own history has changed, in part because I can think of it from a position of safety, and in part because of other experiences I have gathered, including motherhood, that supposed gateway into knee-jerk conservatism.

I'm a caricature, but I'm also a truth, the boner-killing fish-wife who has some serious questions to ask about sex, having once believed the only meaningful answer could be 'yes'. I've become inconvenient, both to myself and to others.

'I don't know why I'm telling you this,' I say to the woman and the man. Then I keep on telling anyway.

Gag reflexes

There's a scene in Emma Cline's novel *The Girls* that beautifully captures the way in which the potential for connection between older and younger women is stretched until it breaks. The narrator Evie, a middle-aged woman with a disturbing

past, is housesitting for a friend when the latter's teenage
son Julian and girlfriend Sasha come to stay. Later they are
joined by Julian's friend Zav. Evie is sensitive to the pressure
Julian and Zav's boorish performances of masculinity place
on Sasha, but also to her own low status as the unfuckable,
off-the-market older woman.

Evie is present when Julian starts telling Zav that Sasha
'doesn't like her tits' and suggests Sasha strips off in order to
let Zav judge their worth:

Sasha's face reddened.

'Do it, babe,' Julian said, a harshness in his voice making
me glance over. I caught Sasha's eye – I told myself the look
in her face was pleading.

'Come on, you guys,' I said.

The boys turned with amused surprise. Though I think
they were tracking where I was all along. That my presence
was part of the game.

'What?' Julian said, his face snapping into innocence.

'Just cool it,' I told him.

'Oh, it's fine,' Sasha said. Laughing a little, her eyes
on Julian.

'What exactly are we doing?' Julian said. 'What exactly
should we "cool"?'

He and Zav snorted – how quickly all the old feelings
came back, the humiliating interior fumble. I crossed my
arms, looking to Sasha. 'You're bothering her.'

'Sasha's fine,' Julian said. He tucked a strand of hair
behind her ear – she smiled faintly and with effort.

It's a wonderfully observed, acutely painful scenario which
we only see through Evie's eyes. Is her reading of the situation
correct? Is she projecting onto Sasha feelings from her own

sexual exploitation as a teenage girl? Who does Evie want to protect from harm: Sasha or her younger self?

As older women we struggle on several fronts, our memories of past sexual experiences coloured and distorted by the passage of time and the accumulation of knowledge. We risk seeing in younger women the selves we would go back to rescue, even if these selves would not want to be rescued at the time. Our low status in the sexual marketplace makes it difficult to communicate with younger women as equals. We might know things they do not, but how can that ever be expressed without it sounding patronising? There is no polite way of saying 'you might one day realise this wasn't what you wanted', especially not when the person who's saying it is a designated loser.

Sasha's decision to comply with Julian's demands, whatever her own desires, is easy to understand. Julian and Zav, as young men, hold the power. From Evie's description, Julian is conscious of his ability to manipulate not just Sasha and Evie as individuals, but the relationship between them. The only way someone such as Evie could hope to maintain any status would be by adopting the role of enforcer rather than disruptor of norms, coaxing the younger woman into compliance. Instead, Evie has tried to bond with Sasha by telling her about her own past, only to find that Sasha has used this against her to gain status with the men, when Julian reveals he knows of Evie's teenage involvement in a murder:

> 'Sasha said you told her so,' Julian went on. 'Like you could have done it, too.'
>
> I inhaled sharply. The pathetic betrayal: Sasha had told Julian everything I'd said.
>
> 'So show us,' Zav said, turning back to Sasha. I was already invisible again. 'Show us the famous tits.'

'You don't have to,' I said to her.

Sasha flicked her eyes in my direction. 'It isn't a big deal or anything,' she said, her tone dripping with cool, obvious disdain. She plucked her neckline away from her chest and looked pensively down her shirt.

'See?' Julian said, smiling hard at me. 'Listen to Sasha.'

To be the Evie in this scenario, having once been the Sasha, and to know how little one has to bargain with – to know that even if, on some level, you understand one another, it is you who is the non-aspirational figure, the one seeking to persuade the woman who still has something with which to trade in the patriarchal marketplace that it will not be worth it – feels like the fate of every older woman trying so hard to weigh her words, to avoid sounding patronising, or bitter, or jealous, to convey that, yes, you know how much a younger woman has to lose.

In 'American Electra', Susan Faludi describes US feminism at the start of the twentieth century being engaged in a kind of custody battle: 'Who was going to win the daughter? Would it be the maternal Victorian reformers, the daughters' former champions, now cast as scolds, hags, and prudes? Or would it be the male expert whose voice became the Oz-like authority lurking behind the curtain of the ascendant commercial culture?' Anyone looking at *Teen Vogue* today would be in no doubt about who has 'won' the daughter. It can feel undignified to keep fighting, particularly if one suspects it may do more harm than good. If, as a young woman, the way you cope with ambivalence, coercion and outright abuse is to sell them to yourself as something else, then of course you will rage at the woman who chips away at your coping mechanism, tugs at the thread which will unravel it all, leading to an admission that you have been hurt and are in pain. She is patronising you, bullying you, suggesting you are not the ultimate authority on what is done to your body. At worst, she is the abuser. If she wasn't there calling it abuse, everything would simply be your free choice.

'You want it to be true that you're free,' the philosopher Jane Clare Jones says, 'and that men are treating you as a human being, and that you're allowed to follow your desire and do exactly as you want, and that there will be no negative repercussions and it's all going to be fine, and you're not being exploited or being objectified. And I'm not going to say there isn't a potential world in which that might be true. But you can't live in a world that you want to be true when it's not true, because it opens up young women to all kinds of horrifying shit.'

It matters to find a way to keep the channels of communication open. One question I increasingly hear regarding feminism and sexual exploitation is 'Why do you even care?' Why should I, having been with the same partner for over twenty years, be bothered about what happens to younger women in the big bad world? It can feel hard to make a move, knowing that any urge to protect could be characterised as interference, prurience, some weird, curtain-twitchy obsession arising from envy and domestic boredom. Empathy and class consciousness should not become absurd propositions because we cannot see the common thread that binds one generation of women to the next.

'People don't always know what's best for them,' Anna-Louise Adams, a radical feminist in her early twenties, tells me. 'And that's why feminists have always taken it upon themselves to at least make sure that there are support systems in place for women who maybe do end up in situations which they thought were autonomous but weren't, because that trajectory was already mapped out before them. And if those support networks aren't still being reproduced through different generations, then that is a concern.'

This is not a wisdom I had at her age. For me, as for others, coming to truly know my own desires has meant a slow, painful acknowledgement of all the desires that were simulated, choice for choice's sake, a giving-away of boundaries in the hope that this proved they were mine to begin with. An acknowledgement that my own body could never be the end point of a struggle that has endured for generations, through other bodies, at variable costs. A realisation that there are worse things than being considered undesirable, including to have one's desires not registered at all. The difficult part now is arguing from a position I already know is discredited, because I once participated in the discrediting myself. I watch my own words going through the 'normal person to prudish, sexphobic hag' translator before I've got to the end of a sentence. Still I speak. It's the difference between fighting a caricature and being a caricature tasked with fighting something that's real.

6

PLOTTING HAG

Feminism is a socialist, anti-family political movement that encourages women to leave their husbands, kill their children, practice witchcraft, destroy capitalism and become lesbians.

Pat Robertson, 1992 anti-Equal Rights
Amendment fundraising letter

The mums on Mumsnet's women's rights forum are constantly complaining about being belittled as 'silly old women' and 'daft housewives.' I agree with them: We underestimate them at our own peril.

Katie J. M. Baker, *The Road to Terfdom*

Women, we are led to believe, are our own worst enemies. Unlike men, who resolve disagreements in a calm, rational manner – say, by beating the crap out of one another, or perhaps even starting a war – women can't help undermining one another, with peer-reviewed academic studies showing that 'mean girl behaviour is hardwired into the female brain'. It's evolution or something, 'going back to the caveman era when women had to learn ways to compete with other females to find suitable males with whom to reproduce'. I'm guessing we might have done this by getting out our cave-tits for the cave-lads.

Given how little help we need in hating each other, it is surprising to see the lengths modern culture will go to in order to remind us to do so. Being confronted with a succession of films, newspaper articles and research studies expounding on our mean girl nature can feel like having an abusive partner constantly whispering in your ear: 'See those other women out there? They all hate you. The only people who'll ever love you are men.' For those of us who have babies, the whispering gets louder the moment we give birth, because of course it has to, lest an experience as dramatic, life-changing and essentially female bring us closer together. It might make us start comparing notes on this whole bitchiness business. Hell, it might even make us band together, and then what would we do? So instead we're drip-fed stories of how the smallest differences demonstrate that all the other new mothers are sitting in judgement on us.

It happens when you're at your most vulnerable. You've just been handed a newborn and allowed – just allowed! – to take that tiny, fragile creature home with you. You've entered that hazy phase of sleepless nights and intrusive thoughts of all the ways in which you could harm him or her. You're cut off from the workplace, just you and the baby all day, and you want to be good enough, all the while knowing you're not. Perhaps you should try to find a group, once you've plucked up the courage to leave the house. But what if you and the other mothers have nothing in common?

Apart, that is, from the baby stuff, but does that count? Is that really enough?

For a moment you're tempted, but then you remember: you had a C-section. Or maybe you didn't have a C-section. Either way, whichever of these is true for you, all the women for whom it's not true hate you. Plus you're breastfeeding. Or maybe you're bottle-feeding. And your baby wears disposable nappies. Or maybe washable ones. You've read that book by Gina Ford. Or maybe you haven't. Eventually, you have an enormous spreadsheet in your head, mapping all the things you've done or not done against the things other mothers have or haven't done and it turns out there's unlikely to be another mother on the planet who's done everything in exactly the same way you have. Therefore all the other mothers think you're a terrible mother. Well, fuck them. I bet they're all terrible mothers, too (and don't get me started on the child-free. They're probably burning effigies of you right this minute.)

Women's mistrust of other women is a vital tool for the maintenance of male power over women at all life stages. It can happen so subtly, so sneakily, that we are led to believe it is all our own fault. If only we were better. If only those other women were better. If only we weren't so useless at getting along. It is one of those areas where coercion has become invisible, and would sound slightly absurd were anyone to point it out. After all, it's not as though a bunch of men would be infused with violent, narcissistic rage the moment women start working together on issues that centre *their* bodies, experiences and priorities. It's not as though there'd be any negative responses to the sight of female collaboration, right? Not in this day and age.

Well, you'd think.

Then along comes Mumsnet.

From liberation to isolation – and thence to Mumsnet

In the olden days – back when people did unsavoury things such as burn the local hag at the stake – female association, particularly among older women, was taboo. According to the *Malleus Maleficarum*, Johann Sprenger and Heinrich Kraemer's fifteenth-century handbook on witchcraft, 'where there are many women, there are many witches'. This was not least because women 'have slippery tongues, and are unable to conceal from fellow-women those things which by evil arts they know'. The only thing for it was to keep women apart, and, failing that, to ensure all congregations were suitably policed. As Anne Llewellyn Barstow writes, 'all women without men were seen as especially vulnerable to the Devil'.

Obviously this is sexist nonsense and nobody believes it now. Still, as a young woman, I took a very dim view of many of the traditional communities – the Mothers' Union, the Women's Institute, even gatherings round the school gates – accessed by women my mother's age. To me they seemed tainted and oppressive: conservative, white, middle-class, low-level religious, ultimately worshipping that great demon, biology-as-destiny. Even when the middle-aged women of Rylstone and District Women's Institute bared all for the calendar later immortalised in the film *Calendar Girls*, I was unimpressed by such twee, non-revolutionary activism.* At the same time, more radical, explicitly feminist communities such as the Greenham Common peace camps held little appeal, seeming not just anti-men and anti-sex, but to involve far too much time spent in the cold and wet. To me, the new

---

* Despite the fact my generation was busy getting our non-ageing, non-breastfeeding-and-gravity-worn tits out and believing it was revolutionary. It was different, because we had better tits.

feminism of the nineties and early noughties was a path away from both the trivialities of church hall mummy culture and the freezing puritanism of old-style feminism. I would keep away from the witches, only I didn't call them witches – that would be anti-feminist, and they were the ones failing at feminism, not me.

One of the greatest achievements of the backlash against second-wave feminism has been the outsourcing of misogyny, so men no longer have to do all that exhausting misogyny-ing themselves. This has been particularly effective in the management of oh-so-threatening female communities, especially those based around domesticity and motherhood. The approach is simple: use the language of feminism to convince younger women that the low status of women who belong to these communities is a result not of oppression but of that very belonging. Replace the old-style sexist tactic of actively denying women any collective memory or shared objectives, and instead insist that acknowledging the very existence of such things could only ever be limiting and 'essentialist'. Do it right, and self-imposed isolation from other women and/or the inclusion of men in female spaces become acts not of compliance but of liberation and inclusion.

'Part of having a resistance to male power,' argued Andrea Dworkin, 'includes expanding the base of that resistance to other women, to women you have less in common with, to women you have nothing in common with. It means active, proselytizing dialogue with women of many different political viewpoints because their lives are worth what your life is worth.' Conversely, part of having a resistance to female liberation includes ensuring women remain isolated from one another, obsessed with supposedly insurmountable differences, to the extent that they may indeed believe other women's lives aren't worth quite as much as theirs. When it comes to motherhood, this is precisely what happened to many of us who thought we could have children without falling into 'the mummy trap'. We mistook the withering of maternal support networks for freedom. We didn't see the serious politics underpinning female organisation or the threat it posed to male authority; we saw only the tea and cakes, the wiped noses, the distinctive hum of female chitter-chatter. We thought it meant nothing to us, the women who knew so much more than those who'd gone before. Whenever people denigrated silly little mummies, we were sure they'd never mean us.

For middle-class women in particular, the insistence that 'motherhood won't change me' – that you will remain a unique individual who just 'happens' to have children, not some PTA clone – can be very attractive. To disassociate from the mummy class becomes a way of convincing yourself that motherhood will not rob you of freedom and individuality because you are nothing like those unfree clone-women over there. That denial of the way in which our identities are constantly reshaped by external relationships, already found in adolescent flights from femaleness, now masquerades as the solution to motherhood's assault on personhood. This is particularly tempting in an age of individualism and dependency-phobia, in which it is easy to confuse the necessary impact of maternity – of course it will change you, as all new relationships and major lifecycle events do – with the disempowerment imposed on mothers by a society that simultaneously appropriates and devalues their work. It is a short step from this to deciding that freedom lies in insisting mothers have nothing in common; they are the exact same people they were before, only with little people somewhere in their vicinity. How much easier life would be if the social, economic and emotional constraints of mothering could be alleviated not by mothers organising as people with shared interests, but by individuals rejecting any group identity whatsoever.

In Elisa Albert's 2015 novel *After Birth*, the narrator Ari compares earlier constructions of maternal experience with her own experience as a middle-class woman in a post-industrialised society who becomes a mother after having been out in the male-defined 'real world':

> Two hundred years ago – hell, one hundred years ago – you'd have a child surrounded by other women: your mother, her mother, sisters, cousins, sisters-in-law, mother-in-law. And you'd be a teenager, too young to have any kind of life yourself [...] Now maybe you make a living, maybe you get to know yourself on your own terms [...] And then: unceremoniously sliced in fucking half, handed a newborn, home to your little isolation tank, get on with it, and don't you dare post too many pictures. You don't want to be one of *those*.

The problem is not that women should not have 'any kind of life' themselves. It is that 'liberated' women are only free to have such a life if they are in no way defined by their responsibility towards dependants. If they are, they can no longer expect support because support belongs to a reactionary, pre-feminist age. And yet the human race continues, a fact which still depends on millions of women becoming mothers, however 'essentialist' and 'reactionary' such a role is now deemed. This is inconvenient, leaving many with the impression that they must choose between having a support network and having an inner life. As is the case with 'sex-positive' feminism, living as if you are no longer constrained by the same old expectations becomes a substitute for genuinely eradicating them. To make matters worse, pointing out that the constraints are still there – suggesting, for instance, that challenging male control of reproduction might involve organising politically around female reproductive labour – instantly makes you responsible for the constraints themselves.* Organise as a mother and you'll only have yourself to blame when people think that's all you are.

It is into this context of post-second wave maternal isolation that online mothering forums arrived in the early noughties. Using online spaces as a new way of forming connections, even from inside the 'isolation tank', they filled a gap carved out, in part, by feminism itself. Middle-class mothers, a starving audience, instantly took to them. It's important to note that these were not grass-roots organisations, for all that recent narratives might cast them as innocent mummy-centred meeting places that have only later been corrupted by darker forces creeping in to 'radicalise' the porridge-brained masses. On the contrary, these were, in their early incarnation, controlled spaces, offering a capitalist simulation of maternal community in return for top tips, freebies and blogger ratings. With their endless offers of 'product review' opportunities and influencer rankings, the early rise of online mothering communities was not unlike the rise of fifties housewife consumerism captured in *The Feminine Mystique*. Betty Friedan described lonely women relegated to the home being pushed to buy more things to gain 'the sense of identity, purpose, creativity, self-realization, even the sexual joy they lack'; fifty years on, mummy blogger culture felt obliged to reassure us that we were career women, too. We didn't just buy, we sold.†

---

* My friend Marina calls this 'she who smelt it dealt it' feminism.
† I have some personal experience of this, having set up a blog when my elder children were two and four. I was not entirely unsuccessful. Not only was I once the finalist in one well-known site's Brilliance in Blogging awards, but I wrote what I consider a great review (with pictures) in return for some eco-friendly household cleaning products. I still have the tea towel and bag for life that came with them.

The trouble only started when we decided to talk and plan as well (as Dworkin said of 'sex-positive' leftist men, 'they started not to have a good time when we started to organize').

In the noughties it was easy to mock those who frequented such sites, even as Mumsnet was starting to draw the attention of politicians. Users could be written off as bored mummies selling their children's privacy in return for a three-month supply of Pop Tarts and a voucher for Alton Towers, scrapping it out over school catchment areas and ratings in the Tots 100 chart.* They were not yet demonised, but ridiculed as deluded, silly little women who'd lost their purpose in life. The politics in which users were meant to engage was strictly mummy politics, benign, fluffy, non-serious. Then Mumsnet appeared to go off-script.

What happened with Mumsnet is fascinating. We are used to seeing feminism appropriated, repackaged, corporatised; we are not used to that which is corporate going grassroots. Mumsnet was altered from the inside, disrupting ideas of both what a modern-day parenting forum should be and what mothers actually are. In early mummy communities, you played with the stereotypes, debunking them a little just to show you weren't 'just some mummy', but there was a nervousness about going too far. Not so with Mumsnet.

Over the past five years, Mumsnet has been increasingly associated with political radicalism, aggression and charges of transphobia. The twee, eminently mockable mummies have, it seems, been led astray by bigoted far-right forces, with critics dubbing the site 'prosecco 4Chan' and putting pressure on advertisers to boycott it. Mumsnet is, in the words of Rebecca Jane Morgan, a trans activist who blogs on history and LGBTQ issues, 'a transphobic swamp' comparable to 'other "alternative" and "free speech" platforms that attract

---

* I'm not explaining Tots 100. If you know, you know.

extremists, such as 4Chan, 8Chan, Parler, and Gab'. There are many theories as to what led to this remarkable fall from grace (Morgan blames 'poor moderation' and 'extremism on social media'). I blame two things: biscuits (more on this later) and older women.

One of the things that makes Mumsnet unlike sites such as Netmums and Britmums is its middle-aged hag quotient. As Sarah Pedersen, author of *The Politicisation of Mumsnet*, tells me, the demographic is different from that of other parenting forums:

> Not many of [the women] are wanting to conceive, not many of them have small babies. It's actually women in their thirties, forties and fifties. Motherhood is not behind them, they have problems, but they are dealing with school-aged children and teenagers as well.

This is not just a site dominated by women, but one in which middle-aged women dominate. It is a site of cross-generational communication, where women share specifically female experiences across life stages, incorporating early and later motherhood through to menopause. This sharing of these experiences is incredibly powerful, and incredibly worrying to those who treat mothers as a group to be controlled via the tactics of divide and rule.

I talk to Kate Williams, former Mumsnet editor, who describes it as a place where corruption does indeed take place, not that of bored, dull-witted mothers by far-right demons, but of women new to motherhood – and reeling from the shock – by those who have been around for longer:

> You see women in that stage of early motherhood, hitting that wall of 'fucking hell, I thought he was a good guy,

he is a good guy, yet here I am doing all the shitwork and actually being treated with contempt for it'. And then there's the old hags in the corner of Mumsnet, putting these women into a kind of full understanding of the nature of their oppression. That is as radical as it's always been. You see it right there. That is how younger women become older women.

This, I think, is the real problem: that if you create a space in which 'mummy politics' can flourish, you create a space in which women who have been taught that sex difference is no longer politically salient – at least for those who no longer wish it to be – will think and talk their way to an understanding of why it still matters. They will reach this understanding because other women – the corrupting hags – will have helped them on the way.

Throughout history there have been concerted, often violent attempts on the part of men to demonise female communities and devalue female experiences, and to persuade women to take on the task of doing this themselves. Ridiculing 'the mummies' has been one way of shaming women out of feeling any connection with one another. But even an artificially constructed community can be one in which women rediscover the thread that connects them, and it's one in which neither biology nor lifecycle experiences are irrelevant. If you don't want women to talk about such things, sticking instead to 'baby food and schools', then you expect too much. Having the right to take to a forum and whinge about domestic injustice isn't enough, not least because whingeing gets boring; explaining and challenging injustice is intellectually stimulating, and, as Pedersen puts it, 'contrary to popular opinion among some sections of Twitter, women do not lose the ability to think once they have had a baby'.

I think when people get angry about Mumsnet they are angry for the same reasons men such as Sprenger and Kraemer were angry about witches. They're angry on the basis that women's speech is evil and can't be trusted; that female knowledge is simultaneously worthless and dangerous; that gatherings without men are gatherings in which the Devil – in the form of female organisation and political thought – corrupts; that, above all, the lowly mummies have slipped out from under their control (they were, after all, allowed to 'discuss anything' – just not the roots of their own oppression).

I know many people think it's different this time. That's what every witch-hunter believes.

Return of the gossips

Women
Rabbit rabbit rabbit women
Tattle and titter
Women prattle
Women waffle and witter
Men talk. Men Talk.

LIZ LOCHHEAD, 'MEN TALK'

Women, as the *Malleus* tells us, have 'slippery tongues' and know 'evil arts'. At the same time, they are quite stupid ('women are intellectually like children'), so you'd think they wouldn't achieve much. This has long been a difficult circle for the average misogynist to square, and it continues to be the case today. Articles denouncing the evils of Mumsnet struggle to explain how a site that is supposed to be 'a forum on which women talk about diaper rash' or somewhere you'd turn to 'for advice on how to descale [your] dishwasher' has been overrun by political schemers whom 'we underestimate [...] at our own peril'. As one middle-aged Mumsnetter describes the problem to me, not without some sympathy, 'Are we all mumsy milk cows, waffling on about our offspring's flute class? Or are we al Qaeda? Because we can't be both yet that's how we're always portrayed, idiot children, but dangerous and evil and abnormal, too.'

One way of binding together notions of female wickedness and maternal stupidity to make 'dangerous' speech has been through the figure of the gossip. 'It is women who "gossip",' writes Silvia Federici, the feminist scholar and Wages for Housework co-founder, 'presumably having nothing better to do and having less access to real knowledge and information and a structural inability to construct factually based, rational discourses.' Women on Mumsnet are treated as classic 'gossips' – 'Madams with nothing better to do than troll the internet ... looking for a bloody argument,' as one critic, quoted by Pedersen, puts it. The removal of women to the domestic sphere justifies their treatment as intellectually inferior and less capable of taking part in debate about the things that matter, which are, by definition, beyond their frame of reference. This prejudice persists, even after women have been permitted entry into spaces and institutions from which they were once excluded. It doesn't matter if you have a postgraduate degree in gender studies (which the Mumsnetter quoted above does). In fact, that makes you more dangerous, having been exposed to ideas that you cannot understand due to your 'structural inability to construct factually based, rational discourses'.

Adrienne Rich wrote of her belief that 'only the willingness

to share private and sometimes painful experience can truly
enable women to create a collective description of the world
which can be truly ours'. The backlash against female-only
gatherings and consciousness-raising forums such as those
found in Mumsnet's feminism section is frequently absorbed
into male-default narratives focused on cancel culture, pitching left against right. This is the wrong story, erasing the
enormous history of male opposition to female speech and
allowing age-old objections to women forming connections
with one another to be justified using misplaced analogies
with Holocaust denial or shouting 'fire!' in a crowded thea-
tre. There is a line that can be drawn from sixteenth-century
images of the 'virtuous woman' who has no head with which
to speak, through anti-suffragette propaganda showing a
woman with a padlock on her lips, to memes describing
superglue as 'lipstick for TERFs'. Free speech does not mean
for women what it means for men.

There is no male equivalent of the scold's bridle, no history
of women using 'nagging' as an excuse for slaughtering their
husbands, no stories of great civilisations in which women
forbade men from speaking at political assemblies. Anxiety
over 'gossiping' women and the need to control them is ever-
present, even when it masquerades as progressive politics. I
didn't notice this in the eighties, when my own 'feminist' aspi-
ration was not to end up like some WI housewife. Unwittingly
I exemplified the very misogyny I sought to flee. I'd absorbed
the beliefs about women, politics and 'unnatural' activism
described by Dale Spender in 1982:

> Men may talk politics in the pub, but women boycotting
> a supermarket are on a 'housewives' jaunt'; the differences
> in power among men are serious and of a political nature,
> but the differences in power between women and men as

conceptualised by women are silly, and of a neurotic nature
[...] Because it is fundamental to the frame of reference in
a patriarchal society that men are the political creatures,
the political activists and theorists, women's activities in
relation to power are denatured, classified as something
else. Either it is denied that the women are concerned
about power (the women have got the issue all wrong) or
else it is asserted that the women are not real women (the
women themselves are wrong), for it is mandatory that the
deficiency be found in the women and not in the means of
interpreting the world.'

If the political woman – like the unfeminine or unavailable
woman – is a contradiction in terms, then that is her fault.

In *On the Perimeter*, her 1984 book on public responses
to the women's peace camp at Greenham Common, Caroline
Blackwood expresses bafflement at the assorted characterisa-
tions of the protestors:

They'd been described as 'belligerent harpies', 'a bunch of
smelly lesbians', as 'ragtag and bobtail', and 'the scream-
ing destructive witches of Greenham' [...] They'd been
described as 'a lot of silly women with nothing better
to do', a merely contemptuous description. They'd been
accused of being 'sex starved', which sounded a lot more
deadly as it made them sound so dangerous. They were also
described as being in the pay of the Soviet Union, and it
was said that many of them were Russian spies.

The Greenham women had been adorned with such a
wealth of unflattering descriptions, it made one start to ask
dizzying questions. Was it worse to be 'sex starved' or to
be in the pay of the Soviet Union?

Several things strike me about both Spender's and Blackwood's descriptions: the frustration at being unable to categorise women engaged in a 'male' activity; the attempts at trivialisation, or to insinuate the women have been led astray; the need to shoehorn female political activism into a template, any template, which 'proves' women are both intellectually and morally unfit to engage in it. Blackwood's 'silly women with nothing better to do' is of a piece with the 'madams with nothing better to do' characterisation of Mumsnetters. It is true that camping out to protest against nuclear weapons in the 1980s is not the same as engaging in online debate regarding reforms to the Gender Recognition Act in the 2020s, but the misogyny in the reactions is timeless.

You can pick any point in the past and find complaints about 'madams with nothing better to do' convening to make trouble when they ought to be putting dinner in the oven/cauldron. In *Feminine Forever*, Robert Wilson complains of menopausal women 'flock[ing] together in small groups of three or four':

Not that they have anything to share but their boredom and trivial gossip [. . .] Typically such women have no trace of humour. Spontaneous laughter is unknown to them, though they are capable of a kind of malicious cackle.

Written in 1966, it nonetheless screams 'Mumsnet'. Going back further, in *From the Beast to the Blonde* Marina Warner reproduces a seventeenth-century broadsheet, *Tittle Tattle, or the several Branches of Gossiping*, which 'depicts the feared sites where women's tongues will wag, where they find themselves alone and able to communicate without supervision':

The places where women gathered alone offered dangerous freedom, this broadsheet warned, in the lively exchange of

news and gossip. At the lying-in, in the hothouse, and then
at the baker's, the well, the alehouse, the river bank for the
laundry, at the market, and in church they mark ordinary
moments of a woman's work (and play). However fighting
and other unruliness results.

Again, it's Mumsnet, and no, I don't think it's accidental
that the author is particularly incensed at women gossiping
'at the lying-in'. That was just the old-fashioned way of calling women biologically essentialist, exclusionary bigots for
organising around anything to do with the female body.

Of course, many of the physical places a seventeenth-
century broadsheet lists would not be visited by women today.
We shop and clean alone, worshipping gods of our choosing
behind closed doors, yet we have found other ways to connect,
other ways to share memories, experiences, knowledge. It is
inevitable, and it is resented. In 1995's rather quaintly titled
Nattering on the Net, Dale Spender was already predicting
the fate of online forums for women, then briefly emerging as
new territories over which men had not yet had time to piss:

> Because they feel as though they do not have free speech in
> the presence of men, many women have set up women-only
> forums [...] But where such safe space has been set up, the
> response from some quarters is predictable. There are men
> who vehemently object and who claim that women-only
> space impinges on their right to free speech. They try to
> over-run, disrupt or destroy the exclusively female forum.

Once more, a pre-Mumsnet voice is already describing
Mumsnet, the site that can no longer even advertise Flora
margarine due to pressure on advertisers not to be tainted by
association with the witches. The 'nice little site, be a shame if

something were to happen to it' insistence that no one would have come for Mumsnet had women refrained from making such outrageous statements as 'being pregnant, giving birth and breastfeeding are the only time in my life that I felt a proper awareness that I am female' is laughable. Mumsnet's card was marked from the word go.

Can women think for themselves?

In late 2021, responding to a male journalist denouncing J. K. Rowling for 'torching her reputation to appeal to the Mumsnet set', one female tweeter recounted an experience familiar to many. 'Back when I first started working,' she wrote, 'men used to say "oh what's this then, a mothers' meeting?" whenever more than two women were talking in the office – as a way of making sure us females knew what we were discussing was a bit of a joke & not important.' It's a tactic women have always noticed. Indeed, one of the brilliant things about Mumsnet is the way in which the intelligent, funny women who gather there have found ways of satirising and subverting the belief that women are too frivolous and trivial to participate in real debate without the guidance of men. In *Gender Trouble*, Judith Butler asks, 'What kind of subversive repetition might call into question the regulatory practice of identity itself?' The answer, as I'm sure Butler knows, is the Mumsnet biscuit question.

This refers to the tradition of politicians who attend Mumsnet Q&A sessions always being asked what their favourite biscuit is – and being judged accordingly. It's funny on several levels. One, those asked about biscuits will pretend that their answers are casual, when they're quite obviously not (what does your biscuit say about your masculinity? Your

patriotism? Your understanding of the common masses?).
Two, those asking about biscuits will pretend that they are
only interested in biscuits, as mummies are, rather than any
serious political matters (thereby enacting a sneaky repli-
cation/subversion of gender norms, which I imagine Butler
might call operating 'within the matrix of power' without
replicating uncritically 'relations of domination'). Three,
Mumsnet denouncers treat the biscuit question as evidence
that there was a time before the site became a hotbed of evil,
sadly recalling it being 'known primarily as a place where
mums could discuss feeding routines, ask politicians about
their favourite biscuits and argue about who is hotter, Ant
or Dec'. That the question itself plays on the expectation that
mothers only care about trivia – that this is, in fact, the main
punchline – is completely overlooked by the third group on
the basis that mummies are too stupid to understand their
own jokes (which is, in turn, part of the joke). It's a joke that
only works because the jokers are playing dumb.

The prejudice might be age-old and joke-worthy, but
today's mothers really are meant to stay in their lane, with
discussions of feeding routines and Ant and Dec. This aggressive downplaying of female intellect – or of the intellect of
a particular group of females – is almost always a warning
that certain women might actually be thinking a little too
much. In A Vindication of the Rights of Woman, Mary
Wollstonecraft noted that 'most of the women, in the circle
of my observation, who have acted like rational creatures, or
shewn any vigour of intellect, have accidentally been allowed
to run wild'. Over two centuries later, Mumsnet provided a
new kind of space in which one such 'accident' could take
place. As ever, the pushback has required much insistence
that neither rationality nor vigour of intellect are anywhere
to be seen.

Regardless of any knowledge or experience they might actually possess, women who frequent Mumsnet are treated as cousins of Facebook Aunts, another group accused of parroting political views they are incapable of understanding and to which they would not have been exposed but for the fact that they have been permitted to 'run wild' online. It's not that women shouldn't have access to public spaces and debate; it's just that a certain set – say, any woman over thirty-five – is too badly educated, domestically minded and set in her ways to cope. The myth of female inferiority which justified female exclusion in Wollstonecraft's day has been replaced with the myth of the 'not-quite-there-yet' woman as discussed in Chapter Four. The same assumptions apply, but they are justified on the basis that they won't apply once women have evolved into using their new-found rights properly.

The insinuation that older women cannot think for themselves – and with it, that the political beliefs we express are not really our own, our education merely brainwashing, the money we spend not really ours – has been a curious accompaniment to responses to female organisation on Mumsnet and offline by groups such as Woman's Place UK. Curious, because it can feel as though the last fifty years of genuine change for women never took place at all, or at least not for older women and mothers, who become honorary members of the group of women who weren't permitted to follow the same career paths as men, acquire the same qualifications or organise their finances independently. On the face of it, the argument that women should be granted the same economic, intellectual and political autonomy as men has been won, even if structural barriers prevent most women from accessing it in its entirety. Nonetheless, in responses to women actually using what education, money and political muscle they now have, we see that what men were expecting when they magnanimously 'gave' us our rights does not correspond to the reality. I suggest there is something cohort-specific as well as timelessly sexist to this.

To understand the backlash, we need to situate it in two contexts: the perpetual panic surrounding women who have aged beyond what male-dominated society perceives to be usefulness and/or compliance, and the cohort-specific panic surrounding women who did not grow up facing the same constraints as their mothers. For Generation X women this is highly significant, given how impactful second-wave feminism was in many spheres. Boomer women achieved gains for women in education, politics, the workplace and finance, but they were not the main beneficiaries – my generation were (despite all our griping about how we'd have done it all better). When we came of age, significant parts of the playing field had, nominally, been levelled. We did not have to fight the same legal battles to formalise our equal participation in education, employment and politics, or for spaces of our own. Today's middle-aged men and women never fought over the 1964 Married Women's Property Act or the 1975 Sex Discrimination Act or the establishment of women's refuges because by the time we became adults the papers had already been signed. Such battles were, however, very recent history, leaving a lingering impression on the attitudes with which we were raised and the beliefs we had about the balance of power between us. In men my age, I detect a sense that my generation of women has not given due consideration to the trauma of being newly divested of the privileges previous generations of men enjoyed. For Generation X women to be 'given' rights for which we never had to struggle ourselves is one thing; for us to have the temerity to use them to promote our own interests even further (rather than just enjoy the idea of them) is quite another.

Woman's Place UK organises to defend sex-based protections for women and girls. Co-founder Kiri Tunks became involved in debates over sex and gender in law after she was approached by members of her union, who said they saw her 'as somebody they trust and who has a record'. Tunks tells me she knew that investigating reform of the Gender Recognition Act would be 'a bit controversial' but that she never expected Woman's Place UK to be 'characterised as this dangerous right-wing hate group. We thought us being recognisable women of the left would make people stop and think.' This is not what happened, with Woman's Place UK being so demonised that in 2020 two out of three Labour leadership candidates signed a pledge declaring the group a 'hate group' whose members should be expelled from the party. The political legacies of Tunks and Ruth Serwotka, her co-founder, were utterly discounted, as were their present words and deeds. The group has since been subject to threats of violence and protests at Labour conferences. That the 'exclusionary' group whose rights they seek to defend in areas such as sports participation, refuges and prisons is the same group once vilified for plotting around the 'lying-in' is not, I think, coincidental.

Tunks tells me that one thing that particularly surprised her in attacks on Woman's Place UK was the assumption that 'we couldn't be organising like this without money, because how would we know how to do that?':

> I was shocked [the critics] were shocked. I thought, well, why wouldn't we? A lot of the women involved in Woman's Place have been active political campaigners all their lives. Why wouldn't we know how to build a campaign on a shoestring? If anybody does, it will be us.

She feels critics have underestimated not just how organised women are but 'how liberated we have become':

> So women have got jobs, they are in positions of influence. They are known in their political parties, some of them are quite high up in positions of authority. You know, it's almost like people think we've just been sitting at home, not actually involved in the kind of political work I've done.

Recognition of experience and authority vanishes the moment women use them to promote the interests of women as a distinct class. It's as though the rights and boundaries we have been granted were only ever meant to be theoretical. 'If we're going to meet,' says Tunks wryly, 'we should meet in ways that people want us to meet, we should be talking about things they want us to talk about, and if we're not going to do that, well, we can't be surprised if we provoke a violent reaction.'

Women are not trusted to act independently, and when they do, it is suspected that they are being guided by someone else. How, then, should one stop them? In 1983's *How to Suppress Women's Writing*, the feminist academic Joanna Russ explored various tactics for erasing and undermining women's work, given that 'a nominally egalitarian society' will still have to give 'members of the "wrong" groups [...] the freedom to engage in literature (or equally significant activities)'. One such tactic she calls denial of agency: 'She couldn't have written it (or painted it, for that matter), she stole it, she's really a man, only a woman who is more-than-a-woman could have done it, or she did write it but look how immodest it makes her, how ridiculous, how unlovable, how abnormal!' I think there are clear echoes of this in responses to women discussing politics on Mumsnet or gathering offline to promote unapproved causes. In 'The Road to TERFdom', Katie J. M. Baker masks her own misogyny – after all, she is morally obliged to grant older women 'the freedom to engage' in politics – by pretending women on Mumsnet are not expressing their own ideas, but are dumb, domesticity-addled victims of brainwashing, desperately in need of salvation. She ends her piece by hoping for a 'movement for gender liberation that sweeps mums in its embrace, leaving toxic forums to wither'. So not, then, a movement led by mums, or one that listens to them, but one that carries them mutely along. This is not about debate; it is about converting the sinners.

Baker will be hoping for a long time. The idea that the child-addled and the menopausal do not think for themselves – and that therefore it's just a case of who wins at capturing them, the goodies or the baddies – has repeatedly been proven wrong. In particular, it's been proven wrong regarding discussions of sex and gender, which are not remotely new. If you allow women a template for political debate that centres their own life experiences, then it is entirely logical that many older women and mothers will focus on the salience of biological sex in relation to their own social and economic status. This is not because, as Baker patronisingly implies, they are lashing out due to 'a sense of isolation that comes during a vulnerable time in their lives' (that is, they've got this crazy, irrational idea that pregnancy and birth are significant in the social construction of female oppression due to their experience of pregnancy and birth being significant in the social construction of female oppression). Mumsnet 'exclusion' is not a bug but a feature of women organising as a reproductive class. Those who attacked earlier gatherings of new mummies and older hags – the spinning circles, the birthing rooms, the washday gatherings – were responding to 'exclusionary' females, too; they just had a different language for it. You can, if you want, pitch current tensions as an old 'behind the times' generation of women failing to understand the importance of inclusion, but that is just another way of shaming the same class of people as before.

It is not weird for mothers and menopausal women who gather online or in real life to get rather angry about the suggestion that femaleness is not politically important, or that female people should not be permitted to organise around their own interests. On the contrary, it would be weird for them not to, which is why they keep doing it, century after century.

Reinventing the coven

In *More Than a Woman*, Caitlin Moran describes the female solidarity that comes in middle age, born of a shared socialised, embodied experience, via the metaphor of the coven:

> Covens are where middle-aged women withdraw from the world to be with those who have, like them, gone through abortion, death, miscarriage, nervous breakdowns, funerals, unemployment, poverty, fear, hospital appointments and broken hearts – where they sometimes weep, and comfort each other, but more often make jokes so pitch black, they can only be laughed at by a fellow Hag. In your coven you attend to your busy, vital Hag Work: drawing up the lists of idiots to curse, and heroes to bless; forming your battle plans and schedules. Scheming the downfall of ass-hats, and the uprising of the righteous. You do this in a place where non-Hags can't hear you, because: Hag Club takes a lifetime to join.

The description is light-hearted, but it carries in it a truth that many find unacceptable. Ageing while female is necessarily exclusionary because it involves the accumulation of experience after experience which male people do not share, and because it repurposes the state of 'being ignored' inflicted on older women into withdrawal by choice. You can attempt to barge your way into Hag Club, but you cannot take a woman's life story and reframe it as yours, just as you cannot ensure that the women you boot out of the public sphere, having served their usefulness, won't make spaces of their own that don't include you. After all, we have to go somewhere.

If women did not have inner lives – if we could simply be whatever is required of us at each individual life stage, untouched by anything that has gone before – things would be easier. Older women would have little to talk about other than ways to meet the needs of others, instead of building up our own histories of strength, love and trauma, histories we might then want to share and pass on. As Kate Williams suggests, what really offends is that we are complete human beings who have been made by what we have experienced as opposed to decommissioned vessels for male progeny or used-up blank slates for male fantasy:

Mumsnet has always been targeted by, on the one hand, 'look at these contemptible, silly women talking about prams', and on the other, 'look at them hating men and churning up misandry'. But of course these two things exist at the same time. Because that's the journey of women. That is what you've made us. We've been sidetracked and now we're not, and the patriarchy is right to find that very problematic [. . .] It's this idea of escaping the marketplace, but rather than being repurposed as enforcers as usually happens in patriarchies, just kind of spilling out in an uncontrolled way.

Older women are told that they are worthless and, through the erasure of body stories, that our pasts do not count. Only the moment patriarchy makes of us an out-group, it creates a group that excludes the not-older and the not-women. Our exclusion from the patriarchal marketplace is supposed to disempower and isolate, not to facilitate the formation of connections through a heightened awareness of shared experience. In her writing about Mumsnet, Pedersen references Nancy Fraser's concept of subaltern counterpublics, environments 'formed in parallel and as a response to exclusion from the dominant public sphere [...] places where members can invent and circulate counter discourses in order to "formulate oppositional interpretations of their identities, interests and needs"'. Anger at modern-day covens is anger at the failure of members to behave as non-people should. It is not rage on behalf of some more marginalised other who has been left out in the cold. It is rage that those out in the cold are still creating stories of their own, stories over which the original excluders have no ownership.

'The deliberate withdrawal of women from men has almost always been seen as a potentially dangerous or hostile act, a conspiracy, a subversion, a needless and grotesque thing,' wrote Rich. Central to this is the question of power and who holds it. Over the past decade, the recasting of female sites of withdrawal and refuge as sites of privilege in which the dominant discourse is replicated has been aided by the concept of cis privilege. This allows, within the category 'woman', an analysis of the power male people hold over female people to be turned on its head (the privileged woman is she who has a vagina, who must therefore cede space to others while remaining silent about the relationship between her sexed body and her own social status). This reassessment of those who must be included in women-only spaces has enabled those who simply do not want women to meet and share knowledge to reframe separatism (the act of the group without power denying access to the group with power) as segregation (in which the group with the power excludes the group without it).

In 'Some Reflections on Separatism and Power', the philosopher Marilyn Frye describes how 'differences in power are always manifested in asymmetrical access':

> Total power is unconditional access; total powerlessness is being unconditionally accessible. The creation and manipulation of power is constituted in the manipulation and control of access.

What we see in the panic surrounding Mumsnet and grassroots organisations such as Fair Play For Women and For Women Scotland is an effort to depict the refusal of female people to be 'unconditionally accessible' as an act of dominance rather than the challenge to 'unconditional access' that it actually is. 'All-woman groups, meetings, projects,' writes Frye, 'seem to be great things for causing controversy and confrontation':

> The woman-only meeting is a fundamental challenge to the structure of power [. . .] The exclusion of men from the meeting not only deprives them of certain benefits (which they might survive without); it is a controlling of access, hence an assumption of power. It is not only mean, it is arrogant.

Frye was writing in 1983, with the advantage of at least being able to use terms such as 'woman-only' in a way that everyone would understand. Today there is such anxiety about the true meaning of 'woman' and 'female' that many feminists seek to fudge the issue, arguing that woman-only spaces are important but that they must be 'inclusive'. It is understandable – who wants to look mean and arrogant when arguing for the very thing that has always led to women being called mean and arrogant? But this is the difference between decorating your open door with a cutesy sign that says 'no boys allowed' and actually closing and locking it.

In early 2019 I spoke at a panel event at Bristol University hosted by the student group Women Talk Back. The topic was not gender identity but the policing of women's speech and writing. Most of the attendees were middle-aged women. The event drew a gaggle of male protestors and required the provision of extra security. On the one hand it was ridiculous to be running the gauntlet of those who seek to demonstrate their progressive, gender non-conforming credentials by enacting the kind of paranoia last seen in the Nicolas Cage remake of *The Wicker Man*. On the other, it was dystopian. These were young men who felt entitled to disrupt feminist events and threaten women with violence not in the name of men's rights' activism but in the name of 'inclusion'. In the end, all I could think was, this is just what it looks like. Nothing more, nothing less. It could have been 1999, 1979, 1959 ... Only the haircuts and insults change.

Germaine Greer famously claimed that 'women have very little idea of how much men hate them'. While I'm not sure this is entirely true – I flatter myself that my partner and sons think I'm all right, really – I think women have very little idea of how violently some men will respond when we step out of line. We might suspect it, and we therefore put off stepping out of line for as long as possible, telling ourselves that the ways we limit ourselves – as Dworkin wrote, 'Women whisper. Women apologize. Women shut up. Women trivialize what we know' – are really just us being nice and kind. You can live in a state of low-level, never fully articulated fear, setting hazy limitations on what you will say, where you will go, whom you might associate with. Motherhood, growing older, being dismissed from the patriarchal marketplace, can put an end to this hesitancy. We do not have infinite time; no one is going to give us intellectual and physical spaces of our own. These have to be claimed, but the moment we make our claims, we are met with aggression and disbelief. 'To be a woman,' writes Marina Strinkovsky, 'is to be permeable, accommodating, open, inclusive':

> Femininity is inclusion. The aggressive hand raised in a gesture of prohibition is the antithesis of femininity, and to see someone like me, who for all other intents and purposes looks and acts like a woman, enact that transgression, is disorienting and potentially frightening. All the more frightening when many women, whole groups of them, communities of women stand up and say: no more. We shall not contain. This is our space and we get to say who comes and goes here.

'Pray you haven't alienated them all'

Ten years ago, if you'd asked me about women-only hostels, I'd have said they might benefit some women but that I wouldn't know. It recently struck me that this is not true. I spent the end of my teens and start of my twenties in one, then promptly decided it was too cringe to think about very much.

It happened when I'd been studying at Oxford. The college I'd chosen had first started admitting women fourteen years before I arrived. Fourteen years is practically a lifetime when you are eighteen, but of course it is no time at all. The residual maleness of the place took me by surprise. I had thought, through denial of the body, hours of study, I had won myself a place in some rarefied church of the mind. No such luck. Male students knew whom that space belonged to, and knew what we, the interlopers, were. Just bodies, just flesh. Midway through my second year, I fell apart, took a break from my studies and left college, moving first into a psychiatric hospital, then onto random floors and sofas, and finally a YWCA hostel.*

The place at the YWCA was assigned to me by someone or other at the benefits office. I don't remember the process clearly, since by that point I'd foolishly adopted the rock 'n' roll cliché of eating nothing and surviving on vodka. In any case, I would not have chosen to move into a woman-only space. Such things – girls' schools, women-only colleges – had always struck me as unnatural. What would you be without the presence of men? How could you possibly learn and grow without that solidity against which to define your floating, fluid self?

Quite easily, as it turns out, not that I was prepared to admit it at the time. On returning to my studies, I carried on living at the YWCA, with women who had mostly come from abroad to study at Oxford's English language schools. In the presence of my university peers, I mocked where I lived, as though there

---

* YWCA stands for Young Women's Christian Association. It is independent of the more famous YMCA though there are some merged associations. It doesn't, as far as I know, have a song, let alone any accompanying actions.

was something slightly insane about it, something quaint, paranoid, old lady-ish and deeply unattractive about living only with women (unless you made lipstick lesbian quips to appease the lads, which, this being the nineties, you could). I could have moved back to the place where I'd had my breakdown, had I wanted to. Two years later, heavier, convinced I now had to be 'normal' and 'available', I finally did.

I should have stayed in the YWCA longer, is what I think now. It was a safe space, not that we ever spoke about it in such terms. There was nothing explicitly feminist about it, but then, there didn't have to be. It was a taste of being out of the game, beyond the gaze, the only intrusions on your boundaries other women's music, their voices, their arguments, their mess. It was solid ground, and there was nothing to fear. There were arguments and tensions; we were not all friends. Nonetheless, this was the place where I learned to feed myself by choice, amid women cooking and eating just for themselves, finally getting the idea that my body might be for me rather than for other people.

The safety I found was more than a question of not thinking anyone might physically or sexually assault me (though that is always a plus). It came from not being compartmentalised, categorised, reduced, from realising I was more than a foil to the default human. To my nineteen-year-old self, so intent on defining myself in terms of how little space I occupied in relation to others, this felt an abnormal proposition, as though women without men were half-women, pictures half-drawn, faint reproductions lacking the original. As though without men, even men who hurt me, I would cease to exist. You cannot know that this is not the case unless you are given the opportunity to test it out. There are lots of men who don't want us to have this chance, who don't want younger women to know.

Internalised misogyny can make us believe that associating with women because they are women is demeaning, as though a group lacks certain human qualities without the addition of males. Part of the fear of ageing felt by many women stems, I now think, from this fear of being cast adrift from the context in which, as a woman, you 'make sense'. Then ageing happens, because we cannot stop it, and it is not what we feared. Whatever we lose in relation to men, as cumulative inequality exerts its drip-drip effect, we gain in terms of our own self-sufficiency and lack of dependency on those who promised much but delivered little. If you are considered to be out of the game, at least as far as the sexual and reproductive marketplace is concerned, or you have realised that the game is in any case rigged, you have less to lose by bonding with others on the bench. Rejecting the metaphorical mother starts to seem less of an entry into maturity than it once did. Your priorities have shifted, and the nature of female friendship is altered, not least by the realisation that you are running out of time. Relationships based on a shared socialised and/or embodied experience no longer seem reductive, a concessionary prioritising of that which has been done to you because you are female at the expense of the unique, self-sufficient individual you actually are.

'Once your social currency to men is of no value as a female, you look around & notice the best people in your life are other women & always have been,' one Twitter user tells me. 'Pray you haven't alienated them all because the sisterhood is your best lifeline & best friend.' Or as Tunks says of the dismissive responses she encountered from people she'd worked with all her life the moment she prioritised the 'wrong' cause, 'You suddenly realise that all the respect that people had for you was actually paper thin [...] but you know the good thing is when working with the sisters you develop a new level of solidarity [. . .] the friends I've got now are worth their weight in gold.'

To misquote Greer, women have very little idea of how much other women don't hate them. That's the biggest secret of all.

Pass it on.

7

PRIVILEGED HAG

This dominance of men by women is experienced by men as real – emotionally real, sexually real, psychologically real; it emerges as the reason for the wrath of the misogynist.

Andrea Dworkin, *Intercourse*

Please don't call the manager on me, Senator Karen

Elon Musk, responding to Elizabeth Warren calling him out on non-payment of taxes

Generational tensions in feminism can resemble those in fairy tales: resourceful orphans versus wicked witches, angry stepmothers versus lost princesses, with fairy godmothers in the wings. Yet if I were to choose a definitive example, it wouldn't involve women, witches or fairies. Mine would be *The Three Billy Goats Gruff*.

We're in the Field of Patriarchy, waiting to cross the bridge to the Field of Equality. Only underneath that bridge lurks a ferocious troll. One by one, we start trip-trapping across and each time, confronted, we lose our nerve. 'Don't eat me!' we tell the troll. 'Eat my sister! She's bigger, older, more privileged, more entitled than me! A total Karen of a goat, if you will!' The first two times, this works; the troll allows us to pass. Then the third time, strong, venerable, experienced, we defeat him. Only alas: there is a plot twist. It turns out that when you get too big, too old, it is decreed that you are the troll yourself. No Field of Equality for you!

The focus of this chapter is privilege and its relationship to ageism and misogyny. On the one hand this is a topic that makes me very nervous. There's nothing like writing about privilege to make one feel as though one's own privilege is under scrutiny, whereupon the desire to bleat an apology before pointing at all the other goats can be overwhelming. It is a legitimately difficult, uncomfortable subject, one which brings all one's hypocrisies to the fore.* On the other hand, there's much I resent about the shape taken by current debates. Not only do they create yet another loophole for men who enjoy telling women who remind them of their mums to shut up, but for some feminists, mitigating the taint of privilege can take precedence over developing a politics which supports the most marginalised women and girls. Several trends already mentioned – such as the 'right side of history' mindset that offloads bigotry and prejudice onto soon-to-be-dead mother-in-law figures, the fetishisation of 'tomorrow's woman' at the expense of today's, the Great Reckoning narrative that demonises the recent past all the better to sanitise the present – feed into the demonisation of Privileged Middle-aged Woman. The recent popularisation

---

* Not least because anyone writing about privilege is probably too privileged to be writing about privilege (unless they offer up a wry quip such as this one, in which case it's definitely okay).

of the Karen figure and the loose application of terms such as 'white feminism' to denote an older, less inclusive style of feminist thought have added to this phenomenon. As someone who is white and middle class as well as middle aged, I realise I am somewhat on the back foot in responding to this (discussing the topic of 'Karen' in any way, shape or form feels rather like constructing my own wicker man, handing a torch to the baying masses and climbing in). However, I don't think it's possible to tackle the subject of middle age and misogyny without facing this head-on. The alternative – to write vaguely about middle-aged women being accused of entitlement and privilege without ever mentioning which women become specific targets – would be to treat middle-class white women as the default women, an approach from which women such as myself benefit quite enough.

I do not expect to approach this topic 'cleanly', and for the limitations and biases of my own perspective, I apologise. I realise a great deal is relative. What, for instance, might the familiar phrase 'when you're accustomed to privilege, equality feels like oppression' mean for the older woman who is white and/or middle-class? That she feels oppressed when she is not? Or that to other people, who expect older women to be inferior, submissive and sidelined, her independence, enabled by freedoms all women should but do not yet have, feels oppressive? How much is behaviour that is dismissed as 'entitled' merely unfeminine? Would a man behaving the same way be deemed obnoxious or simply forthright? While the 'privileged older woman' trope can be a gift to opportunistic misogynists, it also has a basis in reality. She is both/and, part victim, part accomplice. What she must not become is merely an acceptable outlet for hate.

Spoilt madams, entitled Karens

Towards the end of 2013, a series of tweets from the author and television producer Elan Gale went viral. Purporting to be evidence of a 'note war' between Gale and a fellow passenger on a delayed US cross-country flight, it offered an early illustration of a phenomenon that has become widespread: men seeking to rein in entitled, mouthy middle-aged women who are allegedly being rude to serving staff. It is a curious trend, a kind of grassroots activism that seeks to harness the power of mummy-hating to fight the cause of the low-paid and marginalised, albeit on a case-by-case, entirely ineffective basis. You might not want to, say, give up your Amazon deliveries or pay more for your pizza, but bravely calling the stressed woman ahead of you in the post office queue a bitch is the kind of workers' rights activism even the laziest among us can get behind.

In Gale's example, which – following the tradition of the 'pious fraud' encountered in witch trials – turned out to be entirely fabricated, the tweeter depicts himself sending a glass of wine to a woman he's overheard being rude to a flight attendant, along with a note declaring, 'It is a gift from me to you. Hopefully if you drink it, you won't be able to use your mouth to talk.' Ha! Man tells nag to STFU – only righteously, on behalf of those over whom she has power. When, in this imagined scenario, this initial tactic fails to work, Gale escalates things, portraying himself leaving bottles of vodka on the woman's tray, offering to bribe United Airlines to throw her off the flight and, when she tells him he lacks compassion, sending another note stating, 'The person who lacks compassion is you. We all want to get home, particularly the nice men and women who fly your lazy ass around and serve you drinks.' Indeed. How dare this imaginary harridan expect to be flown around and waited on like a passenger in a plane or something! The exchange culminates, predictably, with Gale telling his imaginary adversary to 'eat my dick'. Because women like that don't deserve to have any boundaries (and 'suck/eat/choke on my dick' is something of a rallying cry in anti-hag warfare).

When interviewed about why he invented this story, Gale claimed to have seen a real-life woman being rude to a male flight attendant (why he mentions the flight attendant's maleness isn't clear, other than perhaps to emphasise the iniquity of a woman expecting a man to be the one doling out drinks and sandwiches). He doesn't say whether the real-life woman, like 'Diane', his imagined version, 'is in her late forties or early fifties [...] wearing mom jeans and a studded belt and [...] a medical mask over her idiot face'. Nonetheless, this version – a painstakingly caricatured middle-aged frump – is the one he chooses to use to make a 'hyperbolic point'. Diane is 'a cautionary tale for people like that'. But who is 'like that', and why should someone like Gale – a white, wealthy man – get to sit in judgement over her?

There are some who might argue that I, as a feminist, have only myself to blame if privilege-shaming has come to bite the likes of me on my middle-aged arse. To read some sectors of the right-wing press, you'd think obsessing over privilege was a recent phenomenon, an offshoot of feminism's own preoccupation with victimhood and casting everyone else as the oppressor. I beg to differ. Sometimes I feel have spent my entire life listening to men drone on about how privileged certain women are. The names change – the wife, Diane, Karen – but the story is the same.

As a child, I heard it from middle-class men (usually ones who read those right-wing papers that 'don't do' privilege-shaming). According to them, 'their' women didn't need feminism because to be a middle-class woman was to live life on the easy setting. Middle-class women didn't work – since unpaid domestic and care work didn't count as working – or, if they were in paid employment, the fact that they earned less than their male counterparts proved less was expected of them. Their under-representation in positions of power and authority merely showed they bore none of the weight of life-or-death decisions. Their compliance with fashion and beauty rituals was evidence of their shallowness, while any failure to comply was the ultimate demonstration of laziness. In this reading of the world, feminism constituted a form of ignorant tinkering with the natural order of things, with feminists cast as spoilt children demanding the right to 'do Daddy's job' because something on the telly had convinced them it must be more exciting than going to school. Middle-class men might have been out there earning their privilege, but it was their female counterparts who were cashing it in, too foolish even to appreciate their own advantage (domestic violence, coercive control, financial abuse and sexual abuse were, thankfully, non-existent in middle-class circles. Working-class men abused; middle-class men reasonably chastised.)

I was reminded of this when reading a 2015 article by Paris Lees, in which feminists who question the ethics of the sex trade are described as 'ladies who lunch and feel hard done by because a man held the door open for them on their way in to the Four Seasons'. A similar statement could have been uttered by any one of my male relatives circa 1982, perhaps midway through a news special on Greenham Common, or while watching *The Two Ronnies'* feminist dystopia sketch 'The Worm That Turned'. They might even have followed it up with the classic 'they don't call it harassment when it's someone they fancy' (dutifully replayed by Lees in 2014's

Vice piece 'I love wolf-whistles and catcalls – Am I a bad feminist?') The difference is that Lees self-identifies as a feminist. The traditional male chauvinist's view of middle-class feminists as over-sensitive, self-victimising parasites has been repackaged as a new, more enlightened form of feminism, one which decrees that certain women don't need feminism at all.

In any age, the misogynists with the best comms team have the most success. There are specific and ever-changing formulae for making misogyny sound virtuous, but the basic principles remain the same: one, do not target all women all the time (your aim is to control the majority by assuring them that they can be 'good'); two, insist that the women you do target are powerful in ways that are undeserved and dangerous; three, mitigate the possible appeal/emasculating threat of bad, powerful women by emphasising how much their power depends on them being pathetically in thrall to higher, male-coded authorities. This worked for witch-hunters, it worked for old-style anti-feminists, and it works for those who pretend that calling women they don't like – or whose complaints they find inconvenient – spoilt madams is top-level intersectional feminist praxis.

As Julie Bindel writes, 'Some men find it impossible not to point out that working-class women and women of colour suffer multiple oppressions without suggesting or blatantly stating that white middle-class women have lives of privilege and luxury.' This is anti-feminism in disguise and, to quote the *Observer*'s Sonia Sodha, it empowers men 'to use the fact that all white women are supposedly higher up in the privilege pecking order to tell middle-aged women to shut up or, even worse, accuse them of weaponising their abuse and trauma' (you will have noticed the slippage here from 'white' to 'middle-aged'; keep this in mind).

Feminism needs to engage with the way in which

intersecting oppressions (of which sex and age offer one example) impact individual and shared experiences of misogyny, meaning that solutions for some can fail to be solutions for all. Nonetheless, in place of such an engagement is often found the creation of scapegoats, responsible not just for a flawed or limited feminism but for oppression itself. In recent years this narrative has coalesced around the figure of the 'Karen'. There is a complex background to this, in which good-faith political critique meets misogynist appropriation, but frequently the practical function of Karen as an insult is to rein in the same group once reined in by terms such as nag, harridan and shrew.

The use of a privilege narrative to justify misogyny is not new. 'The stereotype of the Bad Woman is back in style – a modern she-devil who wields enormous power for evil,' declares a *Washington Post* article from 1994, using the term 'Wonder Witch' to describe this new threat. A 2003 *New Statesman* article by Barbara Gunnell focuses on the vilification of middle-class women or 'MCW', targeted by 'feminists and progressives' as well as 'those already predisposed to hostility towards working women'. Middle-class men, argues Gunnell, avoid the same censure as they bask in the sheen of New Labour blokiness: 'We should see this casual unquestioned misogyny towards middle-class women for what it is – a sneer that otherwise thoughtful opinion-makers would not dream of directing at any other group.'

Both these articles describe trends which foreshadow what is happening now with the Karen figure in relation to white, middle-class, middle-aged women. Like Wonder Witch or MCW, Karen 'whips up antipathy towards women' using valid moral discomfort as a starting point. 'Blaming the woman offers quick relief to a society that is anxious about its future,' writes the unnamed author of the Wonder Witch piece. 'And blaming the woman is easy to do because there seem to be so many Bad Women around to blame.'

A significant difference between Karen and MCW/ Wonder Witch is that it is openly, blatantly ageist. As a baby name, Karen was most popular in the mid-sixties, making the average Karen most definitely middle-aged. Describing viral 'Karen' videos, Helen Lewis argues older women are being 'portrayed as witches, harridans, harpies; women who dare to keep existing, speaking and asking to see the manager after their reproductive peak'. Another difference is the way in which the word draws, as Lewis writes, on 'two separate (and opposing) traditions [...] anti-racism and sexism'. Its origins can be traced both to black women's critiques of the racist behaviour of white women and to the r/FuckYouKaren subreddit in which a standard misogynist complains about his ex-wife. The shared name allows a legitimate complaint to be appropriated. This is why a lot of men like Karen. 'Nearly everyone knows that hating women for being women is a bad look,' writes Sarah Ditum, 'but what if they were white women? Presto chango, suddenly you're punching up!' Even black female activists can find themselves accused of being Karens if they question the good faith of men's usage. The use of the term has caused particular distress to real, as opposed to symbolic, Karens, with women called Karen documenting instances of name-based bullying on sites such as Karen Is My Name and Karens United for Respect.

To challenge the misogynist, ageist usage of Karen is to risk engaging in a cross-purposes dialogue in which all the other person hears is that you don't care about racist white women who talk over black women or make false accusations which endanger the lives of black men (or that you don't care about aligning yourself with 'that side', or that

you think Black Lives Matter, but not as much as white
lady feelings). As with conversations on gender identity, it
can reach a point where not mentioning ageism or misogyny
becomes the only way to prove you don't want other people
dead, not because this makes any logical sense, but because
these are the rules of engagement. Indeed, it often feels to
me as though a motte and bailey technique is being deployed
by those who have the least skin in the game (white men),
ramping up the fears of those who have more to lose (the
motte being the basic 'white women shouldn't be racist' or
'trans people shouldn't face abuse', the bailey being 'middle-
aged white women/TERFs want you dead and therefore need
to STFU for ever'). It is easy, therefore, to lose sight of how
blatantly, painfully, *traditionally* sexist so much Karen (and
indeed TERF) talk is.

We have, apparently, 'all met a Karen during our lifetime
but we might not have known it':

> They're asking for your manager, they're telling you how
> much easier you have it than them and their presence on
> Facebook means sharing questionable posts. This is how
> Karen became the catch-all name for rude, middle-aged
> white women.

Or maybe – if you are white, middle-class and in your
late teens/early twenties – it's just a catch-all for all those
annoying female relatives with whom you'd rather not be
associated on social media. When Aja Romano writes in *Vox*
that 'the archetypal "Karen" is blonde, has multiple young
kids, and is usually an anti-vaxxer. Karen has a "can I speak
to the manager" haircut and a controlling, superior attitude
to go along with it', multiple unreconstructed sexism boxes
are being ticked. A mummy with stupid, unfashionable hair!

Incapable of understanding science! Superior and controlling! There is an undercurrent of All-Powerful Mother anxiety behind many Karen descriptions, plus more than a touch of rolling-pin-wielding fishwife panic (the henpecked husband now being represented by the low-paid service worker, the conditions of whose work are improved, in ways we cannot comprehend, by the recreational online misogyny of the righteous).

Advice given to older women on 'how not to be a Karen' can be indistinguishable from traditional guidance on how to be ladylike, selfless, feminine, and to take up less space. In order to avoid the label we are told to 'vent [our] anger elsewhere', 'let someone else take charge', 'have empathy' and get a less offensive haircut ('You might find some hair inspo in celebs like Hollywood stars Michelle Williams and Sandra Oh'). Of course, the flipside of singling out a subset of women whose 'defining essence' is 'entitlement, selfishness, a desire to complain', is the reinforcement of the message that women who fit that profile in other ways should be small, selfless and silent – just to be on the safe side, you understand. Any sign of assertiveness becomes a red flag. For instance, in an article for the *Independent* on vehicle pollution, Rachel Revesz takes care to couch her perfectly legitimate criticism with 'I know it makes me an angry Karen'. Similar anxieties surround the risk of being a 'Covid Karen' who polices the behaviour of others. One can only hope that issuing future warnings about global heating or virus strains is not left to middle-aged white women, lest any fear of looking like an 'angry Karen' stops them from saying a word.

White women can be racist, middle-class women can be classist, but often what is being thrown at them via the popularised version of Karen-shaming is not guidance on reframing their assumptions and dismantling actual material privileges (which is a hard, lifelong task – yet more housework for everyone, white, middle-class men included). Instead it often seems as though a combination of top tips on 'how to please your man' and men's rights activist screeds have been given a cursory search-and-replace treatment (ultimate message: don't be a nag!)

One of the most worrying things about the 'Karen' critique is that it has, for middle-aged white women, stigmatised the act of complaining, regardless of what it is we may be complaining about: a waiter who has irritated us, dangerous driving, lax adherence to social distancing, a *Guardian* obituary for a serial killer, our own experiences of sexual assault. The moment our complaints are heard – whether we are complaining in the House of Commons, at a police station or in the post office queue – we are caught in a double bind. Given the social and political constraints we all know women are under, if you can hear a woman at all she must be privileged in other ways. This instantly invalidates her right to complain. It is yet another patriarchal catch-22 (and one not unrelated to the 'if women's voices were really being silenced, I wouldn't be able to hear any women speaking about women's voices being silenced' fallacy). You can't even complain about not being able to complain because that would be 're-enact[ing] the Karen dynamic'. As the witch-hunter Martin Delrio wrote in his 1599 *Disquisitionum Magicarum Libri Sex*, 'It is evidence of witchcraft to defend witches.' Or, as Ditum writes of 'Karen', it 'is a finger trap insult, where struggling against it only makes it grip tighter'.

Describing the impact of historical witch trials and the climate of fear they provoked, Anne Llewellyn Barstow suggests that 'women began to protest less in general. From having, at the end of the Middle Ages, a reputation for being scolds and shrews, bawdy and aggressive, women began to change into the passive, submissive type that symbolized them by the mid-nineteenth century.' So torturing and burning (mostly older) women for nebulous crimes against humanity had the effect of making them less Karen-y (if more annoyingly damsel-y). While most parts of the world are not at that stage right now, I would suggest that any cultural meme or movement which stigmatises the act of complaining for older women – even if it uses white women as a starting point – ends up drawing on this legacy. The moment the complaint itself no longer matters, just the face of the complainer – wrinkled, shrewish, like Jason Adcock's mask discussed in Chapter One – we are back to a reinforcement of sexist, ageist norms.

Writing about responses to #MeToo, Eimear McBride asks whether 'in an environment in which all-out aggression can no longer be publicly utilised as the first line of defence, might the imposition of taboo provide a promising point of departure for the backlash?' Taboo, argues McBride, 'shifts the argument from the what to the who and, as such, makes it harder to refute in a collective, definitive way'. The shame/taint aspect of privilege has begun to work in concert with a more generalised disgust for older female bodies (Karen is, you will recall, Halloween-level ugly) in a way that is very difficult to refute, especially since our own privileges are not spots to be scrubbed out but realities which can only be dismantled through recognition. If we allow the taint of privilege to become intermeshed with the 'taint' of being a white woman who is neither young nor quiet, it is no longer clear what is to be dismantled – if anything at all. On the other hand, once we reach a stage where white, male multi-billionaire Elon Musk can respond to Senator Elizabeth Warren calling for him to pay his taxes by calling her a Karen, it's clear what is being upheld.

'No one can get me now': reframing independence as entitlement

'I love the ballet,' says Helen Joyce, journalist and author of *Trans*, 'and when you watch the ballet, you know maybe there'll be sixteen people in a plain version of the costume and one person who's in a beautiful version, and everyone on the stage accepts she's the star. It's not like there's seventeen people who each sees themself as the star and everyone else as the supporting parts; everyone knows who the star is. It's a convention you don't even think about when you're watching, so it seems to serve the natural order of things.'

What would happen, though, if 'for some reason one of the girls in the chorus ran to the front of the stage, kicking her legs high and pushing away all the others, even though she's one of the ones in the plain costume'? Joyce compares the incongruity to that which is felt when women assert themselves, refusing to play the part assigned to them in life. They are breaking an unspoken rule which, she says, 'goes through everything, all the conventions of men – the father being on the birth certificate, women taking the man's name on marriage, the idea of head of the household. These things aren't just about extra rights for men. They're an understanding of life as the drama men play, with women in the supporting roles.'

The drama metaphor is not new. Gerda Lerner makes use of it in 1986's *The Creation of Patriarchy*, arguing that 'men and women live on a stage, on which they act out their assigned roles, equal in importance':

Neither of them 'contributes' more or less to the whole; neither is marginal or dispensable. But the stage set is conceived, painted, defined by men. Men have written the play, have directed the show, interpreted the meanings of the action. They have assigned themselves the most interesting, most heroic parts, giving women the supporting roles.

Women notice this, writes Lerner, but it is difficult for them to take on a different part: 'Men punish, by ridicule, exclusion, or ostracism, any woman who assumes the right to interpret her own role or – worst of all sins – the right to rewrite the script.' There are many names such a woman might be called. Point this out, and you will be called those names yourself.

Middle age is a time when women report feeling invisible or being ignored, yet it is also a time when certain women – white and/or middle-class women, women in politics or the media, those with structural privileges – stand accused of being too shouty, too loud, taking up too much space when they ought to be standing back. I find this rather suspicious. If ageing sets in motion a process whereby a woman ceases to be what patriarchal society wants a woman to be then of course it is preferable for her to be neither seen nor heard. Certain women, however, particularly those in positions of relative authority, are better at remaining visible and audible than others. Still others will respond to being ignored by raising their voices. How does one distinguish between this and 'privileged women acting in an entitled manner'? Is it always possible to draw a clear line between the resentment one feels when an older woman genuinely oversteps the mark in relation to someone with less power (however one defines the latter) and the discomfort one feels when any woman steps out of her 'supporting role'? 'To be female is to be deviant by definition in the prevailing culture,' wrote Mary Daly. 'To be female and defiant is to be intolerably deviant.' She didn't add the next stage, which is to be female, defiant and over forty. Then, I suspect, you are off the deviance charts.

True, there's a patronisingly circumscribed, trivial way in which the middle-aged woman is allowed to have her little moment in the spotlight without attracting too much censure. Long before I became middle aged myself, I was aware of a tendency to 'celebrate' the rowdy middle-aged woman who no longer gives a shit. Like the old woman who, in the words of Jenny Joseph's ubiquitous poem, 'shall wear purple' and 'swear in the street', the culturally approved no-shits-given middle-aged woman is a cliché, one which draws on stereotypes of petulance and infantilisation, of grown women with nothing better to do than get together with 'the girls' to cackle at hapless serving staff. It's part of the insidious 'me time'/empowerment marketing message sold to women at every stage of their lives, with face masks, mindfulness exercises and miniature bottles of 'fizz' descending as crumbs from the patriarchal table, casting the progressive economic and emotional exploitation of half the human race as a mere inconvenience from which 'Mum' needs the occasional self-indulgent day – or maybe afternoon – off. It's also a way of mocking older women while pretending to boost their voices. In *The Stranger in the Mirror*, Jane Shilling captures this dynamic brilliantly in her description of noughties television programming that 'represents' older women via 'the *Grumpy Old Women*, and their anodyne daytime cousins, the coy kaffeeklatsch of *Loose Women*'. Shilling notes that while these programmes purport to represent middle-aged womanhood as it really is – 'sluttish, surly, rueful, defeated' – and in a manner for which older women themselves are supposed to feel grateful, other viewers are 'confirmed in their comfortable prejudices about the battiness of women of a certain age'. For many of us, Shilling included, this is not good enough.

It's not that the 'loose cannon' older woman is mythical. I once suggested on Twitter that efforts to denigrate 'entitled' older women could be seen as an attempt to counter the fact that middle age is the time when female socialisation truly starts to wear off. These are some of the responses I received:

It is a fact universally acknowledged that the number of fucks given are in inverse proportion to miles on the clock.

We are also worn out by thirty years of drudgery, by never being slim, pretty or nice enough. By having to juggle kids, jobs and housework and we are finally too exhausted to give any more f.cks. Especially as it is a losing battle.

I thank the perimenopause fairy, I'm pretty sure the drop in oestrogen has something to do with it. It's like a second puberty, rewiring us to look outwards and stop needing the approval of others for our survival.

Our skin is so much thicker, instead of piercing our hearts, their barbs rebound off our hides.

What's striking to me is that while the 'me time' model proposes women temporarily absent themselves from their lowly position in the gender hierarchy, taking a few hours off from inferiority (ideally in 'pampering/relaxing' ways which increase their femininity/fuckability quotient and make them less whiny), the 'no fucks given' ethos of the women I connect with is not about absence but engagement.

'The reason women in middle age and over bother people so much,' argues Sarah Ditum, 'is precisely that they're not willing to put up and shut up any more [...] Add that attitude to the wealth of experience a woman will have accrued over five decades, and she becomes a force to be reckoned with.' Self-styled social justice narratives, which advise women at this stage of life to be quiet, wait your turn, don't complain, never mention your own pain – on the basis that to do otherwise would be 'acting like a Karen' – seek to limit women's scope for self-sufficiency and activism by replacing the stigma of unfemininity with that of privilege. It is ridiculous, if in keeping with the principles of 'just around the corner' feminism, that strength, confidence and independence should be treated as brilliant ideals for future womanhood, but shameful markers of entitlement in the here and now. The punishments for female self-assertion remain ferocious; we should not be surprised if it is women who are older, or who have greater support networks, or both, who are most willing to take risks.

There are several reasons why lifecycle is so important in the construction of the 'entitled' older woman. It may be that older women express different, more 'controversial'/less submissively feminine views – views deemed to reflect privilege, entitlement or a lack of awareness of more progressive politics – because of a combination of life experiences and the 'no more fucks to give' mindset described above. Or it could be that relatively benign views and behaviours are read as aggressive and entitled because of the expectation that older women retreat into the shadows. A third possibility is that older women say and do things some younger women would say and do, too, had they the same level of security and absence of peer pressure. I suspect a combination of all three is in play. For instance, Sarah Pedersen is researching the experiences of gender-critical women in Scotland. 'Older women,' one tells her, 'are more vocal because we can be, and because we have less shits left to give.' Pedersen cites both temporary employment contracts and peer pressure as reasons why younger women may be more reluctant to engage in debate. Retired women or those with permanent jobs are not so dependent on peer (and male) approval to avoid destitution. They also have a different relationship to approval. 'A lot of us just don't care any more,' says one, 'because we've had thirty, forty, fifty years of friendship coming and going, and most of us have lost friends through this, but you just think that's the price you pay.'

Fear of witches is fear of the older woman who is too independent to regulate. This was made abundantly clear during Hillary Clinton's US presidential campaign, when she faced accusations of witchcraft from across the political spectrum. In a *New York Times* article written before the 2016 election, Stacy Schiff drew out the parallels:

> [We] still have few other names for the way a woman's voice unsettles, for the queasy sense that the world must be upside-down if she happens to be running it [...] An older woman moreover knows things a younger woman does not; she can say things a younger woman says with difficulty. Like no.

This is the essence of the 'entitled' older woman: memory and confidence combined with the word no. It is a woman who occupies the wrong position, not because she is at the top of a privilege hierarchy but because she is female and not being crushed underfoot. 'Grown men,' wrote Andrea Dworkin, 'are terrified of the wicked witch, internalized in the deepest parts of memory. Women are no less terrified, for we know that not to be passive, innocent, and helpless is to be actively evil.' The historian Ronald Hutton describes the witch as 'one of the very few images of independent female power that traditional society gives us'. Clinton herself characterised her demonisation as 'rooted in ancient scapegoating, of doing everything to undermine women in the public arena, women with their own voices, women who speak up against power and the patriarchy'. This view is backed up by the definition of 'witch' coming from one 'Hillary for prison' protestor: 'an angry, crotchety old hag who is just out for power'.

Lust for power is one sin; so, too, is being overly clever (the third witch to hang in Massachusetts in 1656 was guilty of 'the capital crime of displaying more wit than her neighbors'). Clinton stood accused of being superior and entitled; her competence and experience worked against her, being read as sinister. There was nothing she could have done to avoid having conservative talk show host Rush Limbaugh dub her 'witch with a B', Trump supporters denounce her (admittedly cool-sounding) 'vagenda of manocide' or Sanders supporters mount calls to 'Bern the witch!' However polarised and extreme political debate becomes, people do not do this to male politicians (besides which, Clinton's witchy nature seemed to be the one thing on which all sides could agree). It tells us something about the enduring, primal nature of misogyny, and the interplay between a genuine fear of women and the performance of fear for political gain. We should be outraged and baffled that, despite our apparent sophistication, this is the ultimate, go-to accusation: you are a witch (both Theresa May and Julia Gillard have faced similar accusations). It should remind us that, at heart, this is nothing to do with how powerful we are, what we say, what we do, whom we hurt. All of us are witches, just most – due to lack of the dreaded privilege – happen to be on reprieve.

In a chapter of her book *Accidental Feminists*, titled 'Hags, crones, witches and mothers-in-law', Jane Caro describes how 'women of a certain age are called names like these in an attempt to shame them into silence. We are superfluous to requirements, meant to accept our invisibility without complaint.' 'Entitlement' is refusing to accept this invisibility, instead existing as a self-sufficient entity in your own right, and not just that but as someone with their own complex inner life, memories and trauma. The more independence to which a woman has access – whether from individual structural advantage or a general broadening of opportunities for women – the more at risk of 'entitlement' she becomes. I would say it is better than the alternative, but then that's forgetting the last part of the entitlement package: the privilege of pain.

Playing the victim

Many years ago, I got into a drunken argument with a PhD history student on the question of whether feminism was 'wrong' and women had 'too many rights'. In addition to the main component of his argument – which seemed to be 'I'm a PhD history student' – he offered the killer line that 'unlike men, women get to fake orgasms'. This was a privilege I had not yet appreciated. Bluffing our way through crap sex! What will we power-hungry bitches think of next? Weaponising our trauma, that's what.

As Helen Lewis argues with regard to the Karen meme, one of the particular tensions it captures is that between victim and aggressor in a political environment in which you can only be one or the other. 'The Karen debate can, and perhaps will, go on forever,' she writes, 'because it is equally defensible to argue that white women are oppressed for their sex, and privileged by their race.' That this is more problematic than the fact that men can be oppressed for their race and/ or their class, and privileged by their sex, relates, I think, to two things: differences in the way sex-based oppression is organised within social groupings, and specifically gendered and age-based expectations in terms of how sympathy and care are given and taken.

Women's personal lives tend to be deeply intermeshed with those of men of their own socio-economic class and race. Most of us grow up with male people in our lives whom we love, or are supposed to. The particular privileges we have in common with these men are visible – our allegiances, compromises and complicity in their actions – whereas the inequalities between us are less so. Indeed, the very personalised nature of men's sexual, domestic and reproductive exploitation of women can make the difference between compromise and coercion blurry even to those at the very centre of it, let alone any outside observers. Gerda Lerner argues that, historically, 'the connectedness of women to familial structures made any development of female solidarity and group cohesiveness extremely problematic', whereas 'other oppressed classes and groups were impelled toward group consciousness by the very conditions of their subordinate status'. This is still true, and still difficult to resolve, with an added complexity arising from the way in which an articulation of the problem within feminism itself risks being treated as interchangeable with a Lees-style dismissal of (white, middle-class) 'ladies who lunch'. Lerner was not suggesting that women who found themselves part of what she termed the 'reciprocal agreement' – 'in exchange for your sexual, economic, political, and intellectual subordination to men you may share the power of men of your class to exploit men and women of the lower class' – were thereby not oppressed as women, but that their oppression was baked into what power they did enjoy. Likewise, in 1991's 'Mapping the Margins', Kimberlé Crenshaw was not claiming that middle-class white women were not really victims of harassment or discrimination, but that a feminism which treats sex as the only meaningful axis of oppression leaves black women caught between narratives of gender 'based on the experience of white, middle-class women' and narratives of race 'based on the experience of Black men'.

In *Jews Don't Count*, David Baddiel describes the position of Jews as 'the only objects of racism who are imagined – by the racists – as both low and high status':

> Jews are somehow both sub-human and humanity's secret masters. And it's this racist mythology that's in the air when the left pause before putting Jews into their sacred circle. Because all the people in the sacred circle are oppressed. And if you believe, even a little bit, that Jews are moneyed, privileged, powerful and secretly in control of the world ... well, you can't put them into the sacred circle of the oppressed. Some might even say they belong in the damned circle of the oppressors.

While whiteness differs in that it is a genuine marker of privilege, I think this leftist construction of a 'high/low status' is often applied white women – not to mention Jewish women – whose suffering is experienced as uncanny and distasteful. Claims to victimhood are written off as calculated moves, ultimate proof of how dominant the would-be victim really is. No one likes sob stories from those who have already been assigned the role of aggressor in the pity economy. Julia Carrie Wong ends her *Guardian* article on the 'year of Karen' (2020) with a quote from Professor Apryl Williams: 'People are not out to get you for the most part, people are not trying to hurt you or harm your property or make you uncomfortable. You're not that special, Karen. You're not that special.' But, sometimes, quite clearly, people *are* out to do that (and often, they're the men with whom

'Karen' is presumed to be in league and whose non-sex-based privileges she shares).

The co-existence of victimhood and complicity is further problematised by gendered and age-based assumptions about who deserves care. To demand pity is to demand recognition that one has an inner life, boundaries, an experience of the world that has as much depth and value as everyone else's. In patriarchal terms, this is untenable, sitting alongside a broader resistance to according female people the same compassion and care as male people, and to seeing their pain as equivalent to theirs, as opposed to a simulation. Going back to Lerner's stage metaphor, demanding compassion on one's own terms – not only when it fits in with the bigger story men want to tell – is a bid to 'rewrite the script'. One way of avoiding openly denying women the chance to write their own trauma narratives is to focus on the privileges that mitigate or undercut these narratives, thereby pushing them back into the male-authored script, in which all female pain is understood in terms of how men might use it.

Added to the expectation of service imposed on older women is the stigma of 'hoarding'. Trauma is about experience and it is about memory. Older women have longer histories of abuse upon which to draw, and the ability to identify links between one historical event and the next, and between what has happened to them and broader attitudes towards female body stories. This very accumulation and application of experience can be deeply uncomfortable to those wedded to the binary thinking of the pity economy. One cannot have privilege and trauma, or the 'wrong' political values and trauma, at one and the same time. The sheer callousness and disbelief with which others respond to older women expressing their pain – the insistence that the motivation can only be to harm others, not to give voice to one's own needs (which one cannot have) – can be remarkable. Judith Butler has accused J. K. Rowling of having 'capitalised on a history of sexual trauma in order to afflict and persecute others', and of indulging in a 'revenge fantasy' when explaining that her own experiences mean she understands the need for traumatised women to have single-sex spaces. This has echoes of what Baddiel describes as the left's antipathy towards Jews for supposedly 'insisting continually on their entitled place at the top of the pain queue'.

One thing I think irritates many people the most about the trauma of older women – and which drives them to conflate middle age with being white, middle class and/or aligned with the values of white, middle-class men – is that the trauma is rarely expressed with recourse to the abstract or the trivial, not even if you are a world-famous millionaire author. It is literal violence, years of actual blood-and-guts abuse and exploitation as opposed to getting slightly ratty with a flight attendant or indulging in some curtain-twitching at the neighbours. In fairy tales older victims become the stepmothers and the witches, the rejects who are dangerous because their rage is fuelled by a long history of damage and promises broken. Think of *Snow White and the Huntsman*'s Ravenna and her hate. The best female victims are the young ones, on the cusp of exploitation, or the dead ones.

Within popular discourse on sexism and misogyny, there is a drive to make female oppression about anything but the desire of male people to exploit female bodies and labour. There is a vague, somewhat culturally imperialistic attempt to suggest that restrictive beliefs about gender arise from white supremacy and capitalism, and that any woman who associates female oppression with sexed bodies is herself an agent of white supremacist capitalist patriarchy. Once you make

misogyny into something simultaneously fuzzy yet rigidly
bound to other, more precisely defined evils, it is easy to turn
on victims of dull, boring, fist-in-your-face male violence.
Their oppression is unsophisticated, their bruises manipu-
lative. The extent of male violence is so overwhelming, the
ubiquity of domestic abuse so staggering, it becomes a trump
card that shouldn't be wielded, lest it be seen as a sneaky
attempt to undermine other claims to victim status (which is
precisely what a bigot would do).

'The tears of a woman,' wrote Sprenger and Kraemer in the
Malleus Maleficarum, 'are a deception, for they may spring
from true grief, or they may be a snare.' The spoilt, prissy
little madam, feigning victimhood to manipulate others, is
a longstanding misogynist caricature. In 2021, the white,
middle-class academic Alison Phipps echoed Sprenger and
Kraemer, complaining that 'bourgeois white women's tears
are the ultimate symbol of femininity, evoking the damsel
in distress and the mourning, lamenting women of myth'.
Yet it is not just 'bourgeois white women' whose stories are
drained of context and meaning by the crass application
of one-sided, bystander-appeasing tropes. In 'Mapping the
Margins', Crenshaw compares the status of Anita Hill, the
black woman who in 1991 brought sexual harassment allegations against Clarence Thomas, a black man and Supreme
Court nominee (who would later be instrumental in the 2022
fall of Roe v. Wade):

> Hill, in bringing allegations of sexual harassment against
> Thomas, was rhetorically disempowered in part because
> she fell between the dominant interpretations of feminism
> and antiracism. Caught between the competing narrative
> tropes of rape (advanced by feminists) on the one hand
> and lynching (advanced by Thomas and his antiracist

supporters) on the other, the race and gender dimensions of her position could not be told.

Crenshaw notes that many white women felt it more liberal to side with Thomas over Hill, as though actively disregarding both Hill's sex and her race would demonstrate their own lack of self-interest. A feminism which takes only victims of the 'right' representative of the patriarchy seriously – the kind of representative whom Helen Lewis describes as 'a white, rich, heterosexual, cisgender bogeyman, cackling and catcalling, probably wearing a monocle' – ultimately fails to take into account the specific locations of all women, not just the most privileged. Even someone such as Hill ends up being relegated to the status of 'damsel in distress' on the basis that 'political whiteness' is not the same as actual whiteness. There is a world – and it is this one – in which white academics might claim to be less politically white than Anita Hill, what with the latter's decision to call the manager all those years ago.

If the means of accessing the redistribution of resources everyone claims to want is by demonstrating you have been unfairly treated and are deserving of redress, it is in the interests of those who still hold power to make sure the criteria for victimhood exclude those upon whose exploitation any proposed utopia might still depend. Just as what is meant by 'entitlement' is often really 'independence', what is meant by 'weaponisation of trauma' is often its contextualisation and subsequent politicisation. Younger middle-class white women, on realising this, may seek other ways of contextualising their pain and making demands. Offering up an older version of themselves as a sacrifice, before couching their own suffering in other, less disruptive terms, can seem the ideal solution.

Purification rituals

Kiran Millwood Hargrave's novel *The Mercies* tells the story of women on a remote Norwegian island who lose their menfolk at sea and have to learn to cope as a self-sufficient, female-centred community. It is not long before this arouses suspicion and the witch-finders arrive. Kirsten, an outspoken, independent herdswoman, finds herself condemned by her peers, even those such as the protagonist Maren, who has previously stood by her:

> 'Witch.'
> Maren watches as the word ripples around the assembled women like a current. One by one they raise their fingers, hatred so bald and terrible on their faces it makes Maren's breath catch in her throat [...] She watches, betrayal thumping its drum in her chest as Kirsten is bound at the wrists and led in the direction of Vardøhus.

What, the reader wonders, would you have done in Maren's situation? Perhaps, if your own life were at risk, the answer is easy, the compromise justifiable, but what if you found yourself playing a (for now) lower-stakes game? What if the cost of speaking out in defence of the accused would not be your life but a job, your social network, the chance of avoiding a torrent of death and rape threats? What if these were the things the accused was facing? Would you say something, or would you find a way to persuade yourself that actually, maybe, the accused was a witch after all, and anyhow, her suffering would not be so bad?

In 2020, the same year *The Mercies* was published, Hargrave refused to sit on the judging panel for a *Mslexia* fiction and memoir competition alongside the older novelist

Amanda Craig. The latter's crime? Signing an open letter con-
demning the misogynist abuse of J. K. Rowling following her
statements on women's rights and transgender politics. Note
that the letter was not in support of Rowling's views per se.
Rather it objected to the dick pics and threats of choking that
followed. For her part, Hargrave objected to the objections.

'To disbelieve in witches,' wrote Kraemer and Sprenger,
'is the greatest of heresies.' No one wants to be the person
challenging the witch-finders, even those most capable of
articulating the human and social cost of failing to make such
a stand. Silvia Federici describes witchcraft accusations as 'the
ultimate mechanism of alienation and estrangement, as they
turn the accused – still primarily women – into monstrous
beings dedicated to the destruction of their communities,
therefore making them undeserving of any compassion and
solidarity'. At the start of the 2020s the publishing and academic communities have been particularly vigilant in warding
off any potential monsters. Communities that ostensibly celebrate original thought and female transgression, in which
members understand and can write with great passion about
the social mechanisms which lead to witch hunts, have preferred to cast the hunted as hunters. The sceptical do believe
in witches, or at least that is what they will say in public. The
more outlandish the accusations, the more vicious the punishments, the more willing the great and good are to conclude
there must be something in it after all.

The impulse, on the part of relatively privileged younger
women, towards denouncing similarly privileged older women
is not new. I, too, once sought to launder my white, middle-
class privilege by pointing my white, middle-class finger at
the white, middle-class women who went before me. It's a
neat way of scrubbing yourself clean of the taint of privilege
because the scrutiny of others can pass for self-scrutiny. Thus

young white women can engage in earnest discussions on 'the trouble with white women' when the people they are actually talking about are older or dead white women whom pretty much everyone already deems to be problematic, but whom they will pretend all other older white women view as Everywoman. It is the outsourcing of self-reflection; even checking one's own conscience and complicity becomes work one hands over to Mummy. Refusing to sit next to her becomes a substitute for asking why a seat was offered to you and not someone else.

Several of the prejudices covered earlier in this book – for instance, the association of domesticity with stupidity and/or conservatism, and the idea that views become outdated and 'second wave' the moment women stop ovulating – contribute to two further misconceptions: first, that older women are intellectually incapable of an educated, sophisticated understanding of intersecting oppressions in a way that younger women are not, and second, that not understanding intersectionality is more or less the same as being privileged. Neither of these is true. Indeed, one could counter this by noting how much these assumptions rely on the privilege of thinking the march of history favours the marginalised. Many US denunciations of British feminists' responses to Gender Recognition Act reform have relied on claiming that 'British feminism's leading voices, writers who had been setting the feminist agenda in Britain's major papers for years' (i.e. they are old hags) exemplify 'the relative insularity and homogeneity of British feminism'. The message is: don't become old, don't presume your opinions matter when you're old, because old women are all the same (and too stupid to realise it), whereas younger ones are more diverse (and far more open to other experiences of womanhood, apart from those of older women).

A further element that feeds into privileged younger
women's disidentification from their older counterparts is
competition for limited resources. This was a feature of historical witch hunts, and remains so in their more modern
iterations. Younger women can – with a degree of justification – consider themselves less privileged than older ones,
at a time when privilege has the aura of sinfulness, due to
genuine intergenerational inequalities and patterns of acquisi-
tion which favour those born earlier (regarding, for instance,
house prices and job security). If you believe you will not benefit from being white and/or middle class to the same degree
that your mother did on the basis that her generation pulled
up the ladder behind them, why not believe yourself more
virtuous? Isn't that all you've got left? At the same time, this
can become a way of trying to claw back the very entitlements
for which you shame others.

Narratives of intergenerational tension, particularly those
pitching Boomers against Millennials, rarely have time to
parse racial, class and gender differences within these groups
(and there is little point in us Gen Xers keeping our heads
down, since members of each group tend to treat us as members of the other anyhow). The older we get, the more we
will simply be read as 'greedy' Boomers who had the same
rights as younger people but none of the economic challenges. Boomer feminists such as Lynne Segal and Jane Caro
have already pointed out the injustice of this with regard
to the cumulative disadvantages of lifelong sex inequality,
while Margaret Morganroth Gullette has identified in such
narratives a form of victim-blaming in the face of the actual
poverty and neglect experienced by so many in old age. The
designation of 'privileged' applied to older people as a group
is, ironically, profoundly anti-intersectional. It also inadvertently reinforces the perception that younger members of

privileged groups are being robbed of a 'birthright', forced to inherit an unfashionable identity without the plentiful perks that once came with it. Privileged older women might be seen to be bestowing on their younger counterparts a shameful inheritance from which the latter can expect too few returns – at least until they can get the older generation out of the way.

Barstow suggests that 'anxieties about inheritance [...] lay at the heart of most [historical witchcraft] accusations':

This was a society designed to keep property in the hands of men [...] Single women and postmenopausal women without sons were especially vulnerable. That in Salem widows were allowed to own property outright may have been the reason that the witch hunt there was espe- cially intense.

Reading this, I cannot help but think of the way in which a generationally coded sex and gender debate has become a means for younger women to try to force older ones out of the way professionally, with unfeminine ambition masquerading as feminine compassion for the most marginalised. I think of the young writers raging at J. K. Rowling, the young journal- ists rounding on Suzanne Moore, or the young dancers who forced choreographer Rosie Kay out of her own company for expressing views on the role of sexed bodies in dance. In her interviews with gender-critical women in Scotland, Sarah Pederson encountered older women who had been denounced by younger women whose careers they had nurtured. The denunciations look ideological – the accused have danced with the Devil by expressing the 'wrong' feminist views – but they have also ascended to ownership of something the denouncers would like for themselves (and for women, there remain few places at the top). Moreover, socio-economic and race-based privileges still exist and remain tremendously powerful, no matter when you were born or how many witches you burn.

'If you disown your legacy,' writes Maureen Freely, 'you do disown yourself. Having disowned yourself, you grow to loathe any mirror that shows the family resemblances that have persisted anyway.' For some younger, white, middle-class women, an alternative to acknowledging both the limitations of their white, middle-class viewpoint and the biological connection that cuts across generations, races and classes has been to set fire to the white, middle-class mother as a form of peace offering-cum-purification ritual. An eagerness to single out their older counterparts for public shaming – particularly via the appropriation of memes and the misrepresentation of intersectional analysis – has spread. It is easier to ignore one's own complicity in environmental collapse, the economic exploitation of others and low-level domestic injustice if one has identified a 'natural' process whereby all spite and fury has been funnelled into the body of a dying breed. Easier, too, to imagine a future in which one does not have to divest oneself of one's own privileges in any practical, meaningful sense on the basis that inequality died out with bad old Mummy. In this way, far from being dismantled, privilege is shored up, and unjust social and economic hierarchies are maintained through the figure of the Privileged Hag.

Women's rights: human rights or outdated, ill-gotten luxuries?

When I am not reading *The Three Billy Goats Gruff* to my youngest son (and, obviously, reminding him of the convoluted feminist analogy Mummy has applied to it), we both like *The Little Red Hen*. This is the story in which a hen finds some wheat and decides to make it into bread. At each stage of the bread-making process she asks her friends the cat, the rat and the pig for help. Every time they refuse. When the bread is finally ready the hen offers it to her friends, who are all too eager to have a slice. She then retracts her offer and eats it all herself. There are various moral and political inter-pretations one can apply to this story – Ronald Reagan even got involved at one point – but I am thinking of the bread as women's rights.* In this version, the cat, the rat and the pig don't help not because they are lazy, but because the little red hen is problematic, perhaps due to her dealings with the baker and the miller (aka The System). Or maybe they are lazy and it's a convenient excuse. In any case, they still want the bread at the end of the process, but are annoyed that there isn't enough for the whole farmyard and because it's a bit too crusty around the edges and why didn't she do a gluten-free version? Whatever: the hen has made rubbish bread and it just goes to show that while everyone should have bread, no one should ever make bread again. Obviously in this version the hen still allows everyone to eat the rubbish bread – she's a feminist – but no one wants the recipe from her. Years later, long after she's been made into roast dinner, the remaining animals think it would be nice to have bread again, but no one knows how to make it. The moral of this story is that it's a pity the hen was such a bitch.

The past work of feminists, like the unpaid work of older women, suffers from a combination of problematisation and invisibilisation. Most of the labour goes unseen and is taken for granted, while that which is noticed is deemed far too

---

* I know, 'rights aren't like pie', so probably not like any other shareable but finite food source either. Apart from when one person's perceived right to one thing impinges on another person's perceived right to a different thing, which is actually quite often. Then someone does indeed have to have less/no pie/bread.

compromised and flawed to teach any fundamental lessons to future generations. As Helen Lewis writes in *Difficult Women*, 'the second wave feminism in the late sixties and seventies is often now derided as privileged and blinkered':

> But it swept away the legal framework which enshrined women's second-class status [...] This was not a ladies' lunch club. If it looks like that in hindsight, it's because the work of thousands of women has been largely forgotten, and the fierce opposition to it has been forgotten too. As a feminist, victory is often bittersweet: the new reality quickly feels normal, obscuring the fight required to get there. Progress erases struggle.

One consequence of this erasure of struggle is that it renders the gains more precarious. If feminist campaigns and those leading them were problematic, perhaps the outcomes were, too. How can we be sure what was won were basic rights and not luxuries targeted at an elite class of women? What could we possibly learn from these women, when we could have done things so much better? Do we really want to keep all the rights they fought for – women-only spaces, abortion access, language and research which centres us – or should we subject them to endless revisions, constantly chipping away at the things we don't need? Should we not even be a little ashamed of them? Isn't the entire concept of women's rights a bit, well, essentialist and entitled?

'During the second wave,' Pedersen tells me, 'there were still people alive who were suffragettes and suffragists and [second-wave feminists] could have actually interviewed them. But, with some honourable exceptions, this did not happen. There was a tendency to dismiss the suffragettes as middle-class white women with selfish goals focused on their own needs. And so they've set up this dynamic that we still have where we ignore the older women, and once women get to a certain age their experiences can't help us. [The older women] were not fighting the same sort of causes that we are now and therefore if they get involved, they'll derail us.' In her memoir of second-wave activism, Susan Brownmiller mentions that associating oneself with the suffrage movement was a provocative move, 'for leftists habitually denigrated the suffrage battle, belittling it as a racist, upper-class white women's campaign'. A movement, one might say, for 'ladies who lunch and feel hard done by because a man held the door open for them on their way in to the Four Seasons'. Or a movement mischaracterised in much the same way Brownmiller's own movement is today.

The hostility is not one-way. In 2015, Brownmiller gave an interview with *New York Magazine*'s *The Cut*. Rather unhelpfully titled '*Against Our Will* Author on What Today's Rape Activists Don't Get', it showed Brownmiller taking a hard, even victim-blaming, stance on women who get drunk, dress provocatively or don't leave abusive partners. I didn't agree with these arguments, though some of Brownmiller's other comments – particularly on the disproportionate focus on college rapes – struck me as perfectly valid. Nonetheless, the retaliatory ageism which characterised some of the responses to the interview was breath-taking. Writing in *Cosmopolitan*, the author and anti-rape campaigner Kate Harding claimed that 'if, forty years from now, someone asks me what I think about young anti-rape activists, I hope my ego will allow me to profess admiration for whatever work they're doing to better the new world they've grown up in':

But honestly, there's just as good a chance that I'll respond like Brownmiller, carping about kids' lack of historical

awareness and respect for their elders, then adding a bunch
of crap that sounds hopelessly outdated to anyone pre-
menopausal. Either way is fine with me, really. If I get to
the point where I have no idea what young activists are on
about, or why they don't seem concerned with what most
concerns me, it will probably mean they've taken what
they needed from my generation's feminism and left the
rest behind. I'm pretty sure that's what progress looks like.

I'm not sure it is, though. I think there is a fine line between
casting a clear eye over the past and recognising that its inhabitants were not untouchable icons but flawed human beings,
and the belief that the work of older feminists does not constitute anything so important – so male! – as a coherent legacy,
but rather a bunch of random ideas. No one wants to listen
to someone 'carping about kids' lack of historical awareness
and respect for their elders', but when the topic is women
as a class, the fact that women as a class have been denied
a history of their own is not irrelevant. Who decides which
aspects of feminism can be 'left behind'? And given that rape
does not just happen to 'anyone pre-menopausal' – despite the
'too old to rape' messages of men's right activists – how can it
be that anyone ages out of being able to make a contribution
to the debate? Feminism should be no place for the belief that
post-fertile women are intellectually and politically obsolete,
yet it can be one in which it thrives. This is damaging to the
principles that women's lives matter at every stage, and that
the rights we have are not passing fashions, constantly ripe for
revision, but fundamental to our status as full human beings.

The path towards the 2022 overturning of Roe v. Wade
provides a stark example of the way in which an 'old' right
can be taken for granted, not least because the women who
won it are deemed irrelevant. Though many factors led to US

women losing constitutional protection of their right to an abortion, they were not helped by the belief among younger feminists that to prioritise abortion rights at all smacked of anti-intersectional, biologically essentialist second-waverism. 'Abortion rights,' wrote Hadley Freeman, in response to a 2019 survey showing that, even under Trump, young women were more concerned with mass shootings and climate change than abortion access, 'are seen by young women as a given – which is understandable, since they have been for their entire lives – and also a bit uncool, something associated with their mothers.'

In 2021, Alexis McGill Johnson, president and chief executive of Planned Parenthood, explicitly stated 'what we don't want to be, as an organization, is a Karen', describing 'organizational Karens' as 'the groups who show up, assert themselves, and tell you where to march. Those who pursue freedom and fairness, but also leverage their privilege in ways that are dehumanizing.' Following the fall of Roe v. Wade, there was much emphasis on how lack of abortion access hits the most marginalised women hardest; prior to that, concern for the most marginalised women could be used to position abortion as a selfish, white-lady concern. 'Young middle-class white women prove their anti-Karen cred by championing less self-centred causes,' writes Janice Turner, 'racial justice, LGBT rights, the climate emergency.' Yet all of these issues intersect with reproductive justice. Not only can a feminist legacy slip through your fingers, but women who have the luxury of prioritising disidentification from the mother over the work of safeguarding sex-based rights – 'the stuff that does not look good on Instagram, but was the means by which now-nameless feminists throughout history slowly heaved that arc towards progress' – end up betraying women and girls with the least privilege.

In her 1911 *History of the Women's Suffrage Movement*, Sylvia Pankhurst predicted that 'the hearts of students of the movement in after years will be stirred by the faith and endurance shown by the women who faced violence at the hands of the police and others in Parliament Square and at the Cabinet Minister meetings, and above all by the heroism of the noble women who went through the hunger strike and the mental and physical torture of forcible feeding'. It is just as well she never lived to see how 'students of the movement' would one day discuss her and her contemporaries on social media (without, one presumes, actually wanting to renounce the right to vote). Discussing her own feminist activism in a somewhat more realistic fashion, Kiri Tunks says 'women always have to choose between the victory or the glory. I'll take the victory.' Even so, I wonder whether, if women could have just a little more glory, a little more legacy, some of our victories could be easier to come by in future, and more firmly fixed. Then we might finally get to the Field of Equality, and stay.

8

DEAD HAG

One lesson we can draw from the return of witch-hunting is that this form of persecution is no longer bound to a specific historical time. It has taken on a life of its own, so that the same mechanisms can be applied to different societies, wherever there are people that have to be ostracized and dehumanized.

Silvia Federici, *Witches, Witch-Hunting and Women*

Let me start by saying that no one is a bigger feminist than me.

Caption to a 2019 *New Yorker* cartoon,
depicting a Puritan holding forth before a
woman about to be burned as a witch

There are times when I'm not sure historical witch burnings ever really happened. This is in spite of ample documentary evidence proving that they did, plus the fact that women are still burned as witches today. It all seems too far-fetched, rather like the idea that a woman might run for US president in 2016 and find herself dealing with cries of 'witch!' from members of both the opposing party and her own. Like that shit would really happen, except it really does.

According to the UN State of World Population report of 2020, the number of missing females has more than doubled over the past fifty years, from 61 million in 1970 to 142.6 million in 2020. In the UK, two women die every week at the hands of a current or ex-partner. The UN reports a rise in women killed for witchcraft over the past decade, with older women in India 'being targeted as scapegoats or as a pretext for seizing their lands and goods'. In *Feminism for Women*, Julie Bindel cites further UN research showing that 'at least eighty-seven thousand women worldwide were killed by men in 2019'. Like so many women who have not lived lives deemed to be particularly high-risk, I have experienced male violence directly, and spent a good deal more time seeking out strategies (a new route home, a new way of dressing, a new, less me-like personality) to avoid it. For all the 'new dawn' feminism I once imbibed, I do not believe what is happening to women and girls today is just a throwback, a very long hangover from past superstitions, whether we are dealing with the man who throws acid into the face of his ex-girlfriend, the parents who leave their baby girl to die or the community that sets an old woman alight. This hatred – this desire to eradicate women – has a long legacy but remains very much alive, and is constantly being renewed. Even so, there's a part of me that feels it's mean to point this out. Why can't I #JustBeKind?

Because male violence against women and girls is the end point of misogyny. Hence this final chapter is about older women and male violence – how the narratives about older women explored in earlier chapters are used to reframe and justify the violence enacted on their bodies, and how these narratives are deployed to trivialise and undercut feminist analyses of male violence as a global phenomenon. I also want to examine how one narrative in particular – that of the so-called 'TERF' – follows a particular pattern of justifying violence against older women as an act of virtue.

My focus here is on acts of violence, but it is also on stories, and the tricky relationship between the two. It's my contention that many of the attitudes covered earlier in this book interact with the under-reporting, misrepresentation and outright excusing of male violence against older women. Messages about the pointlessness and deviousness of older women – those who no longer meet the femininity-fertility-fuckability standards, whose unpaid work is unseen, whose knowledge is viewed as either trivial or dangerously regressive, whose accumulated resources are deemed unearned entitlements, who are expected to provide care but not to receive it – exist in a culture which is, to quote Dr Hannah Bows in the 2020 UK Femicide Census, 'ill-equipped to recognise and prevent violence against older women'. Yet I know these are different things and that correlation is not causation. Indeed, when it comes to male violence against women, it seems essential that women be reminded of this at all times (the risk of taking away a man's recreational hate narratives without just cause being perilously high).

Short of having every perpetrator make, of his own volition, a formal, public declaration of influences, many of which he may not even have consciously recognised as such, there will always be that sliver of doubt as to whether repeatedly telling boys and men that women and girls are worthless actually *makes* them treat us as such. This is one of the reasons why witch burnings, both past and present, can form a useful reference point for feminist analysis, given that they are rare occasions upon which the relationship between murderous, semi-pornographic male violence and socially approved narratives about worthless/demonic older women is made fairly clear. I'll give that to the authors of the *Malleus Maleficarum*: at least they weren't calling themselves feminists.

I am wary of making sweeping assertions and of sounding paranoid. Let me be clear: I don't think those men gathering on social media to bitch about middle-aged Mumsnetters are genuinely hoping for a return to the sixteenth century. Nonetheless, I'm conscious that the very stories we hear about phobic, moral panic-inducing middle-aged women can constitute a highly effective way of frightening women out of making even the most tentative links between socially approved misogyny (such as is found in pornography) and men beating, raping and killing women. The popular misrepresentation of older women as biologically essentialist bigots or sex-hating prudes is, among other things, a way of telling all women that drawing too many conclusions or making too many demands in response to their own fear of male violence will be regarded as misguided and passé. I, too, would rather not be dismissed as a fear-mongering, radicalised housewife. I, too, would like to offer a fancy, academic-sounding analysis of violence which rises above the blood-and-guts basics of who hits whom. I'm sure I could do it, too, but I just don't think we have time.

We are not at risk of organised, large-scale violence against women becoming a global phenomenon; we are already there. It's just that this passes for normal to anyone who isn't a hysterical, misandrist, moral-panic-mongering harpy. So maybe I will sound a bit paranoid. Because witch burnings did, and do, really happen.

'If you don't cure her, I'll kill her': culturally approved scripts

In *Feminine Forever*, Robert Wilson recalls a consultation with a patient who wants to kill his wife:

> 'She's driving me nuts. She won't fix meals [...] Now she tells me to get out and never come back. But I won't. It's my home. And if anyone's going, she is.'
> He reached into his back pocket [...] and quietly laid a .32 automatic on the edge of my desk.
> 'If you don't cure her, I'll kill her.'

Thankfully the story ends happily, with Wilson 'curing' the menopausal, non-meal-fixing wife with doses of HRT (the gun-toting husband is, we are to assume, in no need of treatment himself). But as Wilson goes on to note sadly, 'outright murder may be a relatively rare consequence of menopause – though not as rare as most of us might suppose. Yet the psychological equivalent of murder in the form of broken family relations and hatred between husband and wife is a common result of menopausal change.' Menopausal women, eh? Can't kill 'em (legally), but you can at least hold them responsible for the metaphorical murder of all that you hold dear.

What, do we think, is the connection between this kind of discourse and the so-called 'nagging and shagging' defence for murdering a spouse? The provocation defence, amended in 2010, once allowed men to argue that their wives had 'reasonably provoked' them to murder. It reinforced ideas of how women ought to behave towards men in order not to be seen to be inviting physical violence. Don't, in essence, be a slag or a mother-in-law. It will never be possible to pinpoint just how much the existence of legal defences for killing 'nagging' women interacted with cultural messages about 'shrewish' ones – the sitcoms, the advice columns, the bantz – to modify male and female behaviour. You can't ever know for sure. What we do know is that there is a script in place, one which sets out what women should be and what men might be allowed to do to those who fall short.

Even in the wake of legal reform, the idea that a man might inadvertently kill a woman as a result of her role in his hero's journey persists. For instance, the 'rough sex' defence has been compared to the old 'nagging and shagging' one. In one academic study into defences for murder reliant on the 'sex game gone wrong' narrative, Professor Elizabeth Yardley of Birmingham City University found that 'the normalisation of bondage, domination and sado-masochism (BDSM) provided a "culturally approved script" for men who kill women'. I wonder, though, about the ongoing impact of less superficially edgy cultural content. The attitude expressed by Wilson and his patient hasn't exactly vanished. On the contrary, responses to the deaths of older women are still shaped by prejudices about older women, bolstered by 'acceptable' narratives regarding their questionable place in the world.

If the new, improved woman is just around the corner – if the time of woman is only just beginning – then maybe there's little point in those who are more than halfway through their lives existing all. There is, after all, a collection of perfectly normalised ideas which point in that direction: we are on the wrong side of history; unlike men, we do not add stones to the glorious edifice of human knowledge, but offer waves which crash and recede; we are the beta model women, the over-aged but pre-evolved, the oppressed-but-useless-as-a-consequence class. Also, who'd want to fuck us? What's the point of us any more? 'You know,' says one friend, 'some men just seem really kind of offended that women live longer than about thirty-five.' (And if you're thinking, well, there's always the grandmother hypothesis, sure, but don't you think it's weird that there's been so much academic enquiry essentially framed around the question 'Why haven't these bitches died yet?')

Historical witch-hunters targeted older women deemed to have outstayed their welcome. 'Witch charges,' writes Anne Llewellyn Barstow, 'may have been used to get rid of indigent elderly women, past childbearing and too enfeebled to do productive work [...] The old woman was an ideal scapegoat: too expendable to be missed, too weak to fight back, too poor to matter.' In societies where it is no longer the done thing to murder an older woman for being a witch, narratives which justify the deaths of older women continue to circle the theme of obsolescence. Perhaps she was already fragile; perhaps she put herself at risk because her age had made her desperate; perhaps it was for her own good.

In August 2016, Philip Williamson received a suspended sentence for the manslaughter of his wife of sixty-two years. Josephine, eighty-two, was suffering from dementia when Philip pushed her down the stairs at their home. 'She went before me and something took over me and I pushed her, that's it,' he told responding paramedics. 'I did not want her to become a decrepit old hag. I love her too much for that.' For all the complexity of the case (suffering from terminal cancer, Philip himself did not have long to live) it is difficult not to baulk at the phrasing, leaning as it does towards a disgust perception as opposed to concerns about quality of life.

Mercy killings, says Karen Ingala Smith, CEO of the Nia charity and founder of Counting Dead Women, form a common defence for men's fatal violence against elderly women, particularly in instances where the accused is a spouse or a son. While she concedes that some cases may involve altruism, she points out that this isn't something women tend to be doing to men:

It's something that men do to women. And I think there's a thing around women being socialised to be carers. So when a woman's partner gets ill, women can care for an older partner if he becomes more vulnerable. Some old men would prefer to kill a woman than do that. Some kill her because they think they're ill and that she won't be able to live without them.

The ageing process undermines all the messages we receive about 'natural' gender roles, but rather than conclude that the messages (and the social structures we have built to accommodate them) are wrong, for some it is easier to see the ageing female body as no longer truly itself. It is easier to kill a person who isn't themself any longer. You are not killing them, but the impostor, the decrepit hag.

Bows notes that elderly women have been sidelined in the reporting and analysis of men's fatal violence. Research, she writes, 'has focused on young women as victims and survivors':

we remain 'shocked' when an older woman is killed by a man, believing this to be an unusual occurrence, when in fact my research has identified at least one in four domestic homicides involves a woman aged sixty or older, despite them constituting only 18 per cent of the population.

Until 2018, the murders of women over the age of fifty-nine were not included in the Crime Survey for England and Wales, masking the prevalence of violence against them (the cap has now been raised to seventy-four; life expectancy for women in the UK is 82.9 years). 'When you look at police data on abuse, rape and murder, older women aren't there,' says Bows in an interview with the *Guardian*'s Yvonne Roberts. 'If a crime is looked at, at all, it's treated as a safeguarding issue, gender neutral, "elder abuse" with no perpetrator.' Yet it is not as though the murders of older women appear less violent and hence more ambiguous. On the contrary, older women are more likely than younger women to suffer five or more injuries beyond what would have been needed to kill them (known as 'overkilling'), even in cases that are subsequently regarded as mercy killings. In her article, Roberts even mentions research which indicates the murderers of older women are 'the least likely to express remorse or empathy'.

If the murders of very old women risk being dismissed entirely, those of middle-aged women do not fare much better. In April 2016 the novelist Helen Bailey was murdered by her partner Ian Stewart, whom she had met four years previously at a support group for those grieving dead partners. Throughout Stewart's trial, the press casually patronised Bailey, implying that her attachment to the man who would one day kill her was a sign of typically female midlife desperation. Some examples were provided by the columnist Deborah Orr:

The *Daily Telegraph* has mused that 'a lot of middle-aged women find themselves incredibly lonely'. The *Daily Mail* has pointed out that 'middle-aged single women are incredibly vulnerable', helpfully elaborating on what is meant by 'middle-aged'. It means 'older women' who are 'in the autumn of their years'. Hang on? Autumn? Bailey was fifty-one. At the time she met her murderer, she was forty-seven. One of the many reasons why Bailey's death seems so cruel is that she very clearly had so much life ahead of her, with so much potential for fulfilment and joy.

The very fact of Bailey's ageing, not her partner's violence, is offered up as the tragedy, yet as Orr observes, 'A culture that continues to insist that women lose worth with every year that passes? That's what primes people for emotional or actual annihilation, not "middle age".'

The pressure placed on women not to age, to magically freeze themselves in time in order to continue to make a valued contribution to society, makes the deaths of older women seem less significant, as though these are people who are, to quote Naomi Wolf, not 'entirely alive' to begin with. Or even, perhaps, we are the only truly mortal women in a mass of ethereal, disembodied future women; if anyone is still meant to die these days (another crime against biological non-essentialism), it's us. It's not that this thinking directly translates into the next murder of an older woman, or the next lenient sentence for the loving husband who, as men do, 'just snapped'. It's that we wouldn't even notice if it did. The belief that older women are obsolete, lingering only on sufferance, our bodies, politics, intellectual legacies all set to be burned, makes us things to be tolerated and, if need be, put out of our misery.

'Thou shalt not suffer a witch to live': ageism, misogyny and TERF panic

Burning women at the stake was the ultimate act of punching up. Come on, admit it. Witches were in league with the Devil, and if that's not on a par with being a Nazi, I don't know what is.

Obviously I write this in (sort-of) jest. I don't approve of burning anyone at the stake, or of punching up, down or sideways. Nevertheless, I think it's important to remember that many of those whom history deems the baddies didn't think of themselves as the baddies at the time. Often they have narratives which, on closer inspection, turn out to have much in common with those of the goodies who'd never have allowed themselves to be led so far astray.

Writing on present-day witch burnings in rural communities in Zambia, Silvia Federici argues that older people are hunted as witches today because they are seen as 'dead assets, the embodiment of a world of practices and values that is increasingly considered sterile and nonproductive'. Old women, writes Federici, 'are believed to pose a special threat to the reproduction of their communities, by destroying crops, making young women barren, and hoarding what they have':

> In other words, the battle is waged on women's bodies, because women are seen as the main agents of resistance to the expansion of the cash economy and, as such, as useless individuals, selfishly monopolizing resources that the youth could use. From this viewpoint, the present witch hunts [...] represent a complete perversion of the traditional conception of value creation, which is symbolized by the contempt that witch hunters display for the bodies of older women, whom, in Zambia, they have at times derided as 'sterile vaginas'.

This book is not about rural Zambia, yet reading this, I can't help thinking of many of the themes explored in earlier chapters. Here we find the same disregard for older women's knowledge, the same horror of postmenopausal bodies, the same belief that progress happens when identities are formed via patterns of ownership rather than through mutually negotiated relationships. Above all, the same belief that once *those* women are gone, society will be truly productive, in a pure, progressive way that transcends the squalor of female-ness entirely.

Looking at the treatment of older women on social media, it is striking how well modern-day justifications for dousing a woman with petrol and setting her alight in one part of the world map to justifications for ordering a woman to choke on your dick in another. Every time and place has a batch of hags so repulsive, so superfluous, so dangerous to the social order, they are deserving of violence. While fantasies of misogynist violence/violent misogyny aimed at older women might have similar psychological roots to those aimed at younger women – resentment of female bodies and boundaries, a misplaced sense of victimhood, rage at what are seen to be female 'privileges', the extraction of female-coded services – they also have a particular kind of social acceptability. By selecting a group of women whom even self-styled progressives might deem to be (physically, morally, politically) degraded or even dangerous, the ageist misogynist can tell himself he values women, just not those ones. It is their rotten souls, not their femaleness, with which he claims to have a problem.

There is nothing particularly new about the degree of highly sexualised violence with which 'outspoken', 'enti-tled' or just plain 'superfluous' women are threatened. One only need look at the imaginative tortures devised for women accused of witchcraft, the instruments used to silence 'shrewish' wives or the punishments meted out to suffragettes. It is not simply the case that increasing access to pornography in the digital age has allowed a never before encountered level of misogynistic fantasy to seep out into other areas of discourse. It has always been there. Men of supposedly high moral standing have always been this cre-ative. The differences lie in the ways different communities package their punishments, and in particular how enormous the side order of piety is this time.

In response to a 2013 essay containing the line 'we are angry with ourselves for not being happier, not being loved properly and not having the ideal body shape – that of a Brazilian transsexual', Suzanne Moore received a shocking degree of misogynistic abuse and threats: 'Twitter was full of people telling me how they were going to rape me, decapitate me, ejaculate inside my head, burn me [...] The worst threats were from people who knew where I lived and said that they would give my then eleven-year-old a good fisting.' Abigail Shrier, who in 2020 published a book expressing concerns about the rise in female to male transitions amongst teenage girls, received emails such as the following (which she drily describes as 'thoughtful feedback from someone who undoubtedly considers himself "progressive"'):

> Just wanted to let you know you're a useless fucking cunt. I hope you get hit by a car and don't reproduce so you won't pass on your fucked up ideas of hating trans people into future generations. Pray you never meet me walking down the street you dirty fucking cunt because I'll slit your fucking throat and fuck your newly made neck pussy. You're fucking trash, kill yourself you nasty fucking whore.

While online porn might be an obvious influence on the people making such threats, I'm also reminded of an eighteenth-century woodcut described by Marina Warner as 'a satire against bluestockings, feminists, scolds and other opinionated women':

> 'I will make you good,' declares the doctor Lustucru, as he hammers out a wife's head on the anvil. 'Husbands,

rejoice!' says his assistant, while another woman, with mouth open, waits her turn. The sign outside the smithy, 'A La Bonne Femme', shows a headless woman.

Outspoken women and their hateful heads! No good for anything other than chopping, slicing, hammering, fucking. Or failing that, for a lighter touch, shoving into a scold's bridle. It will be claimed that the impulse to silence is different now, because it is in response to women who are genuinely bad and powerful in a society which isn't silencing all women. This is of course exactly what eighteenth-century woodcut-makers would have said, too (besides which, it's just woodcut bantz).

'Witches,' writes Stacy Schiff, 'tend to be people we didn't like in the first place. They appear suspect in advance of their crimes.' What's particularly insidious is that the more absurd the accusations thrown at them, the more outlandish the punishments, the more deserving of punishment they appear. The ultimate modern-day witch is the TERF, an older woman ascribed ludicrous intentions and powers, her words and actions vastly over-interpreted, any level of violence deemed acceptable in response to her own as-yet-unrealised but certainly unfathomable demonic potential. Like Karen, TERF may have had specific origins in relation to a small subset of women, but today it caters to the broad, unremitting demands of porn-soaked, pious, ageist misogyny.

As the poet Jenny Lindsay, herself a victim of TERF-hunting, writes, '"TERF" stands for "trans-exclusionary, radical feminist" but its usage has expanded over time to include non-feminist women':

The latter may fully affirm current trans rights already enshrined in law by the Equality Act 2010. TERFs may also include women who support actions to further mitigate discrimination faced by trans people [...] The 'exclusionary' aspect comes from defining 'sex' as meaning, simply, the dictionary definition of 'men' and 'women', i.e., 'adult human male' and 'adult human female'. These category definitions are implicitly 'exclusionary'.

Lindsay was denounced as a TERF for objecting to threats of violence against lesbians who do not wish to count male-bodied people as potential sexual partners. 'What happened to me could easily happen to any of you,' she writes. It happened to me when I wrote about my own experiences of dysphoria in relation to anorexia (an impermissible narrative; you either feel at home in your sexed body, or you are not that sex at all). Once the label is there, it is impossible to shed.

In her dissertation on the use of the term, Anna-Louise Adams found TERF to be 'a gendered label, which is utilised by men to legitimise misogynistic language and behaviour':

TERF in itself is used as a word to describe women alongside violent rhetoric such as: punch a TERF, rape a TERF, kill a TERF, highlighting its dehumanising nature. Further, a number of participants reported that they had seen TERF used alongside words which represent uncleanliness, filth, or disease.

Adams tells me the women she interviewed felt it was also conflated with 'old' and 'lesbian'. In a blog post discussing whether or not TERF constitutes a slur, Professor Deborah Cameron lists some examples of usage:

you vile dirty terf cunts must be fuming you have no power
to mess with transfolk any more!

I smell a TERF and they fucking stink

if i ever find out you are a TERF i will fucking kill you
every single TERF out there needs to die

why are terfs even allowed to exist round up every terf and
all their friends for good measure and slit their throats
one by one

if you encounter a terf in the wild deposit them in the
nearest dumpster. Remember: Keeping our streets clean is
everyone's responsibility

The language is necessarily extreme because the 'sins' of
TERFs can only be understood with reference to the misogynistic fantasies of which they are the subject. Without these,
one might otherwise think TERFs are ordinary women with
a basic theory of patriarchy and/or understanding of the
political salience of human reproduction (which is just what
TERFs *want* you to think). 'You get these young women who
start using [TERF] because they see the response first and
they think, these people must be horrible,' says Adams. 'And
there's always such hyperbolic language surrounding women
who are TERFs, like "literally killing trans people", "literally
enacting violence" [...] And it's just this cycle of dismissing
someone's views, legitimising violence against them, thinking
that they're bad, then somebody else comes in and sees you
doing that, then they add to it.'
    In earlier chapters I've suggested older women become
a receptacle for other people's prejudices, symbolic figures

whom it's okay to hate because of all the villainy projected onto them, and who purify everyone else by representing bad, regressive things – mortal bodies, dirt, boundaries – which will soon no longer matter. In the summer of 2020, following her blog post on sex and gender, protestors threw red paint, intended to look like blood, onto an impression of J. K. Rowling's handprints on an Edinburgh street. The message – that she had blood on her hands – was utterly ridiculous, but it didn't matter. The point wasn't to respond to the fact that Rowling was already a monster, but to turn her into one by treating her as such. The sheer magnitude of misogynist aggression directed at Rowling in the form of vandalism, book burnings, rape and death threats were what damned her, not anything she had written. As one anonymous academic tweeted, 'When you're on the outside of the fray on gender issues looking in, it's tempting to say: If someone is hounded for her speech, she must have said or done something horrible':

> The crime and the punishment must match, working back-wards from the severity of the punishment. For example, if the response to what @jk_rowling said is that intense, she must have said something truly terrible – otherwise, no one would make death threats. Because that would be insane.

Ritual witch burnings themselves, writes Barstow, 'taught people that "the woman's crime" deserved the most severe punishment possible, that women, who up to that time had seldom been marked publicly as criminals, were capable of doing the ultimate evil'. The punishment doesn't fit so much as define the crime.

It is very hard to explain to people that neither J. K. Rowling nor the women of Mumsnet – or, by extension, that middle-aged white woman who looked at you a bit funny in the queue at Tesco – are plotting mass murder when so many online voices respond to them as though they are. The misogyny directed at Rowling for what was a compassionate essay, advocating violence against no one, was off the scale. 'Can we stop saying the UK virus?' tweeted one wag during the height of panic over a new Covid variant. 'Her name is JK Rowling.' While Covid-themed woke misogyny is hardly original (remember the 'problematic second wave' joke?), in 2020 it was a go-to, topical way to gain likes and follows. 'It boggles my mind,' confessed one tweeter, in what was perhaps the saddest response to the 'joke', 'that [Rowling] decided to flaunt her controversial views so publicly. She could have been remembered in history as one of the Great British authors but now she has this stigma attached to her. Like why, for what reason??? Mind boggling.' Witch-hunt culture makes women who continue to speak out despite the extreme personal and social costs inexplicable to others.

Misogynists, whatever their style or location, imbue their targets with a power that makes their own threats noble and plucky, the underdog making a stand for what's right. As a hate term, TERF draws on the myth of the entitled, wrong-side-of-history older white woman. By binding accusations of 'biological essentialism' to this all-powerful-but-on-her-way-out has-been, younger women are once again encouraged to cut ties with older ones on the basis that to admit to having any shared experience that excludes male people would be bigotry. Despite the number of prominent older women of colour – Maya Forstater, Linda Bellos, Allison Bailey – who have been publicly denounced as TERFs, there is a reliance on the idea that thinking female biology and female body stories matter is akin to being a white supremacist. In this way, it creates a 'middle-aged white woman loophole' for misogyny by conflating recognition of the biological and political salience of femaleness with 'the fiction of a single female experience'. What women talk about when they recount their body stories and share their experiences of femaleness in a multitude of social and political contexts is misrepresented as a fixed, exclusionary narrative. The story of living in a female body over time – what it means socially, politically, personally, across other axes of oppression, as an individual and in association with other female people – is cast as the property of a mean, bigoted class of hoarding dinosaurs. Thus in the name of 'inclusion' this story is snatched from all female people because it cannot be shared any longer, not across generations, not across socio-economic classes, not across races. By portraying femaleness as a property only ageing, privileged bigots would wish to situate in a political context, TERF-hunters once again make it socially acceptable – nay, virtuous – to hawk the concept of female supremacy, something men's rights activists have been attempting to do for decades and at which old-style witch-hunters excelled.

There is, of course, 'no proof' that people routinely fantasising about hurting and killing TERFs has anything to do with the reinforcement of social norms which justify real-life violence against women. Here, the same rules apply as with porn. As all clever, sophisticated people know, watching violent porn does not make men want to murder women, whereas feminists criticising violent porn creates the stigma that makes men want to murder women in the sex trade. Likewise, men threatening sexual violence against lesbians is not incitement to violence, whereas women objecting to men threatening sexual violence against lesbians is. Words are just words unless women are using them, in which case they're actual violence requiring special acts of self-defence.

A November 2020 article for Rewire News Group (listed

under the category 'human rights') offers advice on how to deal with 'a TERF at your Thanksgiving gathering':

> Throw the turkey at them. If you do not have the upper-body strength to throw the turkey, you can opt for something slightly easier to lift like a handful of mashed potatoes or some stuffing. A pie also works, and offers an added comedic effect.

It's hard to read 'TERF at your Thanksgiving gathering' as meaning anything other than 'older female relative'. Hard, too, to see the 'comedic effect' of a suggestion which brings to mind both femicide census statistics which reveal older women to be victims of homicide not just by intimate partners but by younger male relatives, and that 2001 *EastEnders* Christmas special where Evil Trevor shoves Little Mo's face into her dinner. (At the time we thought it was a hard-hitting illustration of the humiliations of domestic abuse. Turns out we were lacking a sense of humour.)

'Every single civil rights movement,' declared one Twitter account in February 2021, 'has resulted in blood shed, groups don't just move over and accept. Once the terf start being killed the laws will change.' A sixty-year-old feminist was assaulted at Hyde Park Corner because of her (quite simply feminist) views on sex and gender. A member of a punk band who wrote songs about murdering women who misgender others was subsequently outed as a serial sexual abuser. We are not supposed to mention such things because it is viewed as a form of game-fixing. Either there is no evidence you are being harmed, or you are using evidence of harm to misrepresent all of your opponents.

I don't think men who disagree with women on a topic such as sex and gender are necessarily more likely to rape and beat

women. I do suspect men who write songs, make speeches and
send tweets about raping and beating women are more likely
to do so. And they do.

Male violence and feminism: a conspiracy theory

Much of the feminism I encountered as a child, I encountered
as caricature. Literal cartoons – Andrea Dworkin repackaged
as Millie Tant – and phoney wars between women who hated
everything (men, motherhood, families, sex) and those who
loved far too much. The caricatures change, the misogyny
and misrepresentation do not. We now have the screeching
Karens, the dinner-table TERFs, the pearl-clutching Helen
Lovejoys, the plotting mummies all eager to spread their hate.
These are the people you learn to fear. Not the men who
might kill you, but the women who won't.

It is a cheap shot, I know, to point out that the vast majority of assaults, rapes and murders are committed by men.
It feels like cheating, a way of absolving women from their
participation and complicity in the dissemination of beliefs
that incite and legitimise violence. Yet an over-emphasis on
this supposed complicity can be a way of positing an equiva-
lence where there is actually none. Women's words – not even
those of the women we call TERFs – do not wreak the same
damage as men's bodies. However sophisticated our attempts
to reignite panic over women's 'slippery tongues' – whatever
assertions we might make about 'literally' violent language
that, like the Emperor's new clothes, only a simpleton would
fail to see – it is the same old scapegoating.

Like the ageing female body, like care work, like pension
poverty, actual fist-in-the-face male violence is one of those

drudgey, kitchen-sink feminist topics that we're meant to think has had its day. *We've moved on, ladies! We don't say 'male', we say 'gender-based'! And anyhow, broken bones are so, like, essentialist!* In a speech for International Women's Day 2008, the writer Laurie Penny was already proposing that 'misandrist feminism, feminism that is pro-woman but anti-men, is massively out of date':

> The feminism of the sixties and seventies was a political movement which was vital for its time but which is proving dated, anodyne and inappropriate forty years on. In fact, sixties and seventies 'second wave' feminism, having won the most important of its battles years ago, retains only the most questionable and paranoid of its objectives.

We are meant to feel it is 'paranoid' and 'anti-men' to single out men as a class. The right side of history has left behind such old-school thinking; we have thought our way beyond it, albeit in much the same way we have always thought our way beyond male violence against women being plain old male violence against women. It's always far more complicated than that. There's always a deep-seated theological or philosophical or scientific reason why it's not just one easily definable class of people enacting violence on another easily definable class of people. Only the stupid and out of touch – their brains no doubt stuck in the seventies, or maybe even the seventeenth century – would fail to grasp this.

Contemporary caricatures of older women – the nouveau second-waver, the gossiping Mumsnetter, the radicalised Facebook Aunt, the frigid pearl-clutcher, the TERF – play on the idea that these are women in thrall to long-debunked conspiracy theories regarding the threat that male people pose to women and children. Yet this is itself a conspiracy theory, one which falsely positions the naming of male violence – a genuine global crisis – as some confected 'moral panic' led by a hysterical, gullible, ideologically 'violent' league of ageing housewives and lesbians. There is indeed an imaginary, super-hyped threat, but it is not being pushed by older women but projected onto them, just as has been the case in witch trials.

Scapegoating is made easier by the fact that male violence is too widespread, too visible and just too grotesque to be taken seriously. There is no way to take in the blood-and-guts truth of it; representation constantly topples over into cartoonish-ness. The witch-finder wielding the torch, the king disposing of wife after wife, the put-upon husband punishing the nag – all puppets, none of them real. It is little wonder that the commemoration of the murders of real women for witchcraft is still given the theme park treatment; Federici writes of 'sites of famous trials and persecutions [...] now parading in shop after shop doll-like representations of witches [...] reproduc-ing the very stereotypes created by the witch-hunters'. Even when you feel hands around your own throat, it is difficult to categorise what is happening with reference to misogyny. When the victim is you, it's just you.

'I think that's one of the reasons it takes a woman a while to understand what's going on,' Kate, an editor and feminist in her fifties, tells me. 'Because it is so crass. It is so fucking shameless, and exactly what the caricature radical feminist has been saying since Greenham, when we all went, *Okay, well, theoretically, you're talking theoretically, or psycho-analytically, or metaphorically?* And they said, *No, no, we literally mean men hate us and want to kill us*, so then we said, *There must be more to it, a more sophisticated analysis*, but actually, I don't think there is.' She describes her own attitude towards feminism following a path I recognise from my own life:

This is how I thought between the ages of nine and maybe eighteen: men hate women and want to control them, and they will do anything they can to do that. And then you're a young woman, and there's postmodernism, and it has to get more complex and playful, and you're talking about how there needs to be nuance, otherwise how can you possibly participate in your own conceptual death? I'm fifty-three now. You come through, the middle years are kind of a blur, and then you know: it is as straightforward as it seemed at the start.

For many of us, there comes a point at which the degree and consequences of men's violence cannot be endlessly qualified, recontextualised, recategorised, argued into some more comfortably vague 'gender-based' zone. This is, funnily enough, also the point at which we apparently lose our minds, driven mad by the absence of suitably feminine hormones, or perhaps by the housework, or some edgy, not-for-the-likes-of-us political concepts we encountered online. By the time you have enough of a life story to understand that your original impressions of the world of men and women can be confirmed by your lived experience of it – and that the clever fairy tales which seek to overwrite it remain just that – you are not deemed credible. You are the conspiracy theorist, not the people suggesting, with a straight face, that women congregating to discuss the political underpinnings of their childbirth experiences are more dangerous than men getting off on rapes uploaded to Pornhub.

'We don't injure or kill men,' wrote Pauline Harmange in 2020's *I Hate Men*, 'we don't prevent them from getting a job or following whatever their passion is, or dressing as they wish, or walking down the street after dark, or expressing themselves however they see fit. And when someone does give themselves the right to impose such things on men, that person is always a man.' When the original French version of Harmange's booklet was published it led to a threat by a government official to take legal action to ban it. No one was claiming that Harmange's assertions were untrue, but by daring to offer – in what are actually quite restrained terms – a logical emotional response to men's behaviour, she crossed a line. We demonise the women who name the violence we don't want to acknowledge. It's the next step up from raging at Mummy for the fact that the washing-up exists.

Demonisation and scapegoating are short-term measures for managing our fear of things that are real: sickness, weakness, dependency, violence, death. The ageing female – least likely to kill you, most likely to remind you that you're not some immortal, untouchable god – makes the perfect target. As long as rage can be directed towards her, other ways in which we could alleviate pain, suffering and loneliness, and minimise violence, are set to one side. Because we're not aiming for things to be better (a world in which we still die, but in which men are not killing each other and everyone else). We want perfection (no one dies), but in the meantime, we construct narratives which let us pass the blame onto those who won't hit us back.

What this comes down to is not just how much we value older women, but how much we value all people, at all stages of their lives. When we constantly short-circuit the passage of knowledge between generations, or dismiss the importance of the body, or demonise dependency and human connections, or render the formation of communities suspect, we devalue some of the most important things we can do as human beings, male or female. When we downplay the extent and impact of sexual abuse, or approve terminology used to sanitise threats of violence, or reduce a person's worth to a

snapshot of their life, or pretend female speech is the equivalent of male fists, we perpetuate the very wars we claim to
want to end.

You cannot end violence against women if your love for
women is conditional on them remaining at a particular life
stage or holding particular beliefs. If you make a scapegoat
of the older woman – the witch, the harridan, the hag – one
of two things will happen: either you will age into being her,
or the criteria for being her will broaden until they apply to
you, too. You can never kill enough witches to start the whole
project of being human from scratch.

AFTERWORD

Certainly the effort to remain unchanged, young, when the body gives so impressive a signal of change as the menopause, is gallant; but it is a stupid, self-sacrificial gallantry, better befitting a boy of twenty than a woman of forty-five or fifty. Let the athletes die young and laurel-crowned. Let the soldiers earn the Purple Hearts. Let women die old, white-crowned, with human hearts.

Ursula K. Le Guin, 'The Space Crone'

But the truth is I am sick unto death of four thousand years of males telling me how rotten my sex is. Especially it makes me sick when I look around and see such rotten men and such magnificent women, all of whom have a sneaking suspicion that the four thousand years of remarks are correct.

Marilyn French, *The Women's Room*

This is the problem: you know it will, but you don't really believe it will happen to you. No one ever tells you what it's like to be a middle-aged woman. Or rather, plenty of people tell you, but all of them are middle-aged women, so why would you listen to them?

There is something particularly painful about the blend of misogyny and ageism we experience as we enter our forties and fifties, rooted in the fact that we do not have to imagine how we are perceived. We know, we recall it still. Open your mouth and you can hear your own words being translated into middle-aged-woman-ish, a language you used to mock. You're on the wrong side of a thick pane of glass, everything about your inner life – your politics, your fears, your passions – distorted and refracted. You want to tell everyone you've made a terrible mistake.

In *What About Us?*, her 1995 challenge to a burgeoning third-wave feminism and its neglect of mothers, Maureen Freely describes a shopping trip with her ten-year-old daughter and an adult female friend. Freely tries on a dress that her daughter adores so much she asks her mother if she might save it for her to wear when she is older. Both Freely and her friend laugh at this.

My daughter didn't get the joke. I told her she would come to understand it only too well, especially if I kept my promise to her.

'But I want the dress!' she insisted.

'You won't when you're big enough to fit into it.'

'How do you know?'

'I just do.'

'I can't stand it,' she said. 'You think you even know how I'll feel when I grow up. You can't know everything! It's just not fair.' As she stormed out of the room, I smiled again, but as I was turning to my friend, I caught a glimpse of the mirror. And there she was. The image of my mother, smiling just as superciliously, but at me.

Freely describes herself as 'caught between the mother in the mirror who knows me better than I know myself, and the daughter who wants to run away from me because I know why she'll never want to wear my dress. The mother who sees through me. The daughter who can't bear to look.' This is how I have often felt while writing, caught between all the feminists who thought my thoughts so long before me, thoughts I initially rejected (too essentialist! Too shameful! Too damn female!) before arrogantly believing them to be all my own, and all the younger selves who might yet find me patronising, superior, a cautionary tale. In this sense, being middle-aged feels almost akin to being teenaged: transitional, a complex mix of over-confidence and horrendous self-consciousness, littered with mortifying epiphanies.

A difference, though: whereas my teenage self sought resistance, testing out ways to differentiate myself from the common herd, my middle-aged self finds herself drawn to other middle-aged women. Once you've arrived in that most feared place, it becomes easier to shed the internalised misogyny that made it all seem so dreadful. You start to become shameless, in the sense of no longer being haunted by shame at what binds you to other women.

'The system of patriarchy,' wrote Gerda Lerner, 'can only function with the cooperation of women', a cooperation that is secured by, amongst other things, 'the denial to women of their history' and 'the dividing of women, one from the other'. This book is about the hatred of middle-aged women – a particular hatred, one which spreads outwards to undermine all women – but also about love, the love that can exist between women, a love that remains so discomfiting and disruptively terrifying that we are not supposed to congregate on our own terms, to identify and name the threads that connect us, or to look at one another across the generations without suspicion or fear. My younger self might have rejected such a love as being of a low-status variety, but when she is not at my shoulder, asking me what I've become, I am at hers, whispering, badgering, eager to lead her astray.

Just like a real witch.

The feminist lifecycle (in T-shirts)

Allow me to present the four ages – and T-shirts – of feminism:

Stage One: You hate sexism and are eager to smash the patriarchy/live beyond the gender binary/[insert your own vague objective here]. What's more, you're definitely going to win because you are nothing like those mean, useless older women who fucked things up last time. *T-shirt slogan:* Riots Not Diets.

Stage Two: Okay, so you're still nothing like those mean, useless older women who fucked things up last time. That said, you sort of agree with them about some things, only for different reasons, e.g. you worry about choking in porn because it might hurt women, whereas they just have some weird sex phobia thing. Or you think sex matters because you know sex discrimination exists, whereas they think sex matters because they see all women as brood mares. You're still going to win, but you're not going to mention the choking/sex discrimination stuff in public in case it gives the wrong impression. *T-shirt slogan:* Girls Just Wanna Have Fun(damental Rights).

Stage Three: Actually, you hate to admit this, but those mean, useless older women? They were right about many

things, and when you look at it, their justifications make
sense. The trouble is how badly they marketed their arguments. They're appalling at PR, which is why everyone
thinks they're mean, bigoted and essentialist. You, however, will be able to translate for them, making the case
against choking women in sex and telling women their
bodies don't matter in a way that is nuanced, persuasive,
and above all, kind. Those bitches sure are lucky to have
you! *T-shirt slogan:* Eat the Patriarchy.

Stage Four: Bollocks. Turns out that no one cares how
euphemistic your feminism is. The issue was always with
the content, so you might as well express what you believe,
and not on a T-shirt. How come no one – apart from
those useless older women – warned you it would be this
much work?

I'm not saying all women go through these stages in order. I
know some who seem to have been born at Stage Four, others
who never even get to Stage One. There are women who
hit Four then, on witnessing the response, retreat to Three
(though they're never the same again). A significant proportion of mainstream feminism hovers between One and Two
while thinking it's at Three or Four. Nonetheless, the overall
direction of travel is clear, and what's needed is some serious
acceleration. This is why Mumsnet, with its effective methods
of hauling women over to the dark side, has been causing so
much consternation. Most of the time, getting the process to
speed up is a challenge.

'You're asking younger women to form an alliance with an
imaginary future self,' is how my partner describes the plight
of the older feminist. 'You'll get old, too, girls!' is never a
hot sell. Hawking a non-ageist feminism is like hawking life

insurance to people who've been promised eternal life, just as long as they think positive and ignore all those gloomy insurance ads. It may not be sustainable, but an ageist feminism has much more to offer in terms of short-term psychological gains.

It is reassuring to believe that the reason you are treated as inferior is the fault of women who were once in your position and blew it; to insist that it was their moral failings – their privilege, their ignorance, their entitlement – that denied you the utopia your own moral purity will bring about; to believe that your intellect and virtue will win the day, because it can't possibly be that men are consciously choosing not to give you the resources and freedom they award themselves.

I would very much like it if male supremacy were a millennia-spanning misunderstanding, finally on the verge of being resolved by pronoun badges and 'Male Tears' coffee mugs, achieving all that Wonderbras and the Spice Girls failed to do. Non-confrontational, smooth-skinned, pre-menopausal feminism – like the non-confrontational, smooth-skinned, pre-menopausal woman – has such obvious popular appeal. It offers the same hit as buying a new moisturiser or self-help book; you know it's not going to work, but holding it in your hands, you can imagine the self you would be, the life you would have, if it delivered on all of its promises. A feminist scapegoat – the witch with the poisoned apple, plotting against your feisty Snow White – provides you with the victory narrative you want (because she will definitely get old, definitely die, whereas you will live happily ever after).

I thought my generation was the chosen one, ready to see out the End of Patriarchy now that the second-wave mummies had done all the hands-dirty groundwork. We'd drink pints of Stella – full pints! – while waving off every caricature that preceded us, the housewives, the shoulder-padded

ball-busters, the miserable Greenham radicals, the man-
hating eternal victims. *So long, losers! It was never going to
be your time!* How could it be possible for me and my peers to
feel so fully human – so fully in possession of a complex inner
life – were it not for the fact that there had never been women
quite like us before? After all, if there had been, wouldn't we
have treated them as such? And wouldn't the men have, too?

We could tell ourselves discrimination would have ended
years ago, only women hadn't asked before. Or maybe they
had asked, but they hadn't asked nicely. Or they'd asked
nicely, but without providing sufficient evidence to back up
their request. The fact that women of my generation resorted
to 'asking nicely with sufficient evidence while on slutwalks
with our tits out' should have been a sign that desperately
seeking ways to differentiate yourself from the previous generation of women is an expression, not of hope, but denial.
It is feminism as fairy tale, refusing to go beyond a cursory
discarding of the handsome prince. The wicked stepmother/
witch remains, and the options for perfect womanhood – stay
frozen in time, become evil or die – are unchanged. A feminism which refuses to embrace 'the old witch, the Terrible
Mother in myself, or [. . .] the real old women of this world'
is personally and politically unsustainable. It's no feminism at all.

What do middle-aged women want?

Despite having written a book about how much people hate
middle-aged women, I don't wander around every day thinking, Oh no! Everyone hates me! To be a middle-aged woman
is not to live in a state of total misery. Indeed, this is what
makes us such an inconvenience to those who wish to benefit

from our work while treating us as wholly irrelevant. Very few of the attempts to bring us down actually do so.

We're told we're ugly, and that our looks betray our inner badness, yet we don't feel as unattractive as our younger counterparts believe themselves to be; our bodies no longer conform to the patriarchal femininity/fertility/fuckability standards, yet it's through this that we learn to appreciate them in their own right; having become the women from whom we were in flight, we're no longer in flight from one another; the accumulation of compromises and relationships of dependency has taught us to reconsider the supposed 'conservatism' of mothers, grandmas and aunts. For all the attempts to water down the confidence of female middle age into 'liberated to talk about hot flushes while injecting your wrinkles with poison' sloganeering, there is something far more solid that emerges when women lose the assets upon which they were told they must depend in order to function in the world of men. Ageist misogyny decrees that unless we are careful – unless we take the right hormones, engage in the right beautifying practices, utter the correct mantras, show the requisite amount of 'kindness', do anything, anything, to show we still position ourselves solely in relation to the male of the species – then we will cease to be 'proper' women. On the contrary: we are womanhood stripped bare, in all of its physical, experiential and intellectual diversity. The differences between us – differences in socio-economic class, race, life choices, relationships, talents, political allegiances, domestic responsibilities – are only clearer with the artifice swept away. Recognition of that which we truly have in common is a prerequisite to addressing the differences that matter.

Here are some modest proposals for a feminism that sheds itself of the self-hate of ageism:

1. No T-shirts or mugs.*
2. A re-embrace of language that describes female
   embodied experience in all of its continuity, together
   with sex education which covers the menopause and
   beyond. Our bodies are not objects and our lives
   are not lived as a series of disjointed events. A truly
   fluid understanding of human experience does not
   fix us in time or force us to choose between context
   and change.
3. Tracking of the cumulative cost of being female over
   a life course, not just in terms of the gender pay gap,
   but unpaid labour, trauma management and the social
   and economic cost of male violence. 'Great reckonings'
   and 'moments of truth' are all well and good, but the
   spotlight must move back to what living under male
   supremacy means for a lifetime, and how it shapes the
   choices and compromises we make as we age.
4. A feminist investment in intergenerational narratives
   to replace the 'new dawn' narratives of obsolescence
   and replacement which pander to the idea that women
   are only useful for half their lives. If we can identify
   the privileging of the male default in product design,
   medical research and work patterns, we can identify it
   in supposedly 'progressive' political narratives, too.
5. 'Shaming swaps' – every time you are tempted to shame
   an older woman for the crime of navigating a messed-
   up world without clean hands, find a replacement man
   who has said or done the exact same things with zero
   consequences. A database of said men could be created,
   not that it would be necessary (they tend to be the ones
   at the forefront of the latest hag-shaming).

---

* Okay, maybe some tea towels or something.

None of these suggestions are particularly new (apart, perhaps, from the last one). We are more than halfway there in terms of what we know about female lifecycles and how different they could be. Ageism is a story we tell ourselves about who we are and might be; given that every feminist achievement so far has been based on women disbelieving the old stories about ourselves, we are more than capable of doing this in relation to age.

To my old and future self, who will disagree with this book

I am certain that some of the things I have written here will be wrong – if not to me in years to come, then to others, and if not to others, then definitely to a past me. That sudden sense of closing doors, of losing one's place at the table, that arises simply because one is running out of time – the resentment, the outrage of it! – can seep (and I am sure will have seeped) into my own perceptions of structural injustice. Ageist miso-gyny/misogynist ageism is real, but so too is the plain, neutral reality of physical decline and ever-decreasing opportunity. The two are related, as I argued in Chapter Two, but this does not make me any less vulnerable to the lure of blaming the prejudice of others for the less appealing aspects of the human condition. One person's blaming Mummy is another person's blaming the people who blame Mummy. This is one of the many cracks that appear in an attempt to sculpt a pure, feminist truth. You can only write and think and feel from one body, on one timescale. Then again, there is no point in me sharing words and thoughts and feelings at all if there is no possibility, not just that I might change someone else's perspective, but that their response might change mine.

Any truly progressive politics must embrace change, but
the social construction of femininity pushes women towards
resistance to change. 'A woman's character,' wrote Susan
Sontag, 'is thought to be innate, static – not the product of her
experience, her years, her actions [. . .] After a woman's body
has reached its sexually acceptable form by late adolescence,
most further development is viewed as negative.' As suggested
in Chapter Four, one of the comforts of misogynist ageism/
ageist misogyny lies in the way it corresponds to a broader
resistance to future possibilities of personal/political change.
It flatters the impulse to see oneself firmly ensconced on the
right side of history, complete with one's approved set of righteous postures. Certainty – the great, stomping certainty that
means you're so sure of your position you might even threaten
violence to defend it – feels good and pure. What better way to
convince yourself that you are in the right, here, now, and for
ever more, than by vilifying those who represent those lowly,
depressingly human changes across a lifecycle – the decay, the
dust, the accumulation of dependencies? Isn't the only change
that matters the one that comes when you stay just as you are
and the world catches up with you? Isn't the only woman who
matters the woman still emerging, like Maggi Hambling's
Everywoman, from the mulch?

I am not frightened of change. I am frightened of things
staying the same. When I thought change was a given, my
generational birthright, there seemed very little to do other
than wait it out. Indeed, sometimes it felt very important not
to make the slightest movement lest it upset a very delicate
balance. Don't talk to the other girls. Don't copy the conservative mummies. Don't listen to the sex-hating prudes. Don't
empathise with the mothers-in-law. Don't get too close, lest
these creatures taint you. Keep your eyes straight ahead, stay
very still and change will be your reward. It will be given to

you from on high. Don't let them tell you change can only emerge organically from such base phenomena as interactions with women who are not the same as you.

My academic background is in languages.* I think of the feminism I first embraced as akin to learning from a phrasebook, by which I don't just mean learning specific slogans – *no means no, a woman's right to choose, I believe her* – but gathering items that made their own self-contained sense yet would never lead to any fluency. I didn't want to learn the grammar, not really believing that there could be any substantial structures underpinning a political movement just for women. I didn't want rules, because rules were elitist or essentialist or entitled (or something else beginning with 'e'). I found the thought of communicating with other speakers, adapting to their intonation, picking up their nuances, tackling unfamiliar terms, intimidating. I worried that if I allowed women whose destinies I rejected to influence me, I might be weakened in my own resolve to be different. I feared conversations with women I viewed as compromised by their relationships and social roles lest I should become compromised, too. I decided I probably had enough feminism to 'get by'. I ended up talking only to myself, wondering why no one responded.

We don't take the legacies of other women seriously because we don't take women seriously. The alternative to this is not agreeing with everything those who went before us have ever said or written (an impossibility, given the diversity of female experience and thought). It's respecting the idea of female experience and thought, and doing so enough to

---

* With a specific focus on German Romantic literature and fairy tale. As a linguist, I did in fact write some post-grad essays on feminism and language, but in that delightfully airy 'well, what is a woman, anyway, huh? HUH?' manner that no one ever questions despite (or maybe due to) the fact that it says sod all.

recognise that what women have in common does not render us less worthy representatives of the human condition. It is not accidental that the pearl-clutching, ill-educated, bigoted mummy or aunt persists as a personal and political scapegoat, relieving everyone else of the responsibility of recognition – recognition of unpaid labour, of reproductive difference, of male exploitation, of one's own privilege, of millennia of female intellectual work. It is not accidental that middle-aged women are denied the space to transgress – to be messy, to be compromised, to be defined by their relationships with others, to exist beyond the sacred three Fs – when otherwise there is so much we might leave behind. It is not accidental that the middle-aged women who do not become symbols of hate or mockery instead find themselves ignored.

The physical erasure of older women has never been successful, for obvious reasons. What we must fight are the short-circuiting of our conversations, the denial of biological and generational threads, the male-default lifecycle narrative, the constant insistence that 'woman' is a slate that must be wiped clean and written anew with each fresh generation. We know – and we know it more and more, with each passing year – that 'new' woman, the frozen princess in the glass coffin, isn't truly alive, and we cannot throw our lot in with a feminism that wishes us dead.

INGTBI.

NOTES

Introduction

1   *In fairy-tales:* Roald Dahl, *The Witches* (London: Penguin, 2016). p. iii

1   *When we read 'witches' for 'women':* Matilda Joslyn Gage, *Woman, Church and State* (New York: The Truth Seeker Company, 1893). p. 291

1   *legitimate feminist criticism of the film:* Susan Faludi, *Backlash: The Undeclared War Against Women* (London: Vintage, 1993). p. 150

2   *'become invisible':* Sarah Long, 'What 50 Looks like Now: The Invisibility of Middle Aged Women', *Reader's Digest* <https://www.readersdigest.co.uk/culture/books/meet-the-author/what-50-looks-like-now-the-invisibility-of-middle-aged-women> [accessed 10 December 2020].

3   *'the double standard of aging':* Susan Sontag, 'The Double Standard of Aging', in Marilyn Pearsall (ed.), *The Other Within Us: Feminist Explorations of Women and Aging* (Abingdon: Routledge, 1997). pp. 19–24

4   *Research is conducted:* Erica Åberg, Iida Kukkonen, and Outi Sarpila, 'From Double to Triple Standards of Ageing. Perceptions of Physical Appearance at the Intersections of Age, Gender and Class', *Journal of Aging Studies*, 55 (2020), 100876 <https://doi.org/10.1016/j.jaging.2020.100876>.

4   *At forty-seven:* Teresa Perez, 'Earnings Peak at Different Ages for Different Demographic Groups – Compensation Research', *Payscale* <https://www.payscale.com/data/peak-earnings> [accessed 27 September 2021].

4   *A BBC/Ofcom review:* Guy Cumberbatch and others, 'On-Screen Diversity Monitoring: BBC One and BBC Two 2018 Contents Section', CRG – Broadcasting, Media & Social

Policy Research <www.crgbirmingham.co.uk> [accessed 16 August 2022].

4   *As Nicky Clark ... documents:* 'Acting Your Age Campaign 9 Key Aims for Broadcasters, Film Companies & News & Current Affairs', MrsNickyClark.com <http://www.mrsnickyclark.com/-acting-your-age--campaign.html> [accessed 8 December 2022].

4   *'women reach forty and hit their stride':* Rachel Shabi, 'Women Reach 40 and Hit Their Stride ... Only to Be Cruelly Shoved aside at Work', *Guardian* <https://www.theguardian.com/commentisfree/2021/apr/07/women-40-work-sidelined-sexist-standards> [accessed 29 April 2021].

5   *'the worst online trolls':* Esther Walker, 'Middle-Aged Women Can Be the Worst Online Trolls – as Part of That Demographic, I Can Understand Why', *i* <https://inews.co.uk/opinion/middle-aged-women-worst-online-trolls-demographic-i-can-understand-why-1104024> [accessed 14 September 2021]. Zosia Bielski, 'Unravelling to Unwind: Why Middle-Aged Women are Drinking More', *Globe and Mail* <https://www.theglobeandmail.com/life/relationships/why-women-drink/article13436803/> [accessed 14 September 2021].

5   *people make Halloween masks:* Zoe Moore, 'This "Karen" Mask Is Being Called the Scariest Halloween Costume of 2020', *GMA* <https://www.goodmorningamerica.com/living/story/karen-mask-called-scariest-halloween-costume-2020-73000555> [accessed 7 December 2020]. Katherine M. Acosta, 'Vancouver Panel on Gender Identity and Media Bias Encapsulates Conflict between Women and Trans Activists', *Feminist Current* <https://www.feministcurrent.com/2019/11/06/vancouver-panel-on-gender-identity-and-media-bias-encapsulates-conflict-between-women-and-trans-activists/> [accessed 7 December 2020].

5   *'women who dare to keep existing':* Helen Lewis, 'The Mythology of Karen', *The Atlantic* <https://www.theatlantic.com/international/archive/2020/08/karen-meme-coronavirus/615355/> [accessed 19 December 2020].

6   *'I never thought leopards would eat my face':* 'Leopards Eating People's Faces Party', *Know Your Meme* <https://knowyourmeme.com/memes/leopards-eating-peoples-faces-party> [accessed 20 November 2020].

8   *'one woman can often serve as a stand-in':* Kate Manne, *Down*

Girl: The Logic of Misogyny (Oxford: Oxford University Press, 2018). p. 68

8   *there are so many witches:* '... older women [...] detached from patriarchal institutions [...] seen as 'the locus of a dangerous envy and verbal violence'. Lynne Segal, *Out of Time: The Pleasures & Perils of Ageing* (London: Verso, 2014). pp. 42–3

9   *They are 'dinosaurs':* Caitlin Prowle, 'Lammy on Trans Rights: "There Are Some Dinosaurs on the Right" and "in Our Own Party"', *LabourList* <https://labourlist.org/2021/09/anti-trans-members-are-dinosaurs-who-want-to-hoard-rights-says-lammy/?fbclid=IwAR0ta4QeOnZwdwoV9OPC5masWnaIa7F_S3JZyVgOpG1avm4cEqhOvLadfK4> [accessed 28 September 2021]. Joe Roberts, 'Women's Institute Hipsters "at War" with Jam and Jerusalem "dinosaurs"', *Metro* <https://metro.co.uk/2018/04/03/womens-institute-hipsters-war-jam-jerusalem-dinosaurs-7436177/> [accessed 10 May 2021].

10   *'the other within us':* Marilyn Pearsall (ed.), *The Other Within Us: Feminist Explorations of Women and Aging* (Abingdon: Routledge, 1997).

11   *'ritual matricide':* Susan Faludi, 'American Electra: Feminism's Ritual Matricide', *Harper's Magazine* (October 2010), pp. 28–36, 38–42

11   *'problematic second waves':* Twitter <https://twitter.com/mesallyann/status/1329448462820274179#> [accessed 19 December 2020].

11   *'most sexism is down to':* Caitlin Moran, *How to Be a Woman* (London: Ebury, 2011). p. 133

13   *'We're living through the most misogynistic period':* J. K. Rowling, 'J.K. Rowling Writes about Her Reasons for Speaking out on Sex and Gender Issues', J.K. Rowling <https://www.jkrowling.com/opinions/j-k-rowling-writes-about-her-reasons-for-speaking-out-on-sex-and-gender-issues/> [accessed 27 December 2020].

13   *'culturally approved script':* Diane Taylor, 'Rough Sex Excuse in Women's Deaths Is Variation of "crime of Passion" – Study', *Guardian* <https://www.theguardian.com/uk-news/2020/nov/10/rough-sex-excuse-in-womens-deaths-is-variation-of-of-passion-study> [accessed 26 May 2021].

14   *'The generation gap':* Audre Lorde, 'Age, Race, Class, and Sex: Women Redefining Difference', in Julie Rivkin and Michael Ryan (eds), *Literary Theory: An Anthology* (Oxford: Blackwell), p. 632

14   'I was out of touch': Helen Lewis, Difficult Women: A History
      of Feminism in 11 Fights (London: Vintage, 2020). p. 171
15   first batch of young women: Astrid Henry, Not My Mother's
      Sister (Bloomington: Indiana University Press, 2004). pp. 4–6
15   'Becoming the Third Wave': Rebecca Walker, 'Becoming the
      Third Wave', Ms (spring 1992). p. 41.
16   'a low-slung, straight-line bridge': Ada Calhoun, Why We Can't
      Sleep (London: Grove Press, 2020). Introduction, para. 18
16   'being not-young': 'Old people are not, in fact, just like
      middle-aged persons but only older. They are different.
      As is the case with other forms of oppression, we must
      acknowledge and accept these differences, and even see them
      as valuable.' Toni Calasanti, Kathleen F. Slevin, and Neal
      King, 'Ageism and Feminism: From "Et Cetera" to Center',
      NWSA Journal, 18:1 (2006), pp. 13–30 <http://www.jstor.
      org/stable/4317183> p. 17
16   ageism often found in business and advertising: Patricia Lippe
      Davis, 'Women Over 50 Are Often Disregarded by Marketers.
      Here's Why That Needs to End Now', Ad Week <https://www.
      adweek.com/brand-marketing/women-over-50-are-often-
      disregarded-by-marketers-heres-why-that-needs-to-end-now/>
      [accessed 21 October 2021].
16   Not Dead Yet: Susan Hawthorne and Renate Klein (eds), Not
      Dead Yet: Feminism, Passion and Women's Liberation (North
      Geelong: Spinifex Press, 2021).
17   By the time they reach their mid-forties: 'Childbearing
      for Women Born in Different Years, England and Wales',
      Office for National Statistics <https://www.ons.gov.uk/
      peoplepopulationandcommunity/birthsdeathsandmarriages/
      conceptionandfertilityrates/bulletins/childbearingforwomen
      bornindifferentyearsenglandandwales/2018> [accessed 5
      August 2021].
18   'If a woman has kids': Dorthe Nors, 'On the Invisibility
      of Middle-Aged Women', Literary Hub <https://lithub.
      com/on-the-invisibility-of-middle-aged-women/> [accessed 22
      October 2021].
19   'an obnoxious, angry, entitled': 'What Does "Karen" Mean?',
      Dictionary.com <https://www.dictionary.com/e/slang/karen/>
      [accessed 22 October 2021].
20   'if you are good enough, pretty enough': Lorde. p. 633
21   'Class and racial privileges': Gerda Lerner, The Creation of
      Patriarchy (New York: Oxford University Press, 1986). p. 218

22   'Hags are cool, man': Caitlin Moran, More Than a Woman (London: Ebury, 2020). p. 259

22   'a martyr mascot for the women's movement': Kristen J. Sollée, Witches, Sluts, Feminists: Conjuring the Sex Positive (Berkeley: ThreeL Media, 2017). p. 44

22   'the powerless have always wanted to be feared': Susannah Lipscomb, 'What Turns Women into Witches?', UnHerd <https://unherd.com/2021/10/what-turns-women-into-witches/?tl_inbound=1&tl_groups> [accessed 30 October 2021].

23   'women are invoking the witch to find their power': Sofia Quaglia, 'The Resurgence of the Witch as a Symbol of Feminist Empowerment', Quartz <https://qz.com/1739043/the-resurgence-of-the-witch-as-a-symbol-of-feminist-empowerment/> [accessed 6 January 2021].

23   'women are reclaiming this once heretic identity': Sophie de Rosée, 'The Vogue Guide To Being A Modern Witch', British Vogue <https://www.vogue.co.uk/fashion/article/vogue-guide-witch> [accessed 18 November 2020].

23   'feisty independent woman': Ibid.

23   As Mary Beard points out: Mary Beard, Women & Power (London: Profile, 2017). Main text, penultimate para.

24   This book is not a celebration: Although the stories of hags of yore undoubtedly matter from a legacy perspective. Many excellent examples of these can be found in Sharon Blackie's Hagitude (London: September Publishing, 2022).

24   'invoke the witch as a statement': Quaglia.

24   'Like many millennial women': Sollée. p. 5

25   'here for all of the witches': Sam Haysom, 'Emma Watson Ruled the BAFTAs with One Sentence: "I'm Here for ALL of the Witches"', Mashable <https://mashable.com/article/emma-watson-baftas-witches> [accessed 27 June 2022].

27   'the equivalent of a eunuch': Robert Wilson, Feminine Forever (London: W. H. Allen, 1966). p. 15

27   'as close as she can to being a man': 'As the estrogen is shut off, a woman comes as close as she can to being a man. Increased facial hair, deepened voice, obesity, and the decline of breasts and female genitalia all contribute to a masculine appearance, Coarsened features, enlargement of the clitoris, and gradual baldness complete the tragic picture. Not really a man but no longer a functional woman, these individuals live in the world of intersex.' David Reuben, Everything You Always Wanted to

Know About Sex But Were Afraid to Ask (New York: David McKay Company, 1970). p. 292

27   '*much of what is believed*': Janet Radcliffe Richards, *The Skeptical Feminist: A Philosophical Enquiry* (Abingdon: Routledge, 1980). p. 161

28   '*see menopause as the cancellation*': Germaine Greer, *The Change: Women, Ageing and the Menopause* (London: Bloomsbury, 2018). p. 25

28   '*during menopause I slip out*': Darcey Steinke, *Flash Count Diary* (Edinburgh: Canongate, 2019). p. 88

29   '*The days when women of a certain age*': Angela Neustatter, 'Time of Our Lives', *Guardian* <https://www.theguardian.com/world/1999/apr/19/gender.uk2> [accessed 15 December 2020].

29   '*menopause is having a MeToo moment*': Louise Chunn, 'How the Menopause Is Having a MeToo Moment', *Telegraph*   <https://www.telegraph.co.uk/women/life/menopause-having-metoo-moment/> [accessed 19 November 2020].

Chapter 1: Ugly Hag

31   *Is a woman entirely alive:* Naomi Wolf, *The Beauty Myth* (London: Vintage, 1990). p. 235

31   *Of course it's true:* Nora Ephron, *I Feel Bad About My Neck: And Other Thoughts On Being a Woman* (London: Transworld, 2008). p. 7

32   '*persistently reminded of the undesirability*': 'Here be the lesbians in comfortable shoes, the overweight, the old-ish, the busy, the indifferent and the already content. These women – and there are a lot of us – will be persistently reminded of the undesirability of their brand of meatiness, and of just how little the pleasure of going through life without bothering to contort oneself into a more readily acceptable version of femininity makes up for that unpleasant fact.' Eimear McBride, *Something Out of Place: Women and Disgust* (London: Profile, 2021). p. 119

32   '*If it is a gaffe to be plain*': Jane Shilling, *The Stranger in the Mirror* (London: Chatto & Windus, 2011). p. 56

34   '*I who was Snow White*': Elissa Melamed, *Mirror, Mirror: The Terror of Not Being Young* (New York: Linden Press, 1983). p. 10

35   '*your ultimate power and only protection*': *Snow White and the Huntsman*, screenplay by Evan Daugherty, John Lee Hancock

and Hossein Amini, directed by Rupert Sanders, Universal Pictures, 2012.

35   *'double standard of aging'*: Sontag. pp. 19–24

36   *'Men use women'*: *Snow White and the Huntsman*.

37   *Easier by far:* 'Easier by far to hate and reject a mother outright than to see beyond her to the forces acting upon her.' Adrienne Rich, *Of Woman Born: Motherhood as Experience and Institution* (New York: W. W. Norton & Company, 1986). p. 235

38   *memes relating to Hopkins:* Twitter <https://twitter.com/gerrygreek/status/1269988129701797889> [accessed 12 March 2021].

39   *Once upon a time getting a bad haircut:* Emma Rosemurgey, 'Woman Sobs after Paying £215 on Haircut That Leaves Her Looking "like a Karen"', *Mirror* <https://www.mirror.co.uk/news/weird-news/woman-sobs-after-paying-215-25011938> [accessed 24 September 2021].

39   *And woe betide: Mike Wade,* 'Edinburgh Fringe Audience "Harassed by Venue Employee" in Trans Row', *The Times* <https://www.thetimes.co.uk/article/edinburgh-fringe-audience-harassed-by-venue-employee-in-trans-row-90jk2tjpc> [accessed 28 August 2022].

39   *To be fair to the Dahl quote:* 'You can have a wonky nose and a crooked mouth and a double chin and stick-out teeth, but if you have good thoughts it will shine out of your face like sunbeams and you will always look lovely.' Roald Dahl, *The Twits* (London: Penguin, 2013). p. 7

39   *'to look fair and speak fair':* Marina Warner, *From the Beast to the Blonde: On Fairy Tales and Their Tellers* (London: Vintage, 1994). Chapter 3, Section III, para. 3

40   *'When the object of desire raised her voice':* Ibid.

40   *'ugly manly harridans':* Susan Devaney, 'This Is How Misogynists Tried to Stop Women from Winning the Vote', *Stylist* <https://www.stylist.co.uk/visible-women/misogynists-anti-suffragette-illustrations-stop-women-win-vote-history-features/187998> [accessed 14 March 2021].

40   *'It is still the case':* Beard. The Public Voice of Women, para. 17

40   *'I'm guessing late 50s':* Twitter <https://twitter.com/tellthetroof/status/1273310399631417345> [accessed 19 December 2020].

41   *'one of the organisers said of a small group of lesbians':* Julie Bindel, *Feminism for Women* (London: Constable, 2021). p. 123

41   *Twitter is awash with invective:* <https://twitter.com/xonicoleleigh/

status/1105758630652141568>,   <https://twitter.com/_
AAApple_/status/1202935936402608128>,   <https://twitter.
com/adele_leggett/status/931836754386145281>,   <https://
twitter.com/_kgee/status/1303445270114557955> [all accessed
19 September 2021].

41   *In her song 'Better Than You'*: Meghna Amin, 'Jordan Gray
        Praised for Truly Iconic (and NSFW) Friday Night Live
        Performance As She Ends Completely Naked: "What a Finale!"',
        Metro   <https://metro.co.uk/2022/10/21/friday-night-live-
        jordan-gray-praised-for-iconic-naked-performance-17614561/>
        [accessed 30 November 2022].

42   *'in medieval representations'*: Warner. Chapter 3, III, para. 12

42   *'the aged crowd of parts betrays the old woman'*: Sarah Alison
        Miller, *Medieval Monstrosity and the Female Body* (New York:
        Routledge, 2010). p. 23

43   *In 2020 the make-up artist Jason Adcock*: Rachael Dowd, 'This
        Karen Mask Might Be the Scariest Costume for Halloween
        2020', *Alternative Press* <https://www.altpress.com/news/
        karen-masks-2020-halloween/> [accessed 14 March 2021].

43   *'"Karen" is transcendent of all gender and size'*: Moore,
        'This "Karen" Mask Is Being Called the Scariest Halloween
        Costume of 2020'.

44   *Recent books with titles such as:* Jaya Saxena and Jess
        Zimmerman, *Basic Witches: How to Summon Success, Banish
        Drama, and Raise Hell with Your Coven* (Philadelphia: Quirk
        Books, 2017); Katie West and Jasmine Elliott, *Becoming
        Dangerous: Witchy Femmes, Queer Conjurers, and Magical
        Rebels* (Newburyport: Red Wheel, 2020).

44   *'At the nexus of the witch and slut identities'*: Sollée. p. 156

44   *'this is what forty looks like'*: '30th Anniversary Issue / Gloria
        Steinem: First Feminist', *New York Magazine* <https://nymag.
        com/nymetro/news/people/features/2438/> [accessed 12 March
        2021].

45   *'Amazing how different our view'*: Twitter <https://twitter.
        com/FloraEGill/status/1478323538478215168> [accessed 27
        June 2022].

46   *'New possibilities for women'*: Wolf, *The Beauty Myth*. p. 254

46   *slipshod in its use of statistics on anorexia*: Casper Shoemaker,
        'A Critical Appraisal of the Anorexia Statistics in *The Beauty
        Myth*: Introducing Wolf's Overdo and Lie Factor (WOLF)',
        Eating Disorders: The Journal of Treatment and Prevention,
        12:2 (2004).

46   *In its 2019 audit:* 'Cosmetic Surgery Stats: Number of
      Surgeries Remains Stable amid Calls for Greater Regulation
      of Quick Fix Solutions', British Association of Aesthetic
      Plastic Surgeons <https://baaps.org.uk/about/news/1708/
      cosmetic_surgery_stats_number_of_surgeries_remains_stable_
      amid_calls_for_greater_regulation_of_quick_fix_solutions/>
      [accessed 16 March 2021].

47   *'driven by the openness of celebrities':* Ibid.

47   *The US National Organization for Women did:* Patricia Cohen,
      In Our Prime: The Invention of Middle Age (New York: Simon
      & Schuster, 2012). p. 167

48   *'As you progress through the decades':* Moran, *How to Be a
      Woman.* p. 288

48   *'young and pretty women may delude themselves':* Germaine
      Greer, *The Female Eunuch* (London: Paladin, 1971). p. 268

48   *Moran backtracks on having 'work done':* Moran, *More Than
      a Woman.* p. 185

49   *'all angry at all the world':* Twitter <https://twitter.com/
      adele_leggett/status/931836754386145281> [accessed 19
      September 2021].

49   *'changes to facial features that happen naturally':* Phoebe Malz
      Bovy, 'The Curse of Miserable Older White Women', *UnHerd*
      <https://unherd.com/2022/08/the-curse-of-miserable-older-
      white-women> [accessed 29 August 2022].

50   *Nora Ephron wryly termed 'maintenance':* 'Maintenance is
      what they mean when they say, "after a certain point it's just
      patch patch patch".' 'On Maintenance', in Ephron. p. 31

50   Keep young and beautiful: Al Dubin, 'Keep Young and
      Beautiful', from the film *Roman Scandals* (1933).

50   *'the fact that women expend far more time':* Ann E. Gerike,
      'On Gray Hair and Oppressed Brains', *Journal of Women
      & Aging*, 2:2 (1990), pp. 35–46 <https://doi.org/10.1300/
      J074v02n02_05>. p. 38

51   *served 'as looking-glasses':* Virginia Woolf, *A Room Of One's
      Own and Three Guineas* (London: Collins, 2014). p. 33

51   *On the first Women's Liberation March:* Donna Ferguson,
      'The Day That Feminists Took "Women's Lib" to the
      Streets', *Observer* <https://www.theguardian.com/world/2018/
      mar/03/women-liberation-movement-first-march-remembered>
      [accessed 13 September 2021].

52   *'There's this really false idea':* Alex Peters, 'AOC Calls out the
      Patriarchy While Doing Her Make-up', *Dazed Beauty* <https://

www.dazeddigital.com/beauty/head/article/50222/1/aoc-calls-out-the-patriarchy-while-doing-her-make-up> [accessed 17 March 2021].

53 'All the fuss about femininity': Radcliffe Richards. p. 156
54 'The new feminist': Natasha Walter, The New Feminism (London: Virago, 1999). p. 184
54 'scapegoating of femininity': Serano is absolutely right that these are traditionally sexist notions – albeit about women themselves, not the femininity imposed on them. Julia Serano, Whipping Girl: A Transsexual Woman on Sexism and the Scapegoating of Femininity (New York: Seal Press, 2009). p. 5
54 'in those heady days': Henry. p. 124
54 'the old myths about feminists': Walter. p. 5
54 The original, solid feminist critique: '… the fondness for dress, conspicuous in women, may be easily accounted for, without supposing it the result of a desire to please the sex on which they are dependent'. Mary Wollstonecraft, A Vindication of the Rights of Men and A Vindication of the Rights of Woman (Cambridge: Cambridge University Press, 1999). p. 114
55 gender stereotyping in toys and marketing: Elizabeth Sweet, 'Toys Are More Divided by Gender Now Than They Were 50 Years Ago', The Atlantic <https://www.theatlantic.com/business/archive/2014/12/toys-are-more-divided-by-gender-now-than-they-were-50-years-ago/383556/> [accessed 1 November 2021].
55 'as close as she can to being a man', 'castrates': Reuben. p. 292; Wilson. p. 116
55 'From this perspective': Jacquelyn N. Zita, 'Heresy in the Female Body: The Rhetorics of Menopause', in Pearsall (ed.). p. 98
56 'trans women look more like women than they do': Twitter <https://twitter.com/6igantuar/status/1513454560827912194> [accessed 27 June 2022].
56 'In menopause, femininity strains': Steinke. p. 82
56 'an identity tenuously constituted in time': Judith Butler, Gender Trouble (New York: Routledge, 1990). p. 179
57 'The mythology of temptation': Greer, The Change. p. 363
57 'And she answered: Woman?!': Nors.
58 The tender coltishness: Shilling. p. 7
58 'beauty thus acts as a way of disrupting solidarity': Clare Chambers, Intact: A Defence of the Unmodified Body (London: Penguin, 2022). p. 16
58 'In an age that worshipped outward beauty': Anne Llewellyn

Barstow, *Witchcraze: A New History of the European Witch Hunts* (New York: HarperCollins, 1995). p. 137

59   *'the biggest online trolls'*: Walker, 'Middle-Aged Women Can Be the Worst Online Trolls'.

60   *'At some point, middle-aged women'*: Anonymous, 'Why Are the Biggest Trolls Middle-Aged Women?', *Telegraph* <https://www.telegraph.co.uk/women/life/biggest-trolls-middle-aged-women/> [accessed 2 November 2021].

60   *'Sure, I had bad thoughts'*: Walker, 'Middle-Aged Women Can Be the Worst Online Trolls'.

60   *If only we 'fucking cunting jealous cows'*: Twitter <https://twitter.com/romyromes__/status/1122257235688722433> [accessed 19 September 2021].

62   *According to the 2020 Women and Equalities Committee Body Image Survey:* 'Body Image Survey Results', Women and Equalities: House of Commons <https://publications.parliament.uk/pa/cm5801/cmselect/cmwomeq/805/80502.htm> [accessed 2 August 2021]

Chapter 2: Beastly Hag

64   *You can denounce me:* Suzanne Moore, 'Why I Had to Leave The Guardian', *UnHerd* <https://unherd.com/2020/11/why-i-had-to-leave-the-guardian/> [accessed 28 March 2021].

64   *... the traditional status conferred:* McBride. p. 21

65   *'the victim in ourselves'*: Rich. p. 236

65   *'I had no patience for my body'*: Marya Hornbacher, *Wasted: A Memoir of Anorexia and Bulimia* (New York: HarperCollins, 2009). p. 107

66   *'what you are if you assume'*: Maureen Freely, *What About Us? An Open Letter to the Mothers Feminism Forgot* (London: Bloomsbury, 1995). p. 49

67   *the point at which many of use become more invested:* '... the menopause has helped coalesce my thinking [...] I, for one, don't want to be silenced on that equality journey, just at the point where my biology reminds me that as a woman, choice is not always in our hands'. Mandy Rhodes, 'Trans Rights and the Menopause', *Holyrood* <https://www.holyrood.com/editors-column/view,trans-rights-and-the-menopause_10184.htm> [accessed 23 November 2020].

67   *'Outsmart Mother Nature'*: 'Tampax Pearl "outsmart Mother Nature" by Leo Burnett Milan', *Campaign* <https://www.campaignlive.co.uk/article/

tampax-pearl-outsmart-mother-nature-leo-burnett-milan/919105> [accessed 18 November 2020].

68   'her pinched face': Andrew Adam Newman, 'Ads for Tampax Erase a Layer of Euphemisms', *New York Times* <https://www.nytimes.com/2009/03/20/business/media/20adco.htmol> [accessed 24 March 2021].

68   'The body ... has been made so problematic': Rich. p. 40

69   'Feminism ... was always wrong to pretend': Camille Paglia, *Sex, Art, and American Culture* (London: Penguin, 1992). p. 89

69   'if it were up to nature': Laura Kipnis, 'Maternal Instincts', in Meghan Daum (ed.), *Selfish, Shallow and Self-Absorbed: Sixteen Writers on the Decision Not to Have Kids* (New York: Picador, 2015). p. 22

69   'To feel shame': McBride. p. 16

70   'Feminists ... have long avoided putting too much emphasis': Bindel. p. 131

70   'Heaven forbid it might be true': Elisa Albert, *After Birth* (London: Vintage, 2016). p. 139

72   'Motherhood ... is fearsome': Susan Maushart, *The Mask of Motherhood* (London: Pandora, 1999). p. 20

73   By the time they get to my age: 'Childbearing for Women Born in Different Years, England and Wales'.

73   'fifties throwback, maternal revivalist': Freely. p. 49

74   The sharp rise in recent years: Kim Elsesser, 'The Myth of Biological Sex', *Forbes* <https://www.forbes.com/sites/kimelsesser/2020/06/15/the-myth-of-biological-sex/?sh=3086292676b9> [accessed 8 November 2021]. Emma Hartley, 'Why Do so Many Teenage Girls Want to Change Gender?', *Prospect* <https://www.prospectmagazine.co.uk/magazine/tavistock-transgender-transition-teenage-girls-female-to-male> [accessed 8 November 2021].

74   Thousands of daughters: Rich. pp. 235–6

76   'is encouraged to see her body': Katrine Marçal, *Who Cooked Adam Smith's Dinner?* (London: Portobello, 2015). p. 64

76   'A man remains male': Wilson. p. 51

79   'No one calls the female whales roadkill': Steinke. p. 215

80   'increasingly feminists are told': Janice Turner, 'War of Words Risks Wiping Women from Our Language', *The Times* <https://www.thetimes.co.uk/article/war-of-words-risks-wiping-women-from-our-language-djhp2mwjg> [accessed 4 February 2021].

80   'what feminism needs': Martha Nussbaum, 'The Professor

of Parody', *The New Republic* <https://newrepublic.com/article/150687/professor-parody> [accessed 29 March 2021].

83   *'technological and industrial advances'*: Melanie Challenger, *How to Be Animal: A New History of What It Means to Be Human* (Edinburgh: Canongate, 2021). p. 12

83   *'An understanding of the bodies we inhabit'*: Susie Orbach, *Bodies* (London: Profile, 2019). Prologue, para. 3

84   *'To be human'*: Marçal. p. 36

85   *I felt as if I had slipped*: Naomi Wolf, *Misconceptions: Truth, Lies, and the Unexpected on the Journey to Motherhood* (New York: Vintage, 2011). p. 65

85   *'a civil rights and social justice issue'*: Mary Harrington, 'Staying Human in the Meat Lego Matrix', *Reactionary Feminist* <https://reactionaryfeminist.substack.com/p/staying-human-in-the-meat-lego-matrix> [accessed 11 November 2021].

85   *'Women ... because of their visceral'*: Challenger. p. 164; Christina Roylance, Andrew A. Abeyta and Clay Routledge, 'I Am Not an Animal but I Am a Sexist: Human Distinctiveness, Sexist Attitudes towards Women, and Perceptions of Meaning in Life', *Feminism and Psychology*, 26:3 (2016), pp. 368–77 <https://doi.org/10.1177/0959353516636906>.

86   *'so anti-aspirational'*: Michel Faber, 'A Great Divide?', *Guardian* <https://www.theguardian.com/books/2003/may/24/featuresreviews.guardianreview9> [accessed 10 November 2021].

87   *'enhanced by an ideology of sexist ageism'*: Zita. p. 96

88   *'Woman has ovaries, a uterus'*: Simone de Beauvoir, *The Second Sex* (London: Picador, 1988). p. 15

88   *'one is not born, but rather becomes, a woman'*: Ibid. p. 295

89   *of shrinking back, of reserving'*: Hilary Mantel, 'Some Girls Want Out', *London Review of Books* <https://www.lrb.co.uk/the-paper/v26/n05/hilary-mantel/some-girls-want-out> [accessed 13 February 2020].

89   *Language matters*: Deborah Cameron, 'The Illusion of Inclusion', *Language: A Feminist Guide* <https://debuk.wordpress.com/2018/08/05/the-illusion-of-inclusion/> [accessed 11 November 2021].

90   *'The thing I keep coming back to'*: Suzanne Moore, 'What Does the Keira Bell Case Tell Us?', *Letters from Suzanne* <https://suzannemoore.substack.com/p/what-does-the-keira-bell-case-tell?r=cldek&utm_campaign=post&utm_medium=web&utm_source=twitter> [accessed 28 March 2021].

91   *A common argument*: Robin Dembroff and Dee Payton,

'Why We Shouldn't Compare Transracial to Transgender Identity', *Boston Review* <http://bostonreview.net/race-philosophy-religion-gender-sexuality/robin-dembroff-dee-payton-why-we-shouldnt-compare> [accessed 5 August 2021].

91   *'discussions of women, gays and black people'*: Owen Jones, 'Stonewall Is Right to Bring Our Trans Brothers and Sisters in from the Cold', *Guardian* <https://www.theguardian.com/commentisfree/2015/feb/18/stonewall-trans-issues-neglected-progressives> [accessed 31 March 2021].

91   *'a world in which we have all the autonomy to make our own bodies'*: McKenzie Wark, 'Girls Like Us', *The White Review* <https://www.thewhitereview.org/feature/girls-like-us/> [accessed 25 January 2022].

93   *'it seems a pity to have a built-in rite of passage'*: Ursula K. Le Guin, 'The Space Crone', in Pearsall (ed.). p. 251

Chapter 3: Dirty Hag

94   *There would, in fact, be no youth culture:* Barbara Macdonald, 'Look Me in the Eye', from Barbara Macdonald and Cynthia Rich, *Look Me in the Eye: Old Women, Ageing and Ageism* (London: The Women's Press, 1984). p. 39

95   *The most online drama:* Sarah Ditum, 'The Sexism of the Conversation about Cleaners and Covid' *Spectator* <https://www.spectator.co.uk/article/the-sexism-of-the-conversation-about-cleaners-and-covid/> [accessed 8 August 2021].

96   *'the problem that has no name'*: Betty Friedan, *The Feminine Mystique* (London: Penguin, 1992).

97   *'sandwich generation'*: Calhoun. Chapter 3, para. 5

97   *culminating in headlines:* Linda Howard, 'Women Could Face £100,000 Pension Pot Shortfall Compared to Men – and Need to Work Longer', *Daily Record* <https://www.dailyrecord.co.uk/lifestyle/money/pension-shortfall-for-women-23627201> [accessed 7 August 2021]. Marianna Hunt, 'Women Will Be Poorer than Men in Retirement for Another 140 Years Due to the Pandemic', *Telegraph* <https://www.telegraph.co.uk/pensions-retirement/financial-planning/women-will-poorer-men-retirement-another-140-years-due-pandemic/> [accessed 24 November 2020].

97   *'On average women carry out 60 per cent more'*: 'Gender, Work and Care: Explaining Gender Inequality Across the UK', Office for National Statistics <https://bit.ly/2GWMo4D> [accessed 17 November 2021]

98   *more than twice as likely as men':* Ibid.

98   *'it is virtually always the woman':* Linda Scott, *The Double X Economy: The Epic Potential of Empowering Women* (London: Faber & Faber, 2020). p. 24

98   *'older women's challenges accumulate':* 'Tackling Social Norms: A Game Changer for Gender Inequalities', UNDP Human Development Reports <http://hdr.undp.org/en/content/> [accessed 21 April 2021].

98   *'are not so much savings':* Caroline Criado Perez, *Invisible Women: Exposing Data Bias in a World Designed for Men* (London: Vintage, 2019). p. 244

98   *Looking at mixed-sex couples:* Camille Landais and others, 'The Careers and Time Use of Mothers and Fathers', IFS report, 12 March 2021 <https://doi.org/10.1920/BN.IFS.2021.BN0319>. Haroon Siddique, 'Care Worker Shortage after Brexit "Will Force Women to Quit Jobs"', *Guardian* <https://www.theguardian.com/society/2018/aug/06/carer-shortage-after-brexit-will-force-women-to-quit-jobs> [accessed 21 April 2021]. Lee Peart, 'Social Care Facing "Perilously Uncertain Future" after Brexit', *Home Care Insight* <https://www.homecareinsight.co.uk/social-care-facing-perilously-uncertain-future-after-brexit/> [accessed 21 April 2021].

99   *'if you got a group of misogynists in a room':* 'Poverty Causing "misery" in UK, and Ministers Are in Denial, Says UN Official', *BBC News* <https://www.bbc.co.uk/news/uk-46236642> [accessed 17 November 2021].

100   *since debunked the idea (again) that women love cleaning:* Cordelia Fine, *Delusions of Gender* (London: Icon Books, 2010). Deborah Cameron, *The Myth of Mars and Venus* (Oxford: Oxford University Press, 2007).

101   *'gender is an identity':* Butler, *Gender Trouble.* p. 179

102   *'I too shall marry':* Rich. p. 219

104   *'The washing-up. Or the laundry':* Helen Lewis, 'Yes, There Is One Great Contribution Men Can Make to Feminism: Pick up a Mop', *Guardian* <https://www.theguardian.com/commentisfree/2016/jan/14/men-feminism-washing-up-unpaid-labour> [accessed 20 November 2020].

104   *'You know what men could do':* Twitter <https://twitter.com/giagia/status/1462047956174086146> [accessed 20 November 2021].

105   *In articles mocking:* 'Washington Post Opinions on Twitter: 'The Democratic Party Should Stop Wasting so Much Time on

the Lost Cause of Suburban Wine Moms and Start Listening to the Voices That Form the Core of the Party's Base, Writes @lyzl Https://T.Co/Kotrq8g7lm', Twitter <https://twitter.com/PostOpinions/status/1332692621052039172> [accessed 17 May 2021]. '4 Ways to Be As Confident As Someone's White Aunt on Facebook', *Reductress* <https://reductress.com/post/4-ways-to-be-as-confident-as-someones-white-aunt-on-facebook/> [accessed 26 March 2021].

105   *'leaky boobs and the school run'*: Brendan O'Neill, 'How the Trans Ideology Dehumanises Women', *Spiked* <https://www.spiked-online.com/2022/04/23/how-the-trans-ideology-dehumanises-women/> [accessed 27 June 2022].

106   *As the Women's Budget Group reports:* 'Gender, Work and Care: Explaining Gender Inequality Across the UK'.

107   *'high-low duality'*: David Baddiel, *Jews Don't Count* (London: HarperCollins, 2020). p. 114

108   *'Historically, black women'*: bell hooks, 'Revolutionary Parenting', in Andrea O'Reilly (ed.), *Maternal Theory: Essential Readings* (Bradford, Canada: Demeter Press, 2007). Para. 1

108   *'A mother ... typically takes as the criterion'*: Sara Ruddick, 'Maternal Thinking', in O'Reilly (ed.). Para. 5

108   *'Patriarchy ... depends on'*: Rich. p. 61

109   *'Feminist theory ... has a hard time with motherhood'*: Freely. p. 202

110   *Her elderly and confused father:* Giles Fraser, 'Why Won't Remainers Talk about Family?', *UnHerd* <https://unherd.com/2019/02/why-wont-remainers-talk-about-family/> [accessed 18 November 2020].

113   *'There would, in fact, be no youth culture'*: Macdonald, 'Look Me in the Eye'.

113   *Because although people ignore:* Interview with the author.

114   *'Being human ... is experienced precisely'*: Marçal. p. 154

115   *'an independent astronaut'*: Ibid. p. 148

115   *'embodies dependency at the same time she is trapped'*: Martha Albertson Fineman, *The Neutered Mother, the Sexual Family and Other Twentieth Century Tragedies* (London: Routledge, 1995). p. 72

115   *'The first is to be kind'*: Lev Raphael, 'Henry James' Killer Kindness Quote', *HuffPost* <https://www.huffpost.com/entry/a-killer-kindness-quote_b_9063666> [accessed 28 June 2022].

116   *The slogan 'Be kind':* 'Next "Be Kind" Underwear for Young Girls', Mumsnet <https://www.mumsnet.com/talk/

womens_rights/4573763-next-be-kind-underwear-for-young-girls> [accessed 28 June 2022].

116 *'an epidemic of #bekind'*: Suzanne Moore, 'The Kindest among Us Are the Quietest about It', *Telegraph* <https://www.telegraph.co.uk/women/life/kindest-among-usare-quietest/> [accessed 8 February 2021].

116 *'the entrenched belief that women exist primarily'*: Jane Caro, *Accidental Feminists* (Melbourne: Melbourne University Press, 2019). p. 52

116 *'Telling other people to be kind'*: Sarah Ditum, 'Why Snark Is Better than Smarm', *UnHerd* <https://unherd.com/2021/02/why-snark-is-better-than-smarm/> [accessed 4 February 2021].

117 *'much of traditional morality in our society'*: Mary Daly, *Beyond God the Father* (London: The Women's Press, 1986). pp. 100–1

117 *'I wanted to get some kindness out there'*: Annabel Nugent, 'Rupert Grint Reveals Why He Spoke out on JK Rowling's Transgender Row: "I Wanted to Get Some Kindness out There"', *Independent* <https://www.independent.co.uk/arts-entertainment/films/news/rupert-grint-jk-rowling-transgender-harry-potter-b1788500.html> [accessed 28 April 2021].

118 *many saw this as a cynical attempt:* Anna Coote, 'Cameron's "Big Society" Will Leave the Poor and Powerless Behind', *Guardian* <https://web.archive.org/web/20100722171727/http://www.guardian.co.uk/commentisfree/2010/jul/19/big-society-cameron-equal-opportunity> [accessed 28 April 2021].

119 *'a more primitive version of man'*: Barbara Ehrenreich and Deirdre English, *For Her Own Good: Two Centuries of the Experts' Advice to Women* (New York: Anchor, 2005). Chapter 1, para. 13

119 *There is in fact evidence:* 'Empathy Varies by Age and Gender: Women in Their 50s Are Tops', *ScienceDaily* <https://www.sciencedaily.com/releases/2013/01/130130184324.htm> [accessed 13 January 2021].

119 *'The thing about being a middle-aged woman'*: Interview with the author.

120 *'As little girls in our society'*: Maushart. p. 26

120 *'the old woman is one whose labor/energy'*: Baba Copper, 'The View from Over the Hill', in Pearsall (ed.). p. 126

120 *You're Janet, now:* Moran, *More Than a Woman*. p. 6

121 *But think about this:* Marilyn French, *The Women's Room* (London: Virago, 2007). p. 219

121 'asks for or tries to take': Manne. p. 131

122 'the whole education of women': Jean Jacques Rousseau and Williiam Payne, Émile (New York: D. Appleton and Company, 1918). p. 263

122 equivalent to corporate woke-washing: '... brands will gravitate towards low-cost, high-noise signals if these will be accepted as a substitute for genuine reform [...] In fact, let's go further: those with power inside institutions love splashy progressive gestures because they help preserve their power within the institution'. Helen Lewis, 'Woke Capitalism', The Bluestocking <https://helenlewis.substack.com/p/the-bluestocking-woke-capitalism> [accessed 16 December 2020].

123 In February 2021 the cross-party think tank Demos: Danny Kruger MP, 'A New Model of Social Care for England: The Care Commitment', 2021, Demos <www.demos.co.uk> [accessed 28 February 2021].

125 'the vanishing of social services': Judith Butler, 'Why Is the Idea of "Gender" Provoking Backlash the World over?', Guardian <https://www.theguardian.com/us-news/commentisfree/2021/oct/23/judith-butler-gender-ideology-backlash> [accessed 21 November 2021].

126 'in the same way that there is a "second sex"': Marçal. p. 16

127 In 2020 the impact of Covid-19 demonstrated: Helen Lock, 'Half of UK Women Say Progress on Gender Equality Is in Reverse Because of COVID-19', Global Citizen <https://www.globalcitizen.org/en/content/women-uk-gender-equality-backwards-covid-19/> [accessed 25 November 2022].

127 'it turns out, however women identify': Anna Ziggy Melamed, 'When the Mask Slips: Gendered Division of Labour in the Covid-19 Pandemic', The Radical Notion, 3 (spring 2021). p. 75.

127 as the pandemic showed: Joan Costa-Font, 'The Covid-19 Crisis Reveals How Much We Value Old Age', LSE Business Review <https://blogs.lse.ac.uk/businessreview/2020/04/15/the-covid-19-crisis-reveals-how-much-we-value-old-age/> [accessed 21 August 2021].

Chapter 4: Wrong Side of History Hag

129 That perhaps there has been no progress: Dale Spender, Women of Ideas (London: Pandora, 1988). p. 732

129 I can't believe I still have to protest this fucking shit: Alexandra Svokos, 'Viral Photo Of Woman's Abortion Protest

Sign Will Make You Laugh Then Cry', *Elite Daily* <https://www.elitedaily.com/news/politics/woman-abortion-protest-poland/1632496> [accessed 16 October 2021].

131 *'masculinity in crisis':* Justine Picardie, 'Men Who Moan Too Much', *Independent* <https://www.independent.co.uk/lifestyle/men-who-moan-too-much-1575321.html> [accessed 22 August 2021].

131 *lives ruined by false rape accusations:* This particular case, in which male student was acquitted of rape having had his lawyer use as 'evidence' the fact that the accuser had been nominated 'slut of the year' by fellow students, has always stayed with me. 'Student Cleared in Rape Case', *Independent* <https://www.independent.co.uk/news/uk/student-cleared-in-rape-case-1501534.html> [accessed 22 August 2021].

132 *headlines warning of the virtual decriminalisation of rape:* Haroon Siddique, 'We Are Facing the "Decriminalisation of Rape", Warns Victims' Commissioner', *Guardian* <https://www.theguardian.com/society/2020/jul/14/we-are-facing-the-decriminalisation-of-warns-victims-commissioner> [accessed 23 August 2021].

134 *'The mother-in-law figure of my youth':* Caro. p. 35

135 *'society has moved on a lot since then':* Nadia Khomami, 'I Would Not Play Black Person in Remade Little Britain, Says Matt Lucas', *Guardian* <https://www.theguardian.com/tv-and-radio/2017/oct/03/matt-lucas-little-britain-remake-would-not-play-black-character> [accessed 28 August 2021].

136 *'the never-ending jibes against menopausal women':* Greer, *The Change.* p. 28

136 *'What, exactly, [do] the directors':* Hadley Freeman, 'Mother-in-Law Jokes a Thing of the Past? Not at Pixar', *Guardian* <https://www.theguardian.com/commentisfree/2021/jan/23/mother-in-law-jokes-a-thing-of-the-past-not-at-pixar-soul-hadley-freeman?CMP=Share_iOSApp_Other> [accessed 25 January 2021].

138 *'Do you think':* Newsnight, BBC Two, 10 December 2020 <https://www.bbc.co.uk/programmes/m000q5ys> [accessed 16 May 2021].

138 *a piece she had written:* Suzanne Moore, 'Women Must Have the Right to Organise. We Will Not Be Silenced', *Guardian* <https://www.theguardian.com/society/commentisfree/2020/mar/02/women-must-have-the-right-to-organise-we-will-not-be-silenced> [accessed 28 March 2021].

138   *an open letter:* Charlotte Tobitt, 'Suzanne Moore Leaves
       Guardian Months after Staff Send Letter of Revolt
       over "Transphobic Content"', *Press Gazette* <https://www.
       pressgazette.co.uk/suzanne-moore-leaves-guardian-months-
       after-staff-send-letter-of-revolt-over-transphobic-content/>
       [accessed 28 August 2021].

139   *'insecure because a new generation of leftists':* Moore, 'Why I
       Had to Leave The Guardian'.

139   *'Change, youth, and novelty':* Melamed, *Mirror, Mirror.* p. 32

140   *'we can expect a progression towards betterness':* Oliver
       Burkeman, 'The Wrong Side of History Has Become a Crowded
       Place. Time to Rethink', *Guardian* <https://www.theguardian.
       com/lifeandstyle/2019/jun/21/the-wrong-side-of-history-
       has-become-a-crowded-place-time-to-rethink> [accessed 11
       December 2020].

140   *'all attitudes, beliefs and behaviours change':* Bobby Duffy,
       Generations: Does When You're Born Shape Who You Are?
       (London: Atlantic, 2021). p. 14

141   *'The importance of lifecycle effects':* Ibid. p. 214

141   *Until last June:* Andrew Billen, 'Why It's Time to Join
       Generation Woke', *The Times* <https://www.thetimes.co.uk/
       article/why-its-time-to-join-generation-woke-8xmfx3xn8>
       [accessed 20 March 2021].

144   *'student-age women':* Gloria Steinem, *Outrageous Acts and
       Everyday Rebellions* (New York: Open Road Integrated Media,
       2012). p. 230

144   *'conned into believing':* Ibid. p. 234

144   *'a young woman's most radical act':* Ibid. p. 236

145   *'I will not,' he told me:* Billen.

146   *As Andrea S. Kramer and Alton B. Harris reported:* 'Are
       U.S. Millennial Men Just as Sexist as Their Dads?', *Harvard
       Business Review* <https://hbr.org/2016/06/are-u-s-millennial-
       men-just-as-sexist-as-their-dads> [accessed 13 May 2021].

146   *Research in 2020 by the UK Hope not Hate charitable
       trust:* Sabrina Barr, 'Half of Generation Z Men "Think
       Feminism Has Gone Too Far and Makes It Harder for Men
       to Succeed"', *Independent* <https://www.independent.co.uk/
       life-style/women/feminism-generation-z-men-women-hope-not-
       hate-charity-report-a9652981.html> [accessed 13 May 2021].

146   *The 2020 UN Human Development report:* 'Tackling Social
       Norms: A Game Changer for Gender Inequalities'.

146   *'Painting all young people as battling':* Duffy. p. 135

147 *'To hell with the simplistic notion'*: '"Goodbye to All That,"
     by Robin Morgan (1970)', *Fair Use Blog* <http://blog.fair-use.
     org/2007/09/29/goodbye-to-all-that-by-robin-morgan-1970/>
     [accessed 21 December 2020].
147 *'There is no guarantee'*: Rich. p. 274
148 *In* Agewise: 'Whatever happens in the body, and even if nothing
     happens in the body, aging is a narrative,' writes Gullette.
     She describes an 'entire decline system – innocent absorption
     of cultural signals, youthful age anxiety, middle-ageism,
     ageisim – infiltrating our system from top to bottom'. Margaret
     Morganroth Gullette, *Agewise: Fighting the New Ageism in
     America* (Chicago: University of Chicago Press, 2011). p. 5
148 *'smooth continuity'*, *'in ruins'*: Wilson. p. 51
148 *'the old-fashioned women'*: *Ricky Gervais: SuperNature*,
     written by Ricky Gervais, directed by John L. Spencer,
     Netflix, 2022.
149 *'female oppression ... is innately connected'*: Moore, 'Women
     Must Have the Right to Organise'.
150 *'when you boil down a lot of UK political discourse'*: Twitter
     <https://twitter.com/OwenJones84/status/136856797210577
     7154> [accessed 7 March 2021].
150 *'while Generation X ages'*: Henry. p. 34
152 *'brought to mind a Bratz doll'*: Marina Strinkovsky, 'From the
     Ashes of Every Woman, an Everywoman', *The Radical Notion*
     <https://theradicalnotion.org/from-the-ashes-of-every-woman-
     an-everywoman/> [accessed 20 August 2021].
152 *'She has to be naked'*: Robert Dex, 'Artist Maggi Hambling
     Says Critics of Mary Wollstonecraft Sculpture "Missed the
     Point"', *Evening Standard* <https://www.standard.co.uk/
     news/uk/mary-wollstonecraft-naked-sculture-maggi-hambling-
     b63158.html> [accessed 6 September 2021].
152 *According to Mary on the Green:* Geraldine Kendall Adams,
     'Nude Sculpture Dedicated to Mary Wollstonecraft Divides
     Feminist Opinion', Museums Association <https://www.
     museumsassociation.org/museums-journal/news/2020/11/
     nude-sculpture-dedicated-to-mary-wollstonecraft-divides-
     feminist-opinion/#> [accessed 6 September 2021].
152 *dying that most female of deaths:* This is not just some
     historical aside, the kind of thing that would only happen
     to non-pristine Woman Past. According to the World
     Health Organization, 'every day in 2017, approximately 810
     women died from preventable causes related to pregnancy

and childbirth'. 'Maternal Mortality' <https://www.who.int/news-room/fact-sheets/detail/maternal-mortality> [accessed 23 December 2021].

153   'women have basically done fuck all': Moran, How to Be a Woman. pp. 134, 138

154   'women are over, without having even begun': Ibid. p. 135

154   'Women ... are no longer taking a back seat': Twitter <https://twitter.com/UN_Women/status/1368767188706983936> [accessed 8 March 2021].

154   'We raved, we broke down barriers': Eleanor Mills, 'A Woman's Life Doesn't End at 40 – so Why Does Society Make Us Feel That Way?', Guardian <https://amp.theguardian.com/commentisfree/2021/mar/13/woman-life-doesnt-end-40?__twitter_impression=true> [accessed 13 March 2021].

155   'We need to know how patriarchy works': Spender, Women of Ideas. p. 23

156   'beacon lights of what may be attained': Matilda Joslyn Gage, 'Matilda Joslyn Gage Speech at the National Woman's Rights Convention, 1852', National Susan B. Anthony Museum and House <https://susanb.org/wp-content/uploads/2018/12/Matilda-Joslyn-Gage-Syracuse-NY-1852.pdf> [accessed 26 August 2021].

156   'that history was a process of gradual improvement': Spender, Women of Ideas. p. 316

157   To women who believed that the barriers against them: Ibid. pp. 317–18

157   'Many women resist feminism': Andrea Dworkin, Our Blood: Prophecies and Discourses on Sexual Politics (New York: Perigee, 1981). p. 78

Chapter 5: Frigid Hag

159   But surely, we do not want: Stella Browne, 'The Sexual Variety and Variability among Women', British Society for the Study of Sex Psychology, 1917.

159   Women know too much: Rob Warner, Faking It: Jimmy Savile, discovery+, 2020.

160   'an open mouth': Louise Perry, 'Review: Females by Andrea Long Chu', The Critic <https://thecritic.co.uk/issues/january-2020/sissy-porn-and-trans-dirty-laundry/> [accessed 28 May 2021].

161   'the frump at the back of the room': Ariel Levy, Female Chauvinist Pigs (London: Simon & Schuster, 2005). p. 92

162   'the threat [...] posed to male pleasure': Sheila Jeffreys, The

Spinster and Her Enemies (Boston: Pandora, 1985). p. 192

162   '*Can a woman dress like a mannequin*': Walter. p. 76

163   '*As a woman*': Samantha Wood, '"As a Woman, I Don't Feel I Can Own up to Loving Sex": The Taboos That Still Need Breaking', *Guardian* <https://www.theguardian.com/the-last-taboo/2021/may/18/as-a-woman-i-dont-feel-i-can-own-up-to-loving-sex-the-taboos-that-still-need-breaking> [accessed 28 November 2021].

164   '*As the #MeToo stories*': Bindel. p. 51

164   *When I see headlines*: Christina Knight, '#MeTOO – You Will Remember This as a Revolution! – International Alliance of Women', International Alliance of Women <https://www.womenalliance.org/metoo-you-will-remember-this-as-a-revolution/> [accessed 29 November 2021]. Ginia Bellafante, 'The #MeToo Movement Changed Everything. Can the Law Catch Up?', *New York Times* <https://www.nytimes.com/2018/11/21/nyregion/metoo-movement-schneiderman-prosecution.html> [accessed 29 November 2021].

166   '*The 2000s were a very long time ago*': Sirin Kale, '"I Was Worried Lindsay, Paris or Britney Would Die": Why the 00s Were so Toxic for Women', *Guardian* <https://www.theguardian.com/culture/2021/mar/06/why-the-00s-were-so-toxic-for-women> [accessed 7 March 2021].

166   *a young woman might not find it safe to say*: Maddy Mussen, 'We've Been Shaming Women for Being "vanilla" for Years and It Needs to Stop', *The Tab* <https://thetab.com/uk/2021/02/04/weve-been-shaming-women-for-being-vanilla-for-years-and-it-needs-to-stop-193777> [accessed 21 May 2021].

166   '*Many daughters live in rage*': Rich. p. 243

169   '*I can think of no feminist*': Henry. p. 91

169   '*rather than seeing themselves as part*': Ibid. p. 110

169   '*from the failures of men*': Tad Friend, 'Yes.', *Esquire*, 1 February 1994 <https://classic.esquire.com/article/1994/2/1/yes> [accessed 10 September 2021].

170   '*proclaiming victimhood doesn't help project strength*': Katie Roiphe, *The Morning After: Sex, Fear, and Feminism* (Boston: Little, Brown, 1993). p. 44

170   *contemporary warnings*: Alison Phipps, 'Tackling Sexual Harassment and Violence in Universities: Seven Lessons from the UK', *Genders, Bodies, Politics* <https://genderate.wordpress.com/2021/02/05/seven-lessons/> [accessed 7 February 2021].

170   '*set a trap with tears*': Jessica O'Leary, '"Where There Are

Many Women There Are Many Witches": The Social and Intellectual Understanding of Femininity in the *Malleus Maleficarum* (1486)', *Reinvention: An International Journal of Undergraduate Research*, 6:1 <https://warwick.ac.uk/ fac/cross_fac/iatl/reinvention/archive/volume6issue1/oleary/> [accessed 30 November 2021].

170   *In the mid-eighties Andrea Dworkin noted:* '"Well, what we'll do is that we will allow you to have an abortion right as long as you remain sexually accessible to us. And if you withdraw that accessibility and start talking this crap about an autonomous women's movement, we will collapse any support that we have ever given you: monetary, political, social, anything we have ever given you for the right to abortion. Because if your abortion right is not going to mean sexual accessibility for us, girls, you can't have it." And that's what they've been doing to us for the last fifteen years.' Andrea Dworkin, 'Woman-Hating Right and Left', in Dorchen Leidholt and Janice Raymond (eds), *The Sexual Liberals and the Attack on Feminism* (New York: Teachers College Press, 1987). p. 29.

170   *Today one sees the left use similar arguments:* Jennifer Finney Boylan, 'Abortion Rights and Trans Rights Are Two Sides of the Same Coin', *New York Times* <https://www. nytimes.com/2021/10/10/opinion/trans-abortion-rights.html> [accessed 30 November 2021].

170   *In many instances, progress:* David Smith, 'US Supreme Court Agrees to Consider Major Rollback of Abortion Rights', *Guardian* <https://www.theguardian.com/law/2021/may/17/ abortion-case-supreme-court-threatens-roe-v-wade> [accessed 30 November 2021].

171   *as Julie Bindel documents:* Bindel. pp. 25, 32, 42

171   *'When I was a teenager':* Victoria Richards, 'A Man Asked If He Could "Slap" and "Spit on Me" – We Need to Stop Normalising Sexual Violence against Women', *Independent* <https://www.independent.co.uk/voices/sexual-violence- choking-dating-apps-consent-b1790669.html> [accessed 7 February 2021].

171   *Hardcore porn is shaping the defences:* Taylor.

171   *'changing what is normal':* Harriet Grant, 'How Extreme Porn Has Become a Gateway Drug into Child Abuse', *Guardian* <https://www.theguardian.com/global-development/2020/ dec/15/how-extreme-porn-has-become-a-gateway-drug-into- child-abuse> [accessed 5 February 2021].

174   'as anti-sex, prudish': Jeffreys. p. 195

174   'the Puritan camp': Andrea Dworkin, *Intercourse* (New York: Basic Books, 2008). Preface, para. 10

175   'if I condemn pornography': Lori Day, 'Aging While Female Is Not Your Worst Nightmare', *Feminist Current* <https://www.feministcurrent.com/2015/03/10/aging-while-female-is-not-your-worst-nightmare-2/> [accessed 14 September 2021].

176   *In a 2021 lecture for the Scottish PEN Women Writers Committee:* Jenny Lindsay, 'Women's Rights and Women's Writing in a Digital Age', *Bella Caledonia* <https://bellacaledonia.org.uk/2021/02/13/womens-rights-and-womens-writing-in-a-digital-age/> [accessed 13 February 2021].

176   '"progressives" have rewritten': Bindel. p. 26

177   'cold women [who] have a perfect mania': Browne.

177   'the problematic aspects of Victorian maternal protectionism': Faludi, 'American Electra'. pp. 35–6

178   *The pro-sex camp:* Jeffreys. p. 194

178   *Women and girls are the objects:* Ibid. pp. 6–7

179   *Criticising lad mags:* Caron Lindsay, 'Is It Time for Retailers to Lose the Lads' Mags?', *Liberal Democrat Voice* <https://www.libdemvoice.org/is-it-time-for-retailers-to-lose-the-lads-mags-34670.html> [accessed 3 December 2021]. Sean Sutherland, 'OPINION: Pornhub Ban Doesn't Help, Only Harms Sex Workers', *Spoke* <https://spokeonline.com/2021/01/opinion-pornhub-ban-doesnt-help-only-harms-sex-workers/> [accessed 3 December 2021]. Edie Miller, 'Why Is British Media so Transphobic?', *The Outline* <https://theoutline.com/post/6536/british-feminists-media-transphobic?zd=3&zi=6lt4ecvs> [accessed 8 June 2021]. Nick Duffy, 'Mhairi Black Hits Back at Critics of School's Drag Queen Story Time', *Pink News* <https://www.pinknews.co.uk/2020/02/24/mhairi-black-drag-queen-story-time-glencoats-primary-school-flow-snp/> [accessed 3 December 2021].

180   *In a showdown in the final episode:* Patrick Mulkern, 'Russell T Davies on It's A Sin Ending', *Radio Times* <https://www.radiotimes.com/tv/drama/russell-t-davies-its-a-sin-exclusive/> [accessed 3 December 2021].

180   'entrenched in bigotry': 'An Open Letter to All Broadcast Commissioners, Production Companies & Wider Media', MrsNickyClark.com <http://www.mrsnickyclark.com/-5050from45.html> [accessed 8 December 2022].

180   *Davies has said that had the series been longer:* Louisa Mellor,

'It's a Sin: The Single Line That Hints at a Tragic, Unspoken Backstory', *Den of Geek* <https://www.denofgeek.com/tv/its-a-sin-the-single-line-that-hints-at-a-tragic-unspoken-backstory/> [accessed 3 December 2021].

181   *'One of the favourite myths to be propagated'*: Jeffreys. p. 197

181   *'from the spiteful old hag'*: Sollée. p. 11

181   *'Like the witches of legend'*: Ibid. p. 81

182   *In a 2021 article:* Megan Nolan, 'The Rise in Cosmetic Procedures Troubles Me – And It Shouldn't Be Anti-Feminist to Say So', *New Statesman* <https://www.newstatesman.com/politics/feminism/2021/04/rise-cosmetic-procedures-troubles-me-and-it-shouldn-t-be-anti-feminist-say> [accessed 26 May 2021].

186   *'new generations are more proficient'*: Duffy. p. 85

186   *'a parody of the hysteria'*: '"Brass Eye" Paedophilia (TV Episode 2001)', IMDb <https://www.imdb.com/title/tt0330093/> [accessed 29 May 2021].

187   *'it is very tempting to take the side'*: Judith Herman, *Trauma and Recovery* (New York: Basic Books, 2015). p. 7

187   *'We do not really want to know'*: Bessel van der Kolk, *The Body Keeps the Score* (London: Penguin, 2014). p. 11

187   *'powder keg provocation'*: Tim Robey, 'Cuties, Netflix Review: A Provocative Powder-Keg for an Age Terrified of Child Sexuality', *Telegraph* <https://www.telegraph.co.uk/films/0/cuties-netflix-reviewa-provocative-powder-keg-age-terrified/> [accessed 29 May 2021].

188   *'It is no coincidence'*: Helen Walsh, 'So Older Women Don't Have Sex?', *Guardian* <https://www.theguardian.com/commentisfree/2014/apr/13/so-older-women-dont-have-sex> [accessed 28 May 2021].

188   *When, for instance, older women objected:* Dr Em, 'Why Are We Allowing "The Family Sex Show"?', *The Critic* <https://thecritic.co.uk/why-are-we-allowing-the-family-sex-show/> [accessed 30 June 2022].

189   *'Children aren't anxious about the idea'*: Catherine Bennett, 'Beware! Having an Opinion about Sex While Growing Old Has Now Become a Crime', *Guardian* <https://www.theguardian.com/commentisfree/2022/apr/24/beware-having-opinion-on-sexually-inappropriate-theatre-age-you-10-years?CMP=share_btn_tw> [accessed 27 June 2022].

189   *'the most despised and dispensable person'*: Twitter <https://twitter.com/HJoyceGender/status/1355280954496057358> [accessed 7 February 2021].

189   'When anyone stood up to Savile': Louise Perry, 'What
      Mary Whitehouse Got Right', *UnHerd* <https://unherd.
      com/2020/10/what-mary-whitehouse-got-right/> [accessed 18
      November 2020].
190   *In a 1995 update*: '... confronting this abuse and healing its
      effects rarely begin until young women are no longer dependent
      on their families. If the abuse has been severe, this may require
      many years of distance and safety, or begin only after the death
      of the parent or other abuser'. Steinem. p. 238
190   'Now I know I'm a victim': 'Jimmy Savile Whistleblower
      Relives Abuse Ordeal', *Lorraine* <https://www.itv.com/lorraine/
      articles/jimmy-savile-whistleblower-releases-new-memoir>
      [accessed 30 May 2021].
190   *There's a scene in Emma Cline's novel*: Emma Cline, *The Girls*
      (London: Chatto & Windus, 2016). pp. 262–3
192   'Sasha said you told her so': Ibid. p. 263
193   'Who was going to win the daughter?': Faludi, 'American
      Electra'. p. 39
194   'You want it to be true that you're free': Interview with
      the author

Chapter 6: Plotting Hag

196   *Feminism is a socialist*: Associated Press, 'Robertson Letter
      Attacks Feminists', *New York Times* <https://www.nytimes.
      com/1992/08/26/us/robertson-letter-attacks-feminists.html>
      [accessed 15 October 2021].
196   *The mums on Mumsnet's women's rights forum*: Katie J.
      M. Baker, 'The Road to Terfdom', *Lux Magazine* <https://
      lux-magazine.com/article/the-road-to-terfdom/> [accessed 19
      April 2021].
197   'mean girl behaviour is hardwired': Barbara McMahon, 'The
      Science of Being a Bitch', *The Times* <https://www.thetimes.
      co.uk/article/the-science-of-being-a-bitch-gfg50wk25p9>
      [accessed 20 September 2021].
199   'where there are many women': *Malleus Maleficarum* <https://
      pages.uoregon.edu/dluebke/Witches442/442Malleus
      Maleficarum.html> [accessed 23 December 2020].
199   'all women without men': Barstow. p. 142
200   'Part of having a resistance': Dworkin, 'Woman-Hating Right
      and Left'.
202   *Two hundred years ago*: Albert. p. 173
203   'the sense of identity, purpose': Friedan. p. 182.

204   *'they started not to have a good time'*: Dworkin, 'Woman-Hating Right and Left'.

204   *ridiculed as deluded:* As the *Daily Mail*'s Liz Jones memorably put it, 'women have again been duped into thinking the world exists in their tiny, safe, fragrant homes, that life revolves around burps. They might just as well don a burka, and shuffle, so narrow is their vision'. Liz Jones, 'Free? You Blogging Mums May as Well Wear Burkas', *Daily Mail* <https://www.dailymail.co.uk/debate/article-2231184/Free-You-blogging-mums-wear-Burkas.html> [accessed 16 October 2021].

204   *'prosecco 4Chan'*: Mary Harrington, 'Trans Activism Has Mummy Issues', *UnHerd* <https://unherd.com/2021/09/the-trans-war-on-motherhood/> [accessed 9 December 2021].

204   *'a transphobic swamp'*: Rebecca Jane Morgan, 'Mumsnet: How Poor Moderation Created a Transphobic Swamp', *An Injustice!* <https://aninjusticemag.com/mumsnet-how-poor-moderation-created-a-transphobic-swamp-adf391ccf9fc> [accessed 13 December 2021].

206   *'contrary to popular opinion'*: Sarah Pedersen, *The Politicisation of Mumsnet* (Bingley: Emerald, 2020). Introduction, para. 1

207   *'Men Talk'*: Liz Lochhead, *True Confessions & New Cliches* (Edinburgh: Polygon, 1985). p. 134

207   *'women are intellectually like children'*: O'Leary.

207   *Articles denouncing the evils of Mumsnet:* Miller, 'Why Is British Media so Transphobic?'; Baker.

208   *'It is women who "gossip"'*: Silvia Federici, *Witches, Witch-Hunting and Women* (Oakland: PM Press, 2018). Chapter 5, para. 2

208   *'Madams with nothing better to do'*: Pedersen, *The Politicisation of Mumsnet*. Legal issues, para. 1

208   *'only the willingness'*: Rich. p. 16

209   *Men may talk politics:* Spender, *Women of Ideas*. p. 549

210   *They'd been described as 'belligerent harpies'*: Caroline Blackwood, *On The Perimeter* (New York: Penguin, 1985). p. 1

211   *'flock[ing] together in small groups'*: Wilson. pp. 102–3

211   *'depicts the feared sites'*: Warner. Chapter 3, II, para. 17

212   *gossiping 'at the lying-in'*: No, me neither, but to the fevered male imagination, this was definitely A Thing: 'At Child-bed when the Gossips meet, / Fine stories we are told; / and if they get a Cup too much, / Their Tongue, they cannot hold'. Ibid. Chapter 3, II, para. 18

212   *Because they feel as though they do not:* Dale Spender,

Nattering on the Net (North Melbourne: Spinifex Press, 1995). p. 225

212 *can no longer even advertise Flora:* Daniel Farey-Jones, 'Flora Pulls out of Mumsnet Partnership after Transphobia Complaints', *PR Week* <https://www.prweek.com/article/1662358/flora-pulls-mumsnet-partnership-transphobia-complaints> [accessed 16 December 2021].

213 *'being pregnant, giving birth':* Baker.

213 *'torching her reputation':* Twitter <https://twitter.com/EoinHiggins_/status/1470408198444261387> [accessed 14 December 2021].

213 *'Back when I first started working':* Twitter <https://twitter.com/EmilieCope91/status/1470720994230910978> [accessed 14 December 2021].

213 *'What kind of subversive repetition':* Butler, *Gender Trouble.* p. 42

214 *operating 'within the matrix of power':* Ibid. p. 40

214 *'known primarily as a place':* Amelia Tait, 'Mumsnet Moderators Are Struggling to Find the Line between Free Speech and Transphobia', *Wired UK* <https://www.wired.co.uk/article/mumsnet-moderators-trans-rights-debate> [accessed 13 December 2021].

214 *'most of the women':* Wollstonecraft. p. 115

215 *Facebook Aunts:* 'Facebook Launches New "Block Aunts" Feature', *Reductress* <https://reductress.com/post/facebook-launches-new-block-aunts-function/> [accessed 17 December 2021].

217 *This is not what happened:* Michael Savage, 'Labour Candidates Called on to Justify Transphobia Claims', *Guardian* <https://www.theguardian.com/politics/2020/feb/16/labour-candidates-called-on-to-justify-transphobia-claims> [accessed 17 December 2021].

217 *The group has since been subject:* Alix Culbertson and Sophie Morris, 'Labour Conference: Rosie Duffield Appears at Non-Official Fringe Event in Brighton despite Saying She Was Warned to Stay Away on Security Advice', *Sky News* <https://news.sky.com/story/labour-conference-rosie-duffield-appears-at-non-official-fringe-event-in-brighton-despite-saying-she-was-warned-to-stay-away-on-security-advice-12420726> [accessed 17 December 2021].

218 *Women are not trusted to act independently:* In her memoir *Walking to Greenham*, Greenham Common organiser Ann

Pettitt recalls a conversation with a male Labour party activist about the first march in 1981. He cannot believe the women are working alone: 'Because this thing you're talking about, this march thing, is too big to be just ordinary women, like you say you are, doing it. There must be some organisation behind you – I just don't believe you're acting on your own, that's not possible'. Ann Pettitt, *Walking to Greenham: How the Peace Camp Began and the Cold War Ended* (Aberystwyth: Honno, 2006). Chapter 6, para. 7

218   *'a nominally egalitarian society'*: Joanna Russ, *How to Suppress Women's Writing* (Austin: University of Texas Press, 2018). p. 3
218   *'She couldn't have written it'*: Ibid. p. 42
219   *'movement for gender liberation'*: Baker.
219   *'a sense of isolation'*: Ibid.
220   *Covens are where middle-aged women:* Moran, *More Than a Woman.* p. 267
222   *'formed in parallel and as a response to exclusion'*: Pedersen, *The Politicisation of Mumsnet.* Introduction, para. 22
222   *'The deliberate withdrawal of women'*: Rich. p. 105
223   *'differences in power are always manifested'*: Marilyn Frye, 'Some Reflections on Separatism and Power', *Feminist Reprise* <http://feminist-reprise.org/library/resistance-strategy-and-struggle/some-reflections-on-separatism-and-power/> [accessed 19 January 2021].
224   *'women have very little idea of how much'*: Greer, *The Female Eunuch.* p. 263
225   *'Women whisper'*: Dworkin, *Intercourse.* Preface, para. 5
225   *'To be a woman'*: Marina Strinkovsky, 'Radfem Panic: When Demands for Inclusivity Are a Cover for Moral Disgust', *It's Not a Zero Sum Game* <http://notazerosumgame.blogspot.com/2014/09/radfem-panic-when-demands-for.html> [accessed 9 December 2020].
228   *'Once your social currency to men'*: Twitter <https://twitter.com/janesoyp/status/1432846275431452676> [accessed 17 December 2021].

Chapter 7: Privileged Hag
230   *This dominance of men:* Dworkin, *Intercourse.* Chapter 1, para. 24
230   *Please don't call the manager:* Twitter <https://twitter.com/elonmusk/status/1470858546153762819> [accessed 21 December 2021].

231   *The recent popularisation:* Samantha Turnbull, 'How Not to Be a "Karen"', ABC Everyday <https://www.abc.net.au/everyday/how-not-to-be-a-karen/11806882> [accessed 13 January 2021].

233   *turned out to be entirely fabricated:* Leon Watson, 'Elan Gale Thanksgiving Note Battle Played out over Twitter Was a Hoax', *Daily Mail* <https://www.dailymail.co.uk/news/article-2517314/Elan-Gale-Thanksgiving-note-battle-played-Twitter-hoax.html> [accessed 27 April 2021].

234   *When interviewed about why he invented:* Ibid.

234   *chooses to use to make a 'hyperbolic point':* Joanna Stern, 'Why Elan Gale Made Up an Epic 'Note War' on a Thanksgiving Flight', ABC News <https://abcnews.go.com/Technology/elan-gale-made-epic-note-war-thanksgiving-flight/story?id=21099585> [accessed 19 January 2021].

235   *'ladies who lunch':* Paris Lees, 'Ban Sex Work? Fuck Off, White Feminism', *Vice* <https://www.vice.com/sv/article/nn97vk/ban-sex-work-fuck-off-white-feminism-paris-lees-807> [accessed 27 December 2021].

236   *Lees self-identifies as a feminist:* 'I am both white and a feminist. But I am not what you could call a White Feminist, capital letters.' Ibid.

236   *'Some men find it impossible':* Bindel. p. 78

236   *'to use the fact that all white women':* Sonia Sodha, '"White Feminists" are Under Attack from Other Women. There Can Only Be One Winner – Men', *Guardian* <https://www.theguardian.com/commentisfree/2021/sep/26/white-feminists-are-under-attack-from-other-women-here-can-only-be-one-winner--men> [accessed 26 September 2021].

237   *'The stereotype of the Bad Woman':* 'Blame-the-Woman Syndrome', *Washington Post* <https://www.washingtonpost.com/archive/lifestyle/wellness/1994/12/06/blame-the-woman-syndrome/50095e32-280a-441f-94d4-60c7c73eb11a/> [accessed 20 September 2021].

237   *A 2003 New Statesman article:* 'Of "middle-class man" or "father", we hear less, they presumably having taken new Labour's words to heart and, with toffs and blokes, melted into a homogenous, back-slapping football crowd. How strange, then, that their wives and girlfriends are frequently perceived as marooned on an island of anachronistic class privilege.' Barbara Gunnell, 'Thoroughly Bad Behaviour: What's Behind Our Hatred of Middle Class Woman?', *New Statesman*

<https://www.newstatesman.com/node/197963> [accessed 23 December 2020].

237 *Karen 'whips up antipathy'*: 'Blame-the-Woman-Syndrome'.

237 *'Blaming the woman offers quick relief'*: Ibid.

238 *As a baby name, Karen*: Keith Griffith, 'Fewer Newborn Girls in the US Were given the Name Karen in 2020 than in Any Other Year since 1932', *Daily Mail* <https://www.dailymail. co.uk/news/article-9641599/Fewer-newborn-girls-given-Karen-2020-year-1932.html> [accessed 29 December 2021].

238 *'portrayed as witches'*: Lewis, 'The Mythology of Karen'.

238 *'Nearly everyone knows that hating women'*: Sarah Ditum, 'The Sly Sexism of the OK Karen Meme', *UnHerd* <https:// unherd.com/2020/04/the-sly-sexism-of-the-ok-karen-meme/> [accessed 17 November 2020].

238 *Even black female activists*: Twitter <https://twitter.com/ gwensnyderPHL/status/1254783335949152261> [accessed 27 December 2021].

238 *documenting instances of name-based bullying*: <https:// karenismyname.org/> and <https://www.ku4r.org/> [both accessed 08/12/2022].

239 *'all met a Karen during our lifetime'*: Sarah Basford, 'How "Karen" Became The Name For Rude, Middle-Aged White Women', *Lifehacker* <https://www.lifehacker.com.au/2020/05/ how-karen-became-the-name-for-rude-middle-aged-white-women/> [accessed 27 December 2021].

239 *'the archetypal "Karen"'*: Aja Romano, 'Karen: The Speak-to-the-Manager Anti-Vaxxer Mom Turned Meme', *Vox* <https:// www.vox.com/2020/2/5/21079162/karen-name-insult-meme-manager> [accessed 25 June 2021].

240 *Advice given to older women*: Turnbull.

240 *women whose 'defining essence'*: Kaitlyn Tiffany, 'Coronavirus "Karen" Memes Are Everywhere', *The Atlantic* <https:// www.theatlantic.com/technology/archive/2020/05/coronavirus-karen-memes-reddit-twitter-carolyn-goodman/611104/> [accessed 27 December 2021].

240 *'I know it makes me an angry Karen'*: Rachael Reevesz, 'I've Come to Hate Cars with a Passion. I Know It Makes Me an Angry Karen – but You Should Hate Them Too', *Independent* <https://www.independent.co.uk/voices/cars-pollution-noise-mental-health-deaths-accidents-coronavirus-a9636181.html> [accessed 28 December 2021].

240 *the risk of being a 'Covid Karen'*: Tiffany.

241   *stigmatised the act of complaining:* Twitter <https://twitter.
       com/missdaisyfdoo/status/1327680568092467200> [accessed
       24 December 2020]. Alison Phipps, 'White Tears, White Rage:
       Victimhood and (as) Violence in Mainstream Feminism',
       European Journal of Cultural Studies, 24.1 (2021), pp. 81–93
       <https://doi.org/10.1177/1367549420985852>; Reevesz; Tiffany.

241   *'re-enact[ing] the Karen dynamic':* Julia Carrie Wong, 'The Year
       of Karen: How a Meme Changed the Way Americans Talked
       about Racism', *Guardian* <https://www.theguardian.com/
       world/2020/dec/27/karen-race-white-women-black-americans-
       racism> [accessed 27 December 2021].

241   *'It is evidence of witchcraft to defend witches':* Nigel
       Cawthorne, *Witches: The History of a Persecution* (London:
       Arcturus, 2019). Chapter 5, para. 8

241   *'it is a finger trap insult':* Ditum, 'The Sly Sexism of the OK
       Karen Meme'.

241   *'women began to protest less in general':* Barstow. p. 158

242   *'shifts the argument from the what to the who':*
       McBride. pp. 14–15

243   *'men and women live on a stage':* Lerner. p. 12

244   *'Men punish, by ridicule':* Ibid. p. 13

244   *'To be female is to be deviant by definition':* Daly. p. 65

245   *Jane Shilling captures this dynamic:* Shilling. p. 3

245   *For many of us, Shilling included, this is not good enough:* 'I,
       on the other hand, as I passed forty and began to head for fifty,
       wondered whether there might be more to the narratives of
       middle age than hot flushes, absent-minded shoplifting and an
       overwhelming sense of having been cheated by life.' Ibid.

245   *I once suggested on Twitter:* Twitter <https://twitter.
       com/glosswitch/status/1432677361309429773> [accessed 21
       December 2021].

246   *It is a fact universally acknowledged:* Twitter <https://twitter.
       com/harvestlesssea/status/1432691351792013313> [accessed
       23 December 2021].

246   *We are also worn out:* Twitter <https://twitter.com/almu1968/
       status/1432698084052676619> [accessed 31 August 2021].

246   *I thank the perimenopause fairy:* Twitter <https://twitter.com/
       Mumsplainer/status/1432779635335614479> [accessed 23
       December 2021].

246   *Our skin is so much thicker:* Twitter <https://twitter.com/
       AdelaPank100/status/1432684559557017606> [accessed 23
       December 2021].

246   'The reason women in middle age': Sarah Ditum, 'Why Does TV Still Hate Middle-Aged Women?', *The Times* <https://www.thetimes.co.uk/article/46eb247a-5de3-11ec-9d57-254f1e0 40d28?shareToken=8f09870d390d5850642350a53029268e> [accessed 20 December 2021].

247   'Older women': Sarah Pedersen, 'They've Got an Absolute Army of Women behind Them: The Formation of a Women's Cooperative Constellation in Contemporary Scotland', *Scottish Affairs*, 31:1 (2022), pp. 1–20 <https://doi.org/10.3366/SCOT.2022.0394>.

248   *[We] still have few other names*: Stacy Schiff, 'Witchcraft on the Campaign Trail', *New York Times* <https://www.nytimes.com/2016/10/31/opinion/witchcraft-on-the-campaign-trail.html> [accessed 15 December 2020].

248   'Grown men': Andrea Dworkin, *Woman Hating* (New York: E. P. Dutton, 1974). p. 35

248   'one of the very few images of independent female power': de Rosée.

248   'rooted in ancient scapegoating': Michelle Goldberg, 'QAnon Believers Are Obsessed With Hillary Clinton. She Has Thoughts', *New York Times* <https://www.nytimes.com/2021/02/05/opinion/qanon-hillary-clinton.html?smid=tw-share> [accessed 7 February 2021].

249   'an angry, crotchety old hag': Schiff.

249   'the capital crime of displaying more wit': Ibid.

249   'witch with a B', 'vagenda of manocide', 'Bern the witch!': Kim Kelly, 'Are Witches the Ultimate Feminists?', *Guardian* <https://www.theguardian.com/books/2017/jul/05/witches-feminism-books-kristin-j-sollee> [accessed 14 December 2020].

249   *this is the ultimate, go-to accusation*: Madeline Miller, 'From Circe to Clinton: Why Powerful Women are Cast as Witches', *Guardian* <https://www.theguardian.com/books/2018/apr/07/cursed-from-circe-to-clinton-why-women-are-cast-as-witches> [accessed 3 December 2020].

249   'women of a certain age': Caro. p. 25

250   'The Karen debate can': Lewis, 'The Mythology of Karen'.

251   'the connectedness of women': Lerner. pp. 218–19

251   *what she termed the 'reciprocal agreement'*: Personally I am uncomfortable with viewing this as an 'agreement' as such – I think it is more subtle, with less active choice involved. Ibid. p. 218

252   'based on the experience of white, middle-class women':

Kimberlé Crenshaw, 'Mapping the Margins: Intersectionality, Identity Politics, and Violence against Women of Color', *Stanford Law Review*, 43:6 (1991), pp. 1241–99 <https://doi.org/10.2307/1229039>. p. 1298

252 *'the only objects of racism who are imagined'*: Baddiel. p. 18

252 *'People are not out to get you'*: Wong.

253 *'rewrite the script'*: Lerner. p. 13

254 *'capitalised on a history of sexual trauma'*: 'Feminist Icon Judith Butler on JK Rowling, Trans Rights, Feminism and Intersectionality', YouTube <https://www.youtube.com/watch?v=tXJb2eLNJZE&t=1910s> [accessed 27 June 2021].

254 *'insisting continually on their entitled place'*: Baddiel. p. 121

254 *There is a vague, somewhat culturally imperialistic attempt:* Anne Helen Petersen, 'The Trouble with White Women', *Culture Study* <https://annehelen.substack.com/p/the-trouble-with-white-women> [accessed 31 December 2021].

255 *'The tears of a woman'*: *Malleus Maleficarum.*

255 *'bourgeois white women's tears'*: Phipps, 'White Tears, White Rage'.

255 *Hill, in bringing allegations of sexual harassment:* Crenshaw. p. 1298

256 *'a white, rich, heterosexual, cisgender bogeyman'*: Lewis, *Difficult Women*. p. 136

257 *Kirsten ... finds herself condemned by her peers:* Kiran Millwood Hargrave, *The Mercies* (London: Picador, 2020). Chapter 31, final para., Chapter 32, para. 1

257 *Hargrave refused to sit on the judging panel:* Katie Law, 'JK Rowling and the Bitter Battle of the Book World', *Evening Standard* <https://www.standard.co.uk/culture/books/trans-battle-book-world-jk-rowling-a4571221.html> [accessed 30 June 2022].

258 *'To disbelieve in witches'*: *Malleus Maleficarum.*

258 *'the ultimate mechanism of alienation'*: Federici. Chapter 7, final para.

259 *Thus young white women can engage:* Petersen.

259 *'British feminism's leading voices'*: Molly Fischer, 'Who Did J.K. Rowling Become?', *The Cut* <https://www.thecut.com/amp/article/who-did-j-k-rowling-become.html> [accessed 23 December 2020].

260 *Boomer feminists ... have already pointed out:* Segal; Caro; Gullette.

261 *'anxieties about inheritance'*: Barstow. p. 78

261   *forced choreographer Rosie Kay out of her own company:*
      'Rosie Kay: Dancers Write Open Letter to Choreographer
      after Gender Row', *BBC News* <https://www.bbc.co.uk/news/
      entertainment-arts-59584638> [accessed 31 December 2021].

262   *'If you disown your legacy':* Freely. p. 202

264   *'the second wave feminism in the late sixties and seventies':*
      Lewis, *Difficult Women.* pp. 28–9

265   *'for leftists habitually denigrated':* Susan Brownmiller, *In Our
      Time: Memoir of a Revolution* (New York: The Dial Press,
      1999). p. 78

265   *showed Brownmiller taking a hard, even victim-blaming,
      stance:* 'If they can't get out because they don't want to reduce
      their living circumstances, or they don't want to go, or they are
      passive people, then I am supposed to respect that. But I don't.'
      Susan Brownmiller in Katie Van Syckle, *'Against Our Will*
      Author on What Today's Rape Activists Don't Get', *The Cut*
      <https://www.thecut.com/2015/09/what-todays-rape-activists-
      dont-get.html> [accessed 1 December 2021].

265   *the retaliatory ageism which characterised some of the
      responses:* 'I'm not suggesting some sort of *Logan's Run*
      age cut-off for activists or public intellectuals,' wrote Jessica
      Valenti. Well, no, Jessica. But it obviously crossed your
      mind. Jessica Valenti, 'If Feminist Icons Lose Their Way the
      Movement Continues without Them', *Guardian* <https://www.
      theguardian.com/commentisfree/2015/sep/21/feminist-icons-
      movement-continues-without-them> [accessed 29 July 2021].

265   *'if, forty years from now':* Kate Harding, 'When a Feminist
      Trailblazer Turns to Victim-Blaming, It's Time to Let Go of a
      Hero', *Cosmopolitan* <https://www.cosmopolitan.com/politics/
      a46467/susan-brownmiller-rape-victim-blaming/> [accessed 18
      November 2020].

267   *not helped by the belief among young feminists:* Susan Bordo,
      The Destruction of Hillary Clinton (New York: Melville
      House, 2017).

267   *'Abortion rights':* Hadley Freeman, 'American Feminism
      Has Turned its Back on Women', *UnHerd* <https://
      unherd.com/2022/05/american-feminism-has-turned-its-
      back-on-abortion/?tl_inbound=1&tl_groups[0]=18743&tl_
      period_type=3&mc_cid=4747b912d5&mc_eid=e091397603>
      [accessed 27 June 2022].

267   *'what we don't want to be':* Quoted in ibid.

267   *'Young middle-class white women':* Janice Turner, 'I Took

My Rights as a Woman for Granted – We All Did', *The Times* <https://www.thetimes.co.uk/article/janice-turner-i-took-my-rights-for-granted-we-all-did-zk5vbfbrp> [accessed 28 June 2022].

267 *'the stuff that does not look good on Instagram'*: Ibid.

268 *'the hearts of students of the movement'*: E. Sylvia Pankhurst, *The Suffragette: The History of the Women's Suffrage Movement, 1905–1910* (New York: Sturgis & Walton Company, 1911).

Chapter 8: Dead Hag

269 *One lesson we can draw:* Federici. Chapter 7, final para.

269 *Let me start by saying:* John McNamee, 'A Cartoon from The New Yorker', <https://www.newyorker.com/cartoon/a21964> [accessed 20 November 2020].

269 *women are still burned as witches today:* Agence France-Presse, 'Witch-Hunt Murders Surge in Democratic Republic of Congo', *Guardian* <https://www.theguardian.com/world/2021/sep/28/witch-hunt-murders-surge-democratic-republic-congo-women-south-kivu-province> [accessed 17 October 2021].

270 *According to the UN State of World Population report:* <https://www.unfpa.org/sites/default/files/pub-pdf/UNFPA_PUB_2020_EN_State_of_World_Population.pdf> [accessed 9 July 2021].

270 *In the UK, two women die:* Maya Oppenheim, 'These Are the Names of All the Women Killed in the Last Year', *Independent* <https://www.independent.co.uk/news/uk/crime/women-killed-men-jess-phillips-b1815924.html> [accessed 17 October 2021].

270 *'being targeted as scapegoats'*: Miller, 'From Circe to Clinton'.

270 *'at least eighty-seven thousand women'*: Bindel. p. 37

271 *'ill-equipped to recognise and prevent'*: Julia Long and others, Femicide Census. UK Femicides 2009–2018. 'If I'm Not in Friday, I Might Be Dead', 2020, <https://www.femicidecensus.org/wp-content/uploads/2020/11/Femicide-Census-10-year-report.pdf> [accessed 8 January 2021].

273 *'She's driving me nuts'*: Wilson. p. 93

273 *The provocation defence:* 'Timothy Brehmer: From Coercive Control to Loss of Control', *Legal Feminist* <https://legalfeminist.org.uk/2020/10/30/timothy-brehmer-from-coercive-control-to-loss-of-control/> [accessed 9 January 2022].

274 *the 'rough sex' defence has been compared:* Sophie Gallagher, 'Rough Sex Defence: What Will a Change in the

Law Mean?', *Independent* <https://www.independent.co.uk/
life-style/women/rough-sex-defence-ban-domestic-abuse-bill-
government-2020-a9374386.html> [accessed 10 January 2022].

274   *'the normalisation of bondage':* Taylor.

275   *so much academic enquiry:* To be clear, I don't think the
question of where fertility ends in an adult human (and orca)
female's lifespan is not interesting. I just find the frequent
'what are they still doing here, anyhow?' pitching of it rather
telling. Tabitha M. Powledge, 'The Origin of Menopause: Why
Do Women Outlive Fertility?', *Scientific American* <https://
www.scientificamerican.com/article/the-origin-of-menopause/>
[accessed 11 January 2022].

275   *'Witch charges':* Barstow. p. 29

275   *'She went before me':* 'Williamson Did Not Wife to Become
a "Decrepit Old Hag"', *Reading Chronicle* <https://www.
readingchronicle.co.uk/news/14677179.williamson-did-not-
wife-to-become-a-decrepit-old-hag/> [accessed 10 July 2021].

276   *Until 2018, the murders of women over the age of fifty-
nine:* 'National Life Tables – Life Expectancy in the UK',
Office for National Statistics <https://www.ons.gov.uk/people
populationandcommunity/birthsdeathsandmarriages/life
expectancies/bulletins/nationallifetablesunitedkingdom/
2018to2020> [accessed 8 January 2022].

277   *'When you look at police data':* Yvonne Roberts, 'End Femicide:
278 Dead – the Hidden Scandal of Older Women Killed by Men',
Guardian <https://www.theguardian.com/society/2021/mar/07/
end-femicide-278-dead-the-hidden-scandal-of-older-women-
killed-by-men?CMP=share_btn_tw> [accessed 7 March 2021].

277   *older women are more likely:* Long and others. p. 74

277   *'the least likely to express remorse or empathy':* Roberts.

277   *In April 2016 the novelist Helen Bailey was murdered:* At
the time of writing, Stewart is now also awaiting trial for the
murder of his first wife. Martin Evans, 'Man Who Murdered
Children's Author, Helen Bailey, Is Charged with Killing His
Wife Six Years Earlier', *Telegraph* <https://www.telegraph.
co.uk/news/2020/07/06/man-murdered-childrens-author-helen-
bailey-charged-killing-wife/> [accessed 8 January 2022].

277   *Some examples were provided:* Deborah Orr, 'Helen
Bailey and the Lethal Darkness behind This "Middle-Aged
Woman" Myth', *Guardian* <https://www.theguardian.com/
commentisfree/2017/feb/24/helen-bailey-middle-aged-woman-
myth> [accessed 10 July 2021].

278   *not 'entirely alive':* Wolf, *The Beauty Myth.* p. 235
278   *loving husband who . . . 'just snapped':* Ben Quinn and agencies,
      'Pensioner Cleared of Murdering Wife during First Lockdown
      in Wales', *Guardian* <https://www.theguardian.com/uk-news/
      2021/feb/15/pensioner-cleared-of-murdering-wife-during-first-
      lockdown-in-wales> [accessed 11 January 2022].
278   *'Thou shalt not suffer a witch to live':* Exodus 22:18.
279   *'dead assets, the embodiment of a world':* Federici. Chapter 7,
      paras 7 and 9.
280   *Looking at the treatment of older women on social media:*
      boodleoops, 'J. K. Rowling and the Trans Activists: A
      Story in Screenshots', Medium <https://medium.com/@
      rebeccarc/j-k-rowling-and-the-trans-activists-a-story-in-
      screenshots-78e01dca68d> [accessed 7 February 2021].
281   *'Twitter was full of people telling me':* Moore, 'Why I Had to
      Leave The Guardian'.
281   *'thoughtful feedback from someone':* Twitter <https://mobile.
      twitter.com/AbigailShrier/status/1354272038634962949>
      [accessed 7 February 2021].
281   *'a satire against bluestockings':* Warner. Chapter 3, I,
      para. 3
282   *shoving into a scold's bridle:* '. . . with such a frame locking
      their heads and mouth, those accused could be led through
      town in a cruel public humiliation that must have terrified all
      women, showing what one could expect if she did not remain
      subservient . . .' Federici. Chapter 5, para. 10
282   *'Witches . . . tend to be people we didn't like':* Schiff.
282   *today it caters to the broad, unremitting demands:* Writing
      on men who use the term, Helen Lewis suggests 'they still feel
      the old impulse towards woman-hating, but won't admit it,
      and have convinced themselves they are only chastising the
      impure. Witch-finders did something similar.' Helen Lewis,
      'Welcome to the Age of Ironic Bigotry, Where Old Hatreds
      Are Cloaked in Woke New Language', *New Statesman*
      <https://www.newstatesman.com/politics/feminism/2019/05/
      welcome-age-ironic-bigotry-where-old-hatreds-are-cloaked-
      woke-new-language> [accessed 23 December 2020].
282   *As the poet Jenny Lindsay:* Jenny Lindsay, 'Anatomy of
      a Hounding', *The Dark Horse Magazine* <https://www.
      thedarkhorsemagazine.com/anatomy-of-a-hounding-lindsay>
      [accessed 8 February 2021].
283   *'What happened to me could easily happen':* Glosswitch, 'I

Don't Feel I "Match" My Gender, So What Does It Mean to Be Called Cis?', *New Statesman* <https://www.newstatesman.com/uncategorized/2014/02/i-dont-feel-i-match-my-gender-so-what-does-it-mean-be-called-cis> [accessed 12 January 2022].

283   *In her dissertation on the use of the term*: Anna-Louise Adams, '"You should be burnt alive TERF": How a Neutral Descriptor Enables Misogynistic E-Bile and the Obfuscation of Progressive Feminist Ideology' <https://docs.google.com/document/d/1UWL5Dd5eaiHRA28qmYo_-6jmr3PKDi4qu_wPldWX9jA/edit?pli=1> [accessed 25 November 2022].

283   *Professor Deborah Cameron lists some examples*: Deborah Cameron, 'What Makes a Word a Slur?', *Language: A Feminist Guide* <https://debuk.wordpress.com/2016/11/06/what-makes-a-word-a-slur/> [accessed 23 December 2020].

285   *protestors threw red paint*: Indigo Stafford, 'Blood on Her Hands: JK Rowling's Edinburgh Handprints Vandalised with Red Paint', *Edinburgh Live* <https://www.edinburghlive.co.uk/news/edinburgh-news/blood-hands-jk-rowlings-edinburgh-18583199> [accessed 13 January 2022].

285   *'When you're on the outside of the fray'*: Twitter <https://twitter.com/elizamondegreen/status/1354521683126870019?s=20> [accessed 1 July 2021].

285   *'taught people that "the woman's crime" deserved'*: Barstow. p. 157

286   *'Can we stop saying the UK virus?'*: Twitter <https://twitter.com/sarahklop/status/1344467230923268096> [accessed 6 February 2021].

286   *'It boggles my mind'*: Twitter <https://twitter.com/cmcgreevy5/status/1345044546175053824> [accessed 2 January 2021].

287   *'the fiction of a single female experience'*: Ilaria Michelis, 'Re-Centring White Victimhood in the Age of Black Lives Matter: A "Gender Critical" Project?', *Engenderings* <https://blogs.lse.ac.uk/gender/2022/01/12/re-centring-white-victimhood-in-the-age-of-black-lives-matter-a-terf-project/> [accessed 13 January 2022].

287   *cast as the property of a mean, bigoted class of hoarding dinosaurs*: Prowle.

287   *Likewise, men threatening sexual violence*: Lindsay, 'Anatomy of a Hounding'.

288   *'a TERF at your Thanksgiving gathering'*: Caroline Reilly, 'Is There a TERF at Your Thanksgiving Gathering?', *Rewire News Group* <https://rewirenewsgroup.com/article/2020/11/23/is-there-

a-terf-at-your-thanksgiving-gathering/?fbclid=IwAR2TC_YC
xohXQ4TDoM56-xOltdUOS9hcjQa1FLWdzmhGDEFP
rd0zuF0DbZw> [accessed 24 December 2020].

288 *brings to mind both femicide statistics:* Long and others.

288 *'Every single civil rights movement':* Twitter <https://twitter.
com/uktransalliance/status/1359600818664730625?s=20>
[accessed 17 July 2021].

288 *A sixty-year-old feminist was assaulted:* Brittany Vonow,
'Cops Release Pictures of Transgender Activists Wanted
after 60-Year-Old Woman Was Attacked at Hyde Park
Rally', *Sun* <https://www.thesun.co.uk/news/4691455/
cops-release-pictures-of-transgender-activists-wanted-after-60-
year-old-woman-was-attacked-at-hyde-park-rally/> [accessed 8
February 2021].

288 *A member of a punk band:* Twitter <https://twitter.
com/Slatzism/status/1358448150890086408> [accessed 17
July 2021].

289 *the vast majority of assaults, rapes and murders:*
'The Nature of Violent Crime in England and Wales',
Office for National Statistics <https://www.ons.gov.
uk/peoplepopulationandcommunity/crimeandjustice/articles/
thenatureofviolentcrimeinenglandandwales/yearendingmarch
2020> [accessed 5 January 2022].

289 *panic over women's 'slippery tongues':* 'The third reason is that
they have slippery tongues, and are unable to conceal from the
fellow-women those things which by evil arts they know; and,
since they are weak, they find an easy and secret manner of
vindicating themselves by witchcraft', *Malleus Maleficarum.*

290 *'misandrist feminism':* 'Misandry and Hypocrisy: Transcript
of Speech for International Women's Day', *Penny Red* <https://
pennyred.blogspot.com/2008/03/misandry-and-hypocrisy-
transcript-of.html?m=1> [accessed 10 January 2022].

291 *'sites of famous trials and persecutions':* Federici. Introduction,
para. 10

292 *'We don't injure or kill men':* Pauline Harmange, *I Hate Men*
(London: 4th Estate, 2020). p. 20

293 *threat ... to take legal action to ban it:* Kim Willsher, '"We Should
Have the Right Not to like Men": The French Writer at Centre
of Literary Storm', *Guardian* <https://www.theguardian.com/
world/2020/sep/10/french-writer-book-pauline-harmange-i-
hate-men-interview> [accessed 13 January 2022].

Afterword

RESOURCES

Below I'd like to highlight some of the work that is being done to combat both the marginalisation of today's (and future) older women, and to celebrate the legacies of those who have gone before us. This is in no way an exhaustive list – it is intended to give a taste of what is out there. There are many more examples of women of all ages enacting real change at local and national levels, sometimes in collaboration with the groups mentioned here, all of whom are owed a huge debt of gratitude.

Chapter 1: Visibility and representation

Acting Your Age Campaign – Launched in 2018 by Nicky Clark, the Acting Your Age Campaign challenges the marginalisation of middle-aged women on screen and in the creative industries. Clark has compiled a wealth of data to show how older women are edged out and misrepresented in TV and film, winning the support of a wide range of actors and women's organisations. http://www.mrsnickyclark. com/-acting-your-age--campaign.html

Women Over 50 Film Festival – Founded in 2015, WOFFF showcases outstanding work of older women on screen and

behind the camera, while promoting intergenerational networking. In addition to an annual festival, WOFFF hosts
year-round events and film screenings which people of all ages
can attend. https://wofff.co.uk/

Chapter 2: Lifecycle and the body

Gateway Women – This is a support and advocacy network
for women who are childless (whether or not by choice).
Founded by Jody Day, Gateway Women hosts webinars and
offers ways for women to connect with one another, dealing
with issues such grief, ageing while childless and discrimination against women who have not had children. https://
gateway-women.com/
Wellbeing of Women – The website of the women's health
charity provides multiple links to resources on menopause,
from support with symptoms to workplace rights, while
their Menopause Workplace Pledge encourages employers
to make positive changes to support female employees in
midlife.   https://www.wellbeingofwomen.org.uk/campaigns/
menopausepledge/resources

Chapter 3: Work and economics

Women's Budget Group – The WBG is an independent,
not-for-profit organisation that analyses the impact of government policy on women, producing reports, guidance and
campaigning resources. https://wbg.org.uk/
WASPI – The Women Against State Pension Inequality campaign represents women born in the 1950s who lost out due
to the increase in state pension age for women. While this

represents a slightly older demographic than is the subject of this book, the issue is a key example of what happens when cumulative sex-based inequality is ignored and male-default lifecycles prioritised in politics and economics. https://www.waspi.co.uk/

AgeUK – A leading charity representing the needs of older people, as part of its work Age UK offers guidance on age discrimination, how it is defined under the Equality Act and ways in which to challenge it. https://www.ageuk.org.uk/

Chapter 4: Legacy

Women's History Network – The WHN is a national association and charity for the promotion of women's history. Membership is open to anyone with a passion for women's history, and activities include organising an annual conference, distributing a thrice-yearly journal and offering members networking opportunities. https://womenshistory-network.org/

Greenham Women Everywhere – The Greenham Women Everywhere project aims to collate and preserve the archives from those who marched to Greenham Common and/or attended the Peace Camp in the early 1980s. The website includes written, oral and visual testimonies. https://green-hamwomeneverywhere.co.uk/

Spare Rib (1972–93) – The British Library website includes a searchable archive of digitised images from the Women's Liberation Movement magazine. https://www.bl.uk/spare-rib

Chapter 5: Feminist waves and the sexual landscape

The Radical Notion – Launched in 2020, *The Radical Notion* is a not-for-profit online and print magazine run by a collective of radical and socialist feminists. Each issue uses a particular lens through which to analyse sex-based oppression and male dominance, offering a vision of feminist thought and activism which challenges recent liberal repackagings of the movement. https://theradicalnotion.org/

We Can't Consent To This – A campaign set up in response to increasing numbers of women and girls killed and injured in violence claimed to be consensual – the 'rough sex' defence. Many of their stories come from younger women, indicating an increasing 'destigmatisation' of violence in sex despite the promises of the backlash against 'anti-sex' feminists of the past. https://wecantconsenttothis.uk/

SARSAS – SARSAS is a charity based in the South West of England, offering support for 'people affected by rape of any kind of sexual assault or abuse at any time in their lives'. Their 2020 report, *The Chilling Silence*, focused on older women's experiences of sexual violence, both as adults and in the recollection of childhood abuse. https://www.sarsas.org.uk/

Chapter 6: Political organisation

FiLiA – FiLiA is an annual grassroots feminist conference held in different parts of the United Kingdom. One of its key aims is forging intergenerational connections and paying homage to earlier feminists: '"FiLiA" means daughter; we are the daughters of the women who came before us and we fight so that our sisters and daughters may be free'. https://www.filia.org.uk/

Older Feminist Network – Founded in 1982 as an initiative from *Spare Rib* magazine's collective, the OFN has met regularly since, campaigning on issues which particularly impact older women, and offering a strong attendance at Filia conferences in recent years. https://olderfeminist.org.uk/

Woman's Place UK – Woman's Place UK was launched in 2017 by a group of women from left-wing backgrounds, with the aim of ensuring women's voices were heard during consultations on proposals to changes to the Gender Recognition Act. Their work has since evolved into broader women's rights campaigning, often in the face of extreme pushback, misrepresentation and ageist misogyny. https://womansplaceuk.org/

Cambridge Radical Feminist Network and **Women Talk Back!** – Two of an increasing number of groups across UK universities in which younger women engage in consciousness-raising, activism and debating the ideas of earlier feminist thinkers. https://www.camradfems.co.uk/ and https://www.womentalkback.org/

Chapter 7: Privilege and Karen-shaming

Karen is my name and **Karens United for Respect** – Two sites created in response to the use of 'Karen' as an insult/indicator of moral inferiority, explaining the impact on women called Karen, many of whom have experienced discrimination, harassment and bullying simply on the basis of their names. https://karenismyname.org/ and https://www.ku4r.org/

Centre for Ageing Better – The Centre for Ageing Better's reports offer insight into the impact of government policy and economic upheaval on the lives of older people, taking differences such as sex, race and disability into account. As such, they offer a corrective to the popular, undifferentiated image of youthful disadvantages/older privilege often used to pit groups against one another. https://ageing-better.org.uk/

Chapter 8: Violence against women

Femicide Census – Created by Karen Ingala Smith and Clarissa O'Callaghan in response to the limited, decentralised research into men's fatal violence against women, the Femicide Census offers information that is of use to policy-makers and practitioners while also commemorating victims. https://www.femicidecensus.org/

End Violence Against Women Coalition – A group of feminist organisations and experts from across the UK, the EVAW Coalition challenges the belief that male violence is inevitable. Their aim is to drive social change through campaigning and influencing policy, taking an intersectional, anti-racist approach in all their work. https://www.endviolenceagainstwomen.org.uk/

ACKNOWLEDGEMENTS

Many women have helped me in the writing of this book. I owe enormous thanks to my agent, Caroline Hardman, who encouraged me to pursue and develop this idea from an extremely rough outline; to my publisher, Ursula Doyle, for her encouragement and support; to Zoe Gullen, for her thoughtful editorial comments; and to Jess Gulliver, for her work on the book's messaging. It has been hugely reassuring to know that *Hags* has been in the hands of people (fellow hags!) who have really understood what I wish to convey.

The views on feminism, femaleness and relationships between women that shape *Hags* have been developed through conversations and friendships spanning many years. I'd like to give particular thanks to my brilliant friend Marina Strinkovsky, who first inspired me to read the texts my generation was supposed to have left behind, and whose sharp analysis always makes me want to rethink the things I thought I knew. The writing and friendship of Jane Clare Jones has changed my view of the body, dependency and female community. Meetings and online interactions with these women and others – including Rebecca Reilly-Cooper, Anya Palmer, Rachel Hewitt, Sarah Ditum, Michelle Arouet, Juliet Oosthuysen, Karen Kruzycka, Gia Milinovich – have changed my way of thinking, pushing me to replace my earlier view of feminism in terms of exceptionality and tie-cutting with one that conceives of it in terms of female support and shared ideas. I would also like to thank Helen Lewis and Caroline Criado Perez for giving me the confidence to take myself seriously when writing about women's lives and needs.

I am eternally grateful to the women who agreed to speak to me during the writing (despite the discomfort of having been approached with 'I'm writing about hags and thought of you'). These include Esther Parry, Kate Williams, Laura Dodsworth, Emma Burnell, Mary-Ann Stephenson, Sarah Pedersen, Lucy Tatman, Gillian Philip, Helen Joyce, Kiri Tunks, Anna-Louise Adams and Sophie Watson. I'd also like to extend my deepest thanks to the hags of Twitter and Mumsnet, many of whose names I do not know but whose willingness to share their own female experiences, viewpoints and jokes – even when we are supposed to be sticking to earnest discussions of organic baby food and school catchment areas – has transformed my understanding of how lifecycle and relationships make us a force to be reckoned with.

Feminist writing inevitably draws on the intellectual labour and activism of radical feminists, who endure years of being told they are wrong, then that other women will disseminate their ideas 'more nicely', before finally being asked 'Why didn't you say any of this before?' There is no way of adequately expressing my gratitude to these women for holding the line while the rest of us catch up. I would particularly like to express my admiration for Julie Bindel and Karen Ingala Smith, for their tireless work supporting survivors of male violence against women while deepening our understanding of its reach and impact.

At the risk of sounding arse-covering, there are some women whose names I have intentionally not mentioned in order to protect them from professional discomfort – and 'guilt by association' witch-hunts – when it comes to arguments relating to sex and gender. I hope you know that you are appreciated, and that these decisions are a symptom of a problem I hope this book goes some small way to addressing.

Hags would never have been completed without the unflagging support of my partner, Ewan Johnson. From reading drafts and discussing ideas to taking on an unequal share of domestic labour (in order to give me more time to write about inequalities in domestic labour), Ewan made it possible, practically, intellectually and emotionally, for me to think and write. I especially appreciate his generosity in challenging me when I have been unclear in my own arguments, each time knowing I may be reluctant to have my own doubts confirmed, if not tempted to write off his honest questions as mansplaining. He is a true partner and I am incredibly lucky to have him in my life.

While I have not forced my manuscript on our three children, I would also like to thank them for their love and support, and, in particular, my eldest, for his thoughtful conversations about politics and injustice; my middle son, for his incredible enthusiasm in promoting 'Mum's book' to all his friends' mothers; and my youngest, for reminding me that since he writes a book 'every day', I must not get above myself.

When I first thought of writing this book, I did not anticipate how much it would focus on the absence of acknowledgement. Our tendency to cast aside the work of earlier women – denying them accreditation, refusing to pass on their knowledge, forcing ourselves to painstakingly reconstruct their ideas before declaring ourselves the originators – is well-documented, but I did not know how well. The erasure of women's writing about their own erasure is one of feminism's bitterest ironies. 'What gets passed on,' wrote Susan Faludi in 'American Electra', 'is the predisposition to dispossess, a legacy of no legacy.' If there is one thing I would like to stress above all, it is the debt we owe to feminists of the past, not as beta model thinkers laying the groundwork for a more sophisticated present-day feminism, but as co-creators of a rich intellectual heritage that is ours to rediscover. The acknowledgement I refer to here is not specific to this book, but to our position as women in relation to one another.

I am conscious of my own terrible tendency to decide I am the golden mean as far as feminist epiphanies are concerned: no woman could reasonably be expected to reach feminist enlightenment any earlier than I did, but as for those still lagging behind, well, they've got no excuse. In truth there are countless women whose engagement with feminist legacies, and the importance of intergenerational solidarity, started far earlier than mine, and whose ideas I absorbed long before I had the nerve to express them myself. While any mistakes, misapprehensions and bad thinking in this work are my responsibility, I acknowledge that many of the ideas I think of as my own are not. They are shared; they have been passed down; they will be passed down again. Such is the cycle, and I am grateful for it.